IMPROVING PRACTICE

IN PRIMARY CARE

**Practical Advice from
Practising Doctors**

Editors:

Dr Scott Chambers

Dr George Kassianos

Dr Jonathan Morrell

Managing Editor: Dr Scott Chambers
Editorial Controller: Emma Catherall
Production Manager: Julia Potterton
Designer: Chris Matthews
Typesetter: Julie Smith
Publishing Director: Julian Grover
Publisher: Stephen I'Anson

1 Bankside
Lodge Road
Long Hanborough
Oxfordshire
OX29 8LJ, UK

Tel: +44 (0)1993 885370
Fax: +44 (0)1993 881868
Email: *enquiries@csfmedical.com*

www.csfmedical.com

The content of *Improving Practice in Primary Care* is the work of a number of contributors and has been produced in line with our standard editorial procedures. Whilst every effort has been made to ensure the accuracy of the information at the date of approval for publication, the Authors, the Publisher, the Editors and the Editorial Board accept no responsibility whatsoever for any errors or omissions or for any consequences arising from anything included in or excluded from *Improving Practice in Primary Care*.

ISBN: 1-905064-82-9

Typeset by Creative, Langbank, Scotland.
Printed and bound in Thailand.
Distributed by NBN International, Plymouth, Devon.

Contents

Foreword

An introduction to *Improving Practice in Primary Care*

Improving Practice in Primary Care is a compendium of GP-authored articles that have been derived from the medical journal *Drugs in Context*. The authors of these articles were briefed to provide clinical guidance and practical advice on how fellow practitioners might go about improving the management of a variety of different conditions that are frequently encountered in primary care.

Drugs in Context, under the editorship of Dr George Kassianos and Dr Jonathan Morrell, was the first medical journal to review the evidence base surrounding the various drugs that are used routinely in primary care and to place this evidence in the context of the disease or condition concerned and the practical setting where patients with the condition present. Consequently, *Drugs in Context* is now widely regarded as an invaluable clinical management resource, particularly for healthcare professionals working in the primary-care sector.

Feedback from the readers of *Drugs in Context* consistently highlights the Improving Practice component of the journal as one of the most valuable sections of the publication. In addition, we have received numerous requests from practising GPs to publish these articles as a separate compendium in order to create an invaluable reference resource. In response we have decided to publish this first edition of *Improving Practice in Primary Care*. We hope that the guidance and advice it offers will prove useful to you when managing a diverse range of conditions.

Practical advice from practising doctors

Each of the articles that appear in this book are written by practising GPs who have a special interest in a particular disease or condition. As such, each author can relate directly to the pressures of every day primary-care practice but can also draw upon their extensive experience of managing patients with a specific disease and provide empathetic and realistic guidance on the various practical strategies that individual practitioners can employ to the ultimate benefit of their patients. Improving practice can benefit the individual physician too, with the patient–doctor relationship becoming far more rewarding for everyone involved.

Guidance not guidelines

These articles acknowledge that general practice is as much an art as a science, and that the patients that we see in our surgeries on a daily basis do not always fit into convenient 'boxes' who can be readily diagnosed and treated with simple reference to management guidelines. Moreover, each individual practice's starting position may be different and this is also taken into account here. As such, we firmly believe that *Improving Practice in Primary Care* offers empathetic, sensitive and realistic guidance and not just more guidelines!

Realistic advice in a dynamic, evolving environment

Recent years have seen significant changes in the National Health Service, with a concerted drive to put primary care at the forefront of patient management. Initiatives such as the National Service Frameworks (NSFs), the emergence of the National Institute for Clinical Excellence (NICE) and the agreement of a new General Medical Services (GMS) contract are generally welcomed by the majority of practitioners but, on the other hand, have added to the challenges that face GPs on a daily basis. The impact that these initiatives have on the practical management of a particular condition are considered in detail in each of the articles in *Improving Practice in Primary Care.*

The GMS contract in particular has provided a platform for GPs to evaluate their performance on a more formal basis with clinical audit. Whilst once clinical audit was considered by many as a 'stick with which to beat us', by regularly reviewing and monitoring clinical performance we can ensure that patient care is optimised. In addition, suggestions are also made throughout this book on how the entire multidisciplinary healthcare team can be encouraged to become actively involved in improving the management of the condition to the ultimate benefit of the patient.

Improving practice in primary care

Primary care still bears the responsibility for treating the majority of patients in this country. We hope that some of the strategies that are outlined in this book will help you to deliver enhanced care for your patients and make your daily practice a more rewarding and enjoyable experience.

Dr Scott Chambers
Managing Editor

1. Allergic rhinitis

Dr George Kassianos MD (Hons) FRCGP DRCOG LRCPEdin. LRCSEdin.
LRCP&SGlasg. DFP DMedAcup. DMedHypn MILT
General Practitioner, Bracknell, Berkshire

Summary

The symptoms of allergic rhinitis can be particularly debilitating for many patients and can disrupt their day-to-day lives. The importance of the condition should not be underestimated by healthcare professionals, not least because of the impact of the condition on GPs' workload, particularly during the 'allergy season'. Moreover, the condition is becoming increasingly prevalent, possibly due to the adoption of a more modern and westernised lifestyle, although the precise reasons for this remain unclear at present. Successful management of sufferers can lead to significant improvements in their quality of life. By employing appropriate practical strategies, we can also ensure that we can reduce the enormous seasonal burden of the condition on our workload. The availability of new-generation antihistamines and other agents provides us with the opportunity to relieve the symptomatic burden of the condition the first time the patient presents to us in our surgeries.

The challenge in primary care

Spring in Britain is a time when many of us feel our mood lifted by the prospect of longer days, brighter and warmer weather, and the opportunity to spend more time outdoors. However, a substantial number of our patients will be ambivalent about the prospect of summer as they begin to feel the first tingles of their returning hay fever. As GPs, I am sure that we all have great sympathy for our patients when they present with varying degrees of the symptoms of intermittent allergic rhinitis. However, I wonder if, like me, you need to remind yourself sometimes of just how debilitating and life-disrupting these symptoms can be, both for our patients and their families. For us too, the prospect of a season filled with days of high pollen counts can be quite daunting as it usually equates to waiting rooms filled with miserable and often extremely concerned patients whose performance at work or at school is suffering, and who are often deprived of sleep and in real need of any help that we can offer.

To the unaffected, intermittent allergic rhinitis may appear trivial and no more of a nuisance than a summer cold. Some may even be irritated by the constant sniffing, sneezing and moaning of sufferers such that they exclude them from their lives, outdoor activities and social events. Clearly, allergic rhinitis is not a trivial complaint. It can radically change and, on occasion, take over the lives of our patients. Therefore, the challenge in primary care is to manage our patients as best we can so that they regain their quality of life, function properly and return to school or work. Good patient management can significantly improve a child's concentration or an adult's productivity at work. In addition, we could reduce the enormous workload we often experience at this time of year by dealing with our patients as effectively as possible the first time that they present to us in our surgeries.

What is allergic rhinitis?

Depending on the time of exposure to allergens, our patients will either experience symptoms for most of the year, or for at least 9 months (persistent allergic rhinitis), or during a specific season such as the pollen season (intermittent allergic rhinitis). A number of the most severely affected patients suffer from persistent allergic rhinitis but get seasonal exacerbations too.

The nasal mucosa is programmed to stop invasion by foreign bodies such as bacteria. In allergic rhinitis, the nasal mucosa mounts an inappropriate response to a harmless substance. Two critical elements are involved here.

- *A causative allergen.* When an individual becomes sensitised to a particular allergen, an allergic nasal mucosal response will result each time the allergen is encountered. This effect can be immediate or delayed.
- *Inflammation.* The term rhinitis indicates a response of the nasal epithelium. In allergic rhinitis, specific allergens trigger a type-1 hypersensitivity reaction, which can persist for a considerable time after exposure.

Persistent allergic rhinitis

Persistent allergic rhinitis is caused mainly by inhaled or ingested allergens.
- Inhaled allergens include house dust, house-dust mites, pet-animal dander (e.g. fur, feather, skin), indoor moulds and cockroaches.
- Ingested allergens include foods such as nuts, eggs, wheat and milk, and other agents such as drugs that an individual is sensitive to.

Intermittent allergic rhinitis

Intermittent allergic rhinitis is caused mainly by grass, tree, weed or flower pollen. Patients can present with symptoms as early as February and as late as September.

- Tree pollen (e.g. oak, elm, ash, birch and hazel) causes symptoms from February to late May.
- Grass pollens (e.g. rye grass, timothy grass and others) are at their most prevalent from May to September but symptoms peak in the midsummer months of June and July.
- A variety of airborne fungal mould spores are troublesome between May and October, with symptoms peaking in late August and September.
- Increasingly, pollen from the ubiquitous oilseed rape is being blamed by our patients as the trigger for their symptoms, though many farmers will argue that the appearance of fields full of bright-yellow flowers is coincidental with the flowering of the less apparent but real culprits, such as the grasses described above.

The size of the problem

The number of people suffering from allergic rhinitis of one form or another is by no means small – 10–20% of the population suffer from this condition. If we were to look more closely at particular ages, we would find that up to two out of five children can be affected to some degree. By 3 and 5 years of age, one out of five and two out of five sufferers of allergic rhinitis, respectively, will have experienced symptoms. By 20 years of age, four out of five people who go on to suffer regularly are aware of a problem.

At younger ages, we see more boys than girls with allergic rhinitis in primary care but we see no difference between the sexes in adolescence and adulthood. In fact, symptoms tend to improve as we get older, particularly in those with an early onset of symptoms. It is, of course, never too late to develop symptoms for the first time, and these can occur even in old age.

It is perhaps no coincidence that persistent allergic rhinitis has increased in prevalence with an increasingly modern, some say, western lifestyle. Why should this be? We do not know the real reasons behind this, but we can speculate. Obvious factors appear to be environmental, with higher levels of airborne pollution generally. In addition, in our quest to keep our living spaces warm and yet save on heating costs, we have reduced ventilation in our homes and offices, which has led to significant rises in dust and dust-mite populations. We all spend much more time indoors, be it in the office or in our houses. The advent of 24-hour television seems to be entertaining adults and children day and night, and so it is perhaps not surprising that

> The number of people suffering from allergic rhinitis of one form or another is by no means small – 10–20% of the population suffer from this condition.

> Allergic rhinitis has increased in prevalence with an increasingly modern, some say, western lifestyle.

cases of persistent allergic rhinitis among children have doubled over the past 20 years.

Identifying patients

Nobody can miss the person who walks into the consulting room suffering from nasal congestion. The challenge here is to make the correct diagnosis and prescribe appropriate and effective therapy.

A person presenting with a streaming nose, itchy eyes and nose and sneezing is typical of a patient who is affected seasonally, whereas a patient whose main symptom is a blocked nose will typically be suffering from persistent allergic rhinitis.

Not infrequently we also see patients who find their symptoms persist after the pollen season, usually as a response to other nasal mucosal irritants such as tobacco smoke, changes in temperature, various smells and exercise.

All of these troublesome symptoms can lead to chronic problems such as fatigue, low energy, disturbed nights, and even inability to concentrate at work or to learn whilst at school. These patients must be helped and we have the appropriate therapies to do so if we choose and prescribe well.

The most important part of a consultation is to obtain a detailed clinical history. The aim is to identify the allergens and their seasonality and to advise on how best these might be avoided. Many sufferers have associated evidence of atopy such as asthma and eczema, and in some instances allergic skin reactions and a history of drug or food allergies. Relying on skin-prick tests is not generally recommended because they are not widely available and can be time-consuming to perform. Where such tests are available, up to one in five tests give false positive results.

A good physical examination, particularly of the nose, is mandatory. In allergic rhinitis, the nasal mucosa has an oedematous appearance and characteristically is covered by a thin layer of watery secretion. It is important to look for any septal wall abnormalities that would compromise the nasal cavities, and also to check for hypertrophy of the turbinates, nasal polypi or tumours, and foreign bodies.

In general practice, we should never forget that many other local factors (e.g. infection, atrophic rhinitis) or general factors (e.g. pregnancy, hypothyroidism, drugs [antihypertensives, oral contraceptives, non-steroidal anti-inflammatory drugs, aspirin]) as well as environmental factors (e.g. occupational allergens, temperature changes, industrial smells) may be causes of allergic rhinitis.

The most important part of a consultation is to obtain a detailed clinical history. The aim is to identify the allergens and their seasonality and to advise on how best these might be avoided.

Goals and management

What patients want most is freedom from their symptoms and a rapid return to normality. In addition, there is a need to improve other concomitant conditions such as asthma and eczema.

Allergen avoidance

The mainstay of the treatment of allergic rhinitis is avoidance of allergens or reduction of exposure to them. This implies a definite identification of the culprit allergens, which can often be achieved whilst taking the patient's history.

Not all patients are willing to comply with our recommendations. Giving up a pet in order to remove animal dander may be necessary and good practice but can be emotionally upsetting. On the other hand, recommending that someone else cuts the grass may be welcomed by some pollen-sensitive sufferers! Avoiding suspected food allergens can be inconvenient, but is always possible.

Pollen sufferers know that leaving windows open can make them feel worse in the morning when they get up, but few of our homes have air conditioning and this has to be balanced against the downside of sleeping in a hot, stuffy bedroom. Remember, the objective is to restore normality, not to incarcerate our patients. Vacuum cleaners with special filters, air pollen filters and other measures in the house can prove very helpful. A very important step is to have an environment that is free of cigarette smoke, both at work and at home. Table 1 lists some useful advice that can be given to parents for reducing sensitivity to house dust mites in affected children. Many cars these days have effective pollen filters fitted as part of their air-conditioning units, which can provide patients with a certain amount of freedom.

Desensitisation injections

A good number of us can remember the time when we routinely treated pollen allergy with desensitisation injections. The aim was to produce a blocking IgG antibody that would prevent antigen binding to IgE. I must say, this method was often successful, but the risk of anaphylaxis has caused it to be more or less abandoned in primary care. We are hoping that, in the future, special vaccines will produce similar and possibly better results with significantly fewer side-effects.

> The mainstay of the treatment of allergic rhinitis is avoidance of allergens or reduction of exposure to them.

Table 1. Advice to parents for reducing sensitivity to house-dust and house-dust mites.

- Keep the child out of the room while cleaning.
- Use a damp/dust-attracting cloth to clean surfaces.
- Replace feather pillows and eiderdowns/duvets with synthetic alternatives.
- Pillows manufactured since 1985 are washable; wash them at least every 6 months.
- Enclose the top and sides of the mattress in a dust-proof cover and dust the cover regularly.
- Use sheets and blankets that can be washed at over 55°C, hot enough to kill mites.
- Vacuum the mattress, pillows, base of the bed and floor thoroughly; if you are using dust-proof covers, simply damp dust them when the sheets are changed.
- Change and wash pillowcases, sheets and underblankets weekly. Wipe all surfaces (pelmet tops, window sill, cupboards) with a cloth.
- If the child is attracted to a stuffed toy, put that toy in the freezer for 6 hours once a week.
- Replace woollen blankets with synthetic or cotton cellular quilts or blankets and wash them frequently.
- Use light washable curtains and wash them frequently. Roller or vertical blinds are an alternative.
- Use plastic or woollen rather than upholstered furniture.
- Have synthetic/nylon rather than woollen carpets.
- Consider the use of a house-dust-mite control spray (e.g. Actomite) for the carpet, settee, curtains and mattress in the child's room.
- Use a vacuum cleaner with disposable paper bags, ideally with a special fine filter that retains dust mites and their particles.
- Vacuum upholstered furniture twice a week, particularly headrests, arms and edges of seats.
- Keep clothes in a closed cupboard.
- Keep dust-gathering objects such as ornaments, books, cassettes, toys and wall hangings to a minimum.
- Do not shake rags indoors.
- Do not use room humidifiers, and keep humidity below 50% if possible.
- Sleep with a window open. Mites need humidity to thrive, so opening the window at night and airing the bed during the day is good practice.
- Keep animals out of the child's bedroom.

Pharmacological therapies

Pharmacological therapies are effective overall, and work mainly by preventing mast cell degranulation or inhibiting/blocking the effect caused by released mediators. Patients find these therapies generally easy to administer topically or systemically.

Topical corticosteroids administered as sprays or drops are popular because they effectively control symptoms of rhinorrhoea, sneezing, nasal blockage and itching, with some of them achieving control with a single daily administration. As such, they form the mainstay of conservative treatment of allergic rhinitis. If topical corticosteroids are used in children, we need to monitor the height of the children and general growth if use is prolonged. In addition, because of their possible systemic absorption of varying degrees, particularly when used in high doses or when treatment is prolonged, a number of GPs try children on topical sodium cromoglycate.

Topical antihistamines are generally less effective than topical steroids but are more effective than topical sodium cromoglycate. Where allergic rhinitis is associated with vasomotor rhinitis (predominance of the non-allergic parasympathetic autonomic nerve supply of the nasal mucosa), the addition of topical nasal ipratropium bromide can reduce rhinorrhoea.

Oral antihistamines have the advantage of convenient administration so they are most welcome by patients who do not wish to or are not so good at applying topical nasal treatment. They are effective in reducing runny, itchy noses and sneezing but only relatively effective in unblocking congested noses. They are therefore particularly useful in controlling intermittent allergic rhinitis. Side-effects are more common with the older oral antihistamines. The newer antihistamines are less able to cross the blood–brain barrier and thus are generally non-sedating, which is a distinct advantage in patients who drive, work or attend school.

Some patients have greater needs than others. What do you do for a pupil/student with allergic rhinitis who is taking important examinations, or for individuals getting married? Furthermore, what about patients who must have quick relief for one reason or another, or who are starting a course of a topical corticosteroid therapy when there is a need first to relieve severe mucosal oedema and allow the spray to penetrate the nasal cavity? These are cases where a short course of *systemic corticosteroids* will do nicely!

Finally, not infrequently we are consulted by patients using complementary therapies, usually in the form of herbal medicine/remedies, nutritional supplements, homeopathy or acupuncture. We have no clinical evidence that these complementary therapies work, but if the patient experiences no side-effects I see no reason to discourage them from using these. If anything, they are at least benefiting from the placebo effect.

Conclusion

Allergic rhinitis is a troublesome condition which affects patients' lives in varying degrees. Recognition and management rely heavily on obtaining a good clinical history and examination. Effective therapies are available but these must be carefully selected for the individual patient. In intermittent allergic rhinitis, consideration should be given to starting treatment 1–3 weeks before the anticipated onset of symptoms whilst in persistent allergic rhinitis, treatment may have to be prolonged.

Recognition and management rely heavily on obtaining a good clinical history and examination.

Key points

- Allergic rhinitis should not be regarded as a trivial complaint. Its symptoms can be particularly debilitating for a substantial number of patients and it can disrupt education and lead to lost productivity at work.

- The seasonal nature of a substantial number of cases of allergic rhinitis imposes a major burden on GPs' surgeries. By employing appropriate practical strategies, we can strive to improve patient care, and ultimately reduce this addition to our workload.

- Allergic rhinitis is highly prevalent and is becoming even more common, with the spread of more modern lifestyles.

- Patient management should begin with a good clinical history and appropriate physical examination.

- Symptoms can be controlled by reducing exposure to the precipitating allergen (for example using air pollen filters and vacuum cleaners with special filters).

- A number of drug treatments are also available to control symptoms and are reasonably effective in this regard. The newer generation antihistamines combine good efficacy with good safety profiles and are non-sedating.

2. Alzheimer's dementia

Dr Ian Greaves MBChB BDS BMsc MRCGP
General Practitioner, Gnosall, Stafford

Summary

Dementia is a debilitating condition which impacts greatly on patients and their families. Although the prevalence of dementia is increasing as a result of increased longevity and social demographic changes, most family physicians may only encounter one or two new cases annually. As a result, many GPs are unaware of how to diagnose and manage the condition effectively, despite being ideally placed within the patient community to identify early signs of the illness. Although these may be difficult to define, physicians should look for signs of deterioration of cognitive (short-term memory) and non-cognitive abilities (depression, delusions, behavioural changes) and difficulties in performing activities of daily living (dressing, shopping). The acetylcholinesterase inhibitors offer effective relief from the symptoms of dementia with the greatest benefit observed for those patients in whom treatment is initiated rapidly following formal diagnosis. Although the improvement following drug treatment can be dramatic, some patients continue to steadily deteriorate. In spite of this, long-term data suggest that continued treatment may benefit all patients by improving quality of life and delaying nursing home placement. Patients and their carers should be well advised of the many support groups and facilities available within the community and should be kept fully informed as to the likely course of disease progression and treatment expectations.

The challenge of dementia in primary care

Family physicians with an interest in dementia are few and far between. The Audit Commission in their *Forget Me Not* report of 2000 have shown that more than half of the GPs surveyed admitted that they did not know enough about dementia. Only 48% of those surveyed felt that they had received sufficient training to help them diagnose and manage dementia effectively and only 54% recognised the importance of actively looking for early signs of dementia.

More than half of GPs surveyed admitted that they did not know enough about dementia.

Negative attitudes persist amongst many family doctors with regard to the reporting of an early diagnosis of dementia, partly due to the distress that is evoked in patients and their families when they receive a positive diagnosis. However, a clear message needs to be communicated to family physicians: patients with dementia are interesting, challenging and rewarding to treat, and a proactive caring approach can greatly enhance their patient's and their family's or carer's quality of life.

The majority of patients diagnosed with dementia are managed in the community. It is therefore vitally important that this problem is seen as one that principally affects people who live in the community and who only rarely visit healthcare professionals for advice or management. As such, the primary healthcare team are probably best placed to identify patients with early signs of dementia.

Dementia has an enormous impact not only on the patient but also on their family and carers and society as a whole. Indeed the social pathology of dementia can dominate the management of these patients and can enhance or restrict their care plans. The stigma associated with dementia and its negative image as a chronic debilitating disease that has no cure with only very limited therapies has an enormous effect on both the public perception of the condition and the attitude of healthcare professionals.

Dementia is a syndrome with many causes. It may be easier to think of it as 'brain failure' in order to overcome some of the negative perceptions that exist amongst healthcare workers. Dementia then becomes comfortable and manageable rather than foreboding. Healthcare workers are used to dealing with patients who have heart failure and most family doctors feel comfortable with its diagnosis and management despite its multiple causes and poor prognosis.

There is also a significant misconception by a lot of community healthcare workers that dementia is only a problem where the patient has memory lapses. Given that the brain is an essential organ, failure of function produces dramatic effects beyond memory lapses.

Practical strategies in dementia care

Expressions of dementia

There are three main features that GPs should be aware of when establishing a diagnosis of dementia. These are outlined below.

Cognitive deficits

Cognitive expressions of dementia initially begin as a reduction in short-term memory, euphemistically referred to as 'senior moments'. Most people develop compensation mechanisms such as confabulation, social ritual or become grumpy. As such, it can be extremely difficult to spot early changes. There are also changes in the ability to perform and interact socially. The reduction in verbal reasoning and loss of language skills can also result in social isolation.

Non-cognitive features

Non-cognitive features associated with dementia include depression, hallucinations, delusions, misidentifications and behavioural disturbances. Such features may be accompanied by agitation, aggression, wandering and sexual disinhibition, or these symptoms can occur independently. Behavioural changes with wandering, aggression and inappropriate behaviour usually herald a stage where coping at home becomes impossible, leading to a need for structured care in an appropriate setting.

Declining function

Further deterioration of brain function impacts on activities of daily living (ADLs), increasing the dependence of the patient upon others to look after them to survive. The patient presents with difficulties in feeding, dressing, toileting and activities such as using money, shopping or making telephone calls.

The burden of dementia in primary care

Most family physicians with a list of about 2000 patients will see about one or two new cases of dementia each year. As such, it is by no means a common condition. However, increased longevity and social demographic changes mean that dementia is going to become an increasing problem in the future. As a rule of thumb, the incidence of dementia doubles every five years in patients over 60 years: only 1% of the 60–64 year age group are affected, whereas dementia can be diagnosed in approximately 30% of all people aged 90 years.

Although its incidence is relatively low compared to say chest infections or cardiovascular disease, the problem of dementia represents an enormous drain on our resources and time. Several agencies are usually involved in the care programme and therefore the care plans set up to manage our patients demand good communication and multidisciplinary working practices.

Dementia management

Early diagnosis of dementia is essential as there is a new range of drugs available – the acetylcholinesterase inhibitors – that have been shown to have symptomatic benefit (in terms of cognition, behaviour and function) in this debilitating condition. These drugs seem to work better if we can introduce them at the earliest stage possible. Unfortunately the average time between suspicion of dementia and formal diagnosis can be several years.

Early diagnosis is also helpful in planning services for individuals including the initiation of other treatments for non-cognitive symptoms. These interventions should include psychosocial approaches and maintenance of patients' independence by environmental manipulation. Social interaction can be improved with activity programmes and other interventions. It is important that a thorough assessment is also made to distinguish between dementia, depression and other confusional states. However, the differential diagnosis between dementia and other conditions is usually completed by secondary care services. The GP can help by checking the results of a full blood count, a biochemical screen and midstream specimen of urine. The results of these should be included in the referral letter.

The National Institute for Clinical Excellence (NICE) insists that only specialists should initiate acetylcholinesterase inhibitor treatment in patients with Alzheimer's disease. In contrast the Scottish Intercollegiate Guidelines Network (SIGN) encourages GPs to diagnose dementia and prescribe acetylcholinesterase inhibitors in straightforward cases. In addition, if GPs are to be involved in repeat prescribing, the guidance recommends they should do so only under an agreed shared care protocol with a clear end point. This means that monitoring and prescribing of acetylcholinesterase drugs in the community needs a carefully constructed integrated approach that uses group protocols and shared care arrangements. One of the milestones of the National Service Framework (NSF) for Older People is the production and implementation of shared care protocols for dementia. Most patients find access to secondary care more difficult than primary care and a more integrated service could therefore reduce the delay in diagnosis and thereby improve outcomes and compliance.

Although the labelling for the acetylcholinesterase inhibitors states that this class of drugs is indicated for symptomatic treatment there is a growing body of evidence to suggest that additional non-cholinergic actions may have additional benefits. Mild Alzheimer's disease is usually associated with a mini-mental state examination (MMSE) score of 21–26 and moderate disease with a score of between 10 and 20. Severe disease is considered to exist when the MMSE is below 10. Donepezil, rivastigmine and

> Most patients find access to secondary care difficult and a more integrated service could therefore reduce the delay in diagnosis and thereby improve outcomes and compliance.

galantamine are all licensed for the treatment of mild-to-moderate Alzheimer's disease. It is currently recommended by NICE that treatment should not continue in patients in whom the MMSE has fallen below 12, although this guidance is due to be reviewed in 2005. However, withdrawal of these drugs can be problematic when we consider the expectations of a patient's family and carers. Such concerns can be minimised by the use of an explicit care plan that sets out the benchmarks of treatment interventions. It is best to avoid sudden changes and inform all individuals concerned of proposed changes in treatment.

Practical strategies for early diagnosis

Early diagnosis of dementia in routine care is difficult but not impossible. Firstly we need to get the message out to the community that early presentation helps. Obviously, the target population is the elderly. In our area we often go and talk at older people's clubs and social functions. If doctors cannot afford the time then there are plenty of volunteers in the Alzheimer's Society. The message needs to be upbeat and exciting to combat the negative image that prevails at present. We already do a lot of things well. For example, we can manage cardiovascular risk factors, encourage mental exercises, review medications to minimise the use of drugs with cholinergic side-effects and can treat concomitant conditions.

We can also use our position as family doctors to identify the early clinical signs of dementia. The elderly are seen much more often than other patients, and if doctors don't see them there are others in the primary healthcare team who do. The over 75s get seen by someone at least once a year. It's a case of having appropriate suspicion and knowing the patients well. What you are looking for is change. Remember some of the brighter people can exhibit a considerable change in their cognitive powers whilst others may have less of a change, but the fall off takes them below the coping level and becomes noticeable.

The advent of the new GP contract means we are now screening everyone for cardiovascular disease. Those at a high risk of arteriosclerosis are also at a high risk of vascular dementia. These high-risk patients regularly get examined and have bloods taken for baseline renal and lipid levels. They may even undergo an electrocardiogram (ECG), as it is easy then to spot the difference when they have an acute event. This affords us an opportunity to add in a cognitive test to the cardiovascular assessment to spot changes when they do occur. Remember though that vascular dementia has a pattern of sudden decline and plateaus, whereas decline in Alzheimer's disease is gradual and progressive.

The Royal College of General Practitioners strongly recommend that GPs should be at the forefront of identifying dementia in older patients. In general they recommend that cognitive function be assessed in a systematic way. They recommend the following assessments, with a warning of cultural specificity:

- ask the patient the time to the nearest hour (orientation)
- give the patient an address to recall at the end of the test; the patient should repeat the address to ensure that it has been heard correctly (recall)
- ask the patient to count backwards from 20 to 1 (attention)
- ask the patient to draw the face of a clock with the fingers pointing at ten to eleven.

If the patient fails any of these initial assessments it is then necessary to move on to a full assessment.

The facilities for looking after the elderly and especially those with dementia vary across the globe. In affluent countries the state offers both financial and physical help through the social services agencies. This can range from care plans designed to keep the patient at home through to some form of assisted, residential or nursing home accommodation.

In poorer countries the responsibility for care of the elderly falls entirely on the family. It is perceived as their responsibility to look after their relatives and this can cause an enormous strain. However, this model is fine as long as there are sufficient numbers of younger family members to support their elders.

Unfortunately, in richer countries the burden of eldercare is falling onto a smaller workforce, necessitating a greater role for the family in patients' care. This is borne out of the marked change in social demography as the population lives longer. Moreover, we have yet to experience the consequences of the post-war baby boomers reaching retirement age and the likely impact this will have on healthcare services.

Drug treatment

The rationale for early initiation of acetylcholinesterase inhibitor treatment is to delay the debilitating effects of this disease, improve quality of life for both patient and carer and to keep the patient in the community for longer. Intergenerational tensions arise as families struggle with the competing demands of a busy work life, childcare and eldercare. As a result there is a greater need for state provision often involving a complex series of care agencies. Therefore, not only are there sound clinical reasons for early intervention with acetylcholinesterase inhibitors, but economic arguments also exist supporting such an approach.

The prescription and monitoring of acetylcholinesterase inhibitors is an essential element of the care plan for dementia. The guidance from NICE indicates that patients' prescriptions should only be renewed if they are stabilised or continue to show improvement and this, therefore, demands an assessment of the patient's condition. The standardised MMSE for all its faults is still considered to be the best tool for this purpose. However, most clinicians feel that the MMSE alone does not give a good picture of the function of the patient and they therefore combine it with a good history taken from the patient's carer and an assessment of ADLs. The 'clock draw' test (discussed previously) is another good addition when monitoring a patient, and by comparing previous attempts of this task, it is an excellent visual assessment of disease progression.

The response to drug treatment can be dramatic, but some patients continue to deteriorate in a steady decline. Others show an initial response followed by deterioration below baseline.

Recent long-term data suggest that, as with many other conditions, there are continued benefits with continued treatment even if there is a decline in an individual's symptoms. We don't withdraw treatment when a patient's blood pressure starts to rise again or if diabetic control is lost. Even in the face of decline in dementia, continued treatment is associated with slower rate of decline, better quality of life and a delay to nursing home placement.

Patients treated with acetylcholinesterase inhibitors may experience a range of side-effects but common ones include gastrointestinal symptoms of dyspepsia, nausea and vomiting and diarrhoea, and the central neurological symptoms of fatigue, insomnia and dizziness. Most patients tolerate these side-effects or can be managed with appropriate dose titration. In some cases treatment discontinuation or a switch to an alternative cholinesterase may be necessary. The GP is also ideally placed to take into account other medical conditions in which cholinergic stimulation may have an effect. Such effects are common in the elderly population and include supraventricular cardiac conduction disorders, asthma and reversible airways disease, bladder outflow disorders and seizures. Patients with these comorbidities should be reviewed more regularly and in more detail. The renal function of the patient should also be monitored, as patients with moderate renal impairment will require lower daily doses.

Donepezil can be given in a once-daily regimen and, as such, this may improve patients' compliance. The side-effect profile is dose related but the maximum dose is 10 mg. The dose range of rivastigmine is more complex and requires twice-daily dosing and a gradual titration. However, it has dual

The rationale for early initiation of acetylcholinesterase inhibitor treatment is to delay the debilitating effects of this disease and to keep the patient in the community for longer.

inhibitory effects on both acetylcholinesterase and butyrylcholinesterase in the brain. Unlike the other acetylcholinesterase inhibitors, rivastigmine has minimal potential for drug–drug interactions. Galantamine inhibits acetylcholinesterase and also modifies nicotinic cholinergic receptors. Thus, although all agents increase levels of acetylcholine in the brain, they also exhibit different individual non-cholinergic pharmacology.

Other services for patients with dementia

Drug treatments are only one arm of the therapeutic management of Alzheimer's disease. Any treatment plan should also include a comprehensive assessment of all the patients and their carer's needs.

Admiral nurses (specialist dementia nurses, working in the community, with families, carers and supporters) and community care teams that include mental health nurses, social workers and other support agencies offer carer support and it has been shown that timely intervention can prevent social breakdown. These teams can add focused and appropriate support required by patients' families.

Care plans should include the provision of respite and day-care services. The reduction in the financial viability of nursing homes has caused a lot of these facilities to close and has reduced the availability of good respite care. This is short sighted as the burden of care on the relatives rather than the severity of the dementia is often the determinant of permanent residential care admission.

The voluntary agencies are an invaluable resource in managing the care of dementia patients in the community. They provide a range of services from patient and carer education, support and advocacy through to befriending and sitting services. The voluntary workers frequently have a wealth of experience as they may have cared for their own relatives with dementia. Charitable societies such as the Alzheimer's Society provide a vast range of skilled and informed people to help with dementia.

Occupational therapists can assess the home of patients with dementia to provide aids and adaptations that manipulate the environment to help maintain independence. There has been an enormous amount of research that focuses on the abilities rather than the disabilities of people suffering from dementia. Dementia patients seem to do best in a friendly and familiar environment. Such things as the use of good lighting and primary colour decoration can be particularly beneficial. Familiar furniture contemporary with the time that the patient was at the peak of their performance has also been shown to be helpful.

Although communication through written and verbal language is reduced, patients with dementia can be stimulated with music and other art forms. The brain is a complex organ and there are many alternative ways of compensating for a reduced function. Such therapies certainly have a place in the rehabilitation of patients in the community.

The primary–secondary care interface

All patients who have been diagnosed with dementia in the community are referred to secondary care and in the majority of cases the service they get is excellent. It is very important that young patients with cognitive impairment (<60 yrs) should be referred to secondary care as a matter of urgency as the likelihood of non-dementia pathology is far higher. Secondary care services are not dissimilar to primary care in that they are stretched to breaking point. It is unfortunate that over a third of the family doctors in the UK surveyed in the *Forget Me Not* report felt that they did not have ready access to specialist advice. Specialist teams for older people with mental health problems were fully available in less than half of all areas and partly available in a further third. Additionally, the majority of secondary care teams did not have a full complement of recommended core team members. NICE imposes a further burden on these services by only allowing specialists to initiate cholinesterase inhibitors.

The common sense approach to overcome these problems would seem to be to help each other. The 'carve out' model where a consultant assumes the care of a patient until they eventually die cannot be sustainable. Nor does the prevalence of the disease justify the transfer of memory clinics into primary care. Domiciliary visits increase costs and, whilst giving the consultant first hand experience of the social arrangements of the patient, may actually serve to lengthen waiting times. So the future of dementia care may be to come together to produce clearly defined pathways of care. This will serve to break down the tribal barriers of service provision improve consistency and rapidity of diagnosis and set out best practice for management. This does not necessarily mean us doing anything different – just smarter.

In my own family practice the adult psychiatrists run the outpatient clinics at our surgery. This has reduced the stigma of the condition and brought the services closer to the patient. Moreover, the failures to attend have reduced from 30 to 1%. As family doctors we have gained in confidence in the diagnosis and treatment of a lot of other common psychiatric problems – it is amazing how much is diffused subconsciously into a doctor's brain over a cup of coffee with a consultant colleague. Similarly the background information we can offer to specialists is vital and is much better given verbally than in a three-page letter of referral. It is easy for us to help to prepare the patient for a consultant opinion both in the physical work-up with the blood tests and other things that need to be done. We can also use our position as the trusted family doctor to help them understand the process and guide them through the multidisciplinary assessments that lie in front of them. We already share resources – our practice nurses, community nurses, health visitors and their community psychiatric nurses (CPNs), elderly mentally infirm (EMI) beds, respite services, day hospitals and other therapeutic options.

Surely this is best way forward for the elderly mentally ill. I am convinced we would use joined up thinking to agree mutual pathways of care with family doctors doing the things we are good at and get the best out of our consultant colleagues. It does not have to be as formal as outreach clinics. Perhaps we can agree to look at particular groups to get earlier identification of patients with suspected dementia and improve the quality of referral with all the basic investigations done. We can then monitor consultant-initiated therapies and enact treatment plans. We already do this for diabetics and for patients with cardiovascular disease. In turn the consultants would see our new referrals more quickly and bail us out if we phone them in a panic. However, Primary Care Trusts would have to acknowledge the effect of the change of prescribing on the drug budgets of GPs, given that the cost of treatment is approximately £800–1000 per patient per year.

Key points

- It is important that the primary healthcare team, as the first point of contact for many elderly patients, is able to recognise the early signs of dementia and instigate an effective programme of management.

- The deterioration of short-term memory and verbal reasoning, mood changes, behavioural abnormalities and difficulty performing activities of daily living all represent characteristic features of dementia.

- A proactive caring approach can greatly enhance patients' and caregivers' quality of life and can be both rewarding and interesting for the physician.

- Patients' families in particular may benefit from the level of specialist support offered by Admiral nurses and community care teams, which represent an invaluable resource in disease management.

- Addressing elderly audiences through social and community groups will increase the awareness of dementia and its early symptoms and may help to combat the negative image associated with mental illness.

- Early diagnosis can be aided by initiating a full blood count, a biochemical screen and a midstream specimen of urine, the results of which should be incorporated into the referral letter.

- Combining the MMSE with a clock-drawing exercise provides a more visual representation of disease progression.

- Drug treatment may dramatically slow disease progression in some patients whilst others may continue to deteriorate. Continued treatment may still benefit the patient, even if there is a decline in their symptoms.

- The discontinuation of drug treatment following a sudden deterioration in mental status, in line with current guidelines, should be fully explained in advance to the patient's family and carers.

3. Angina

Dr John Pittard BSc MSc BM BCh
Hospital Practitioner, Cardiology, St Peter's Hospital,
Chertsey General Practitioner, Staines, Middlesex

Summary

New models of care are constantly evolving within general practice. This is perhaps best exemplified by the management of chronic conditions such as coronary heart disease (CHD) and angina, particularly with the emergence of nationwide strategies such as the National Service Framework (NSF) for CHD and the introduction of the new General Medical Services (GMS) contract. Given the symptomatic nature of angina, the condition is likely to present initially to a GP, and then patient care will be managed according to protocols agreed between primary and secondary care. However, the size of the practice is likely to be a major determinant in how a patient is managed in reality. Angina is a common condition, with the average primary-care practice expecting to see about 10 new cases a year in addition to managing up to 100 patients with existing disease. Treatment of the condition focuses on symptom control and reducing the risk of future occlusive thrombotic events. Management should include lifestyle advice and a range of pharmacotherapies including lipid-lowering agents, antithrombotics and antihypertensives. The GMS contract demands that such details are recorded on the practice computer systems when managing patients with angina.

The primary care environment

The traditional model of the doctor–patient process has been supplemented over the past decade by the evolution of the primary-care team and the availability of systematic disease management plans. Perhaps this is best exemplified by the management of CHD and angina. An individual patient with suspected angina will engage in the doctor–patient model initially, but further investigations and diagnosis will increasingly follow care pathways that are agreed between primary and secondary care. Prevention programmes will then be initiated. Whilst there is no prescriptive model for primary care, these general principles remain universal.

The introduction of the new GMS contract in 2003–4 will reinforce and develop the systematic identification, diagnosis and management of patients with CHD and angina.

Local considerations, such as practice size, staffing, professional training and professional interests, will determine how the pattern of management is implemented. The introduction of the new General Medical Services (GMS) contract in 2003–4 will reinforce and develop the systematic identification, diagnosis and management of patients with CHD and angina. The new GMS contract has substantial overlap with existing arrangements, for example the National Service Framework (NSF) for CHD in England and its variants in Scotland and Wales.

Angina in primary care

Case finding in symptomatic diseases like angina is generally easier than that for largely asymptomatic conditions such as hypertension. Thus, the majority of angina cases will declare themselves rather than us having to seek them out, though a small proportion imagine that they have indigestion! Where chest pain occurs against a background of risk factors, for example smoking or type 2 diabetes, there should be a high index of suspicion.

The incidence, and thus prevalence, of angina will be determined by social and demographic data. The Standardised Morbidity Ratio (SMR) will range from around 80 in rural communities to around 140 in urban deprived areas of northern parts of the UK. From these national figures, an individual practice population of around 2000 patients would be predicted to generate about 5–10 new cases annually, with about ten times as many chronic cases.

Recent primary care computer-based audits in most good or average practices indicate that around two-thirds of CHD cases are presently collated on computer-based CHD registers. As the new GMS contract becomes more familiar, this proportion is likely to expand.

The usual methods of searching for cases include records of chest pain and ECG, or computer entries for hospital attendance. Drug searches for nitrates, β-blockers, calcium-channel blockers and nicorandil will also assist in identifying further cases. New patient medical notes and their histories in addition to hospital cases should also be added to the computer-based CHD register. Full practice staff meetings and training can help all members of the primary care team look for opportunities to add to and validate the CHD register.

Individual clinical case management

Angina is essentially a symptom rather than a disease *per se*. For practical purposes, asymptomatic reversible heart ischaemia is unlikely to be a concern in primary care, unless the patient has breathlessness upon effort but without chest pain.

Established cases of angina may typically be quite stable whilst on medication and only require repeat prescriptions or perhaps annual blood tests and regular medical review. Where hypertension or diabetes is comorbid with angina, patients should also be monitored according to the protocols for these associated conditions.

The practice size is likely to determine the type of clinical review system. For example, in smaller practices a typical model will often involve shared risk-factor management, and will involve practice nurses or nurse practitioners working with a GP with an interest in the field, to common and agreed care plans. The systematic aspects of the NSF for CHD (or its national equivalent), together with targets for risk registers and therapy goals from the new GMS contract, will harmonise the clinical management of cases across primary care.

New-onset cases will usually require a resting electrocardiogram (ECG) and the use of secondary care services (Table 1). In stable angina, the resting ECG can often be normal, though further tests may indicate coronary insufficiency. For suspected new-onset stable angina, rapid-access chest pain clinics will be the usual route of referral. Currently, over half of all district general hospitals operate these clinics, representing welcome and tangible evidence of government investment translating into clinical care. Usually, suitable cases will be seen within 2 weeks of referral. A specialist cardiac history and an examination to exclude uncontrolled serious hypertension and aortic stenosis will be followed by an exercise test. Local referral protocols will have guidance on which are the most suitable cases to send to chest pain clinics. However, exclusion of young females (<40 years and without a family

> The systematic aspects of the NSF for CHD will harmonise the clinical management of cases across primary care.

> For suspected new-onset stable angina, rapid-access chest pain clinics will be the usual route of referral.

Table 1. Elements of rapid access referral work-up for stable angina in primary care.	
Family history	Early coronary artery disease (<60 years)
	Hypertension
	Diabetes
	Hyperlipidaemia
Useful investigations	Full blood count
	Fasting blood sugar
	Fasting lipid profile
	Resting ECG (if available)
Record	Current medication (whether unsuccessful or poorly tolerated)
	Cardiovascular therapy

history of stable angina) and the elderly immobile is usual, as exercise testing is inappropriate in such cases. Patients unable to walk on a treadmill can be referred for consultant advice on possible thallium scanning assessment. Direct referral to a consultant rather than a rapid-access chest pain clinic would, however, be more likely to result in optimum clinical management.

Irrespective of the route of referral, the essential need is to confirm a diagnosis of suspected angina. The expert secondary opinion will attempt to decide upon ischaemia as a cause of the chest pain. Severe cases will have ST-depression on ECG after modest exercise. Suitable cases will proceed to coronary angiography. In older patients (75 years or older), the risks of invasive testing and lack of evidence for an improvement in prognosis by coronary artery bypass graft (CABG) suggests that maximal medical management is the first-line action. Refractory symptoms may be suitable for surgical intervention, particularly where angioplasty can avoid serious complications from CABG procedures.

Established angina cases

The GMS contract and latest treatment guidelines place a lot of emphasis on the diagnosis and management of new cases of angina. However, primary care registers will already include large numbers of stable diagnosed cases. Some of these cases may require review if the original diagnosis is unsupported by further clinical investigation. Others may develop worsening symptoms, which may also necessitate review. In either case, the bulk of these established cases will be managed in primary care.

Elderly patients with stable angina (75 years or older) can usually be safely reviewed by the primary-care practice team, and this is always preferable. Practice-nurse led clinics can review lifestyle and secondary prevention medication effectively, whilst GPs will usually review and adjust patients' symptomatic treatment.

Primary care treatment options

The primary goals of treatment are to reduce symptoms and reduce immediate and future risks of thrombotic vascular occlusion. A number of clinical trials and treatment guidelines provide recommendations which focus on both these goals.

There are a number of drug classes available for symptomatic management of stable angina, ideally involving β-blockers, nitrates, calcium- and potassium-channel blockers. However, the use of multiple drugs places a compliance challenge on these patients. Wherever possible, combination therapy such as diuretic/antihypertensive drugs and the use of nicorandil in place of nitrates and calcium-channel blockers should be considered in order to reduce the tablet burden.

The preventive programmes for angina patients are identical to all high-risk post-MI cases. Indeed, many patients will have both histories. Modifications of diet and exercise, and smoking cessation are critical, but in many cases are difficult to achieve. Nicotine replacement therapy (NRT) should be approached with caution as angina can be worsened. However, the paramount need to quit smoking may require specialist support to prescribe NRT where the patient is fully informed of its risk–benefit relative to a failure to quit.

Systematic angina management in primary care: the new GMS contract

The new GMS contract has shifted funding away from capital projects towards primary care to provide an incentive to pursue systematic process objectives. What this means for data collection and the management of CHD secondary prevention is summarised in Table 2.

Angina cases are at an equivalent risk to established post-MI cases, where the risk is greater than 30% over ten years. All cases will require the recording of smoking status, together with a record of the support offered for cessation. The other parameters that should be documented are all evidence based and concern the appropriate use of lipid lowering agents, antithrombotics, blood pressure management, and β-blockers and angiotensin-converting enzyme (ACE) inhibitors. The main evidence base has been the Scottish Intercollegiate Guidelines Network (SIGN) guidelines. These are web based and accessible at *http://www.sign.ac.uk/ guidelines/fulltext/51/index.html*

Angina has been given specific mention for new cases (post-April 2003) in the new GMS contract. Thus, exercise testing and/or specialist referral is given GMS points from 25% through to 90%. The current funding will be £75 per point rising to £120 per point in 2006. These funds will come directly into the practice and support the increased staff costs related to implementing systematic care and patient review. In the GMS contract, angina is specifically identified as requiring specialist confirmation of diagnosis together with prognostic assessment. In general, younger and fitter patients require assessment for their suitability to undergo angiography. Those with triple vessel disease can be offered CABG or angioplasty when the risk–benefit favours this action. Beyond the age of 75, the prognosis is not improved with these procedures, principally due to the downside of procedural complications. All cases will require intensive

All cases will require intensive lifestyle and secondary prevention measures.

Table 2. Secondary prevention in coronary heart disease (CHD): the new GMS contract (adapted from The New GMS Contract 2003: Investing in General Practice at *http://www.bma.org.uk/ap.nsf/Content/NewGMSContract/$file/gpcontractannexa.pdf*)

Indicator	Points	Maximum threshold
Medical records		
CHD1. The practice can produce a register of patients with CHD.	6	
Diagnosis and initial management		
CHD2. The percentage of patients with newly diagnosed angina (after 1/4/03) who are referred for exercise testing and/or specialist assessment.	7	90%
Ongoing management		
CHD3. The percentage of patients with CHD, whose notes record smoking status in the past 15 months, except those who have never smoked where smoking status needs to be recorded only once.	7	90%
CHD4. The percentage of patients with CHD who smoke, whose notes contain a record that smoking cessation advice has been offered within the last 15 months.	4	90%
CHD5. The percentage of patients with CHD, whose notes have a record of blood pressure in the previous 15 months.	7	90%
CHD6. The percentage of patients with CHD, in whom the last blood pressure reading (within the last 15 months) is 150/90 mmHg or less.	19	70%
CHD7. The percentage of patients with CHD whose notes have a record of total cholesterol in the previous 15 months.	7	90%
CHD8. The percentage of patients with CHD whose last total cholesterol (within the last 15 months) is 5 mmol/L or less.	16	60%
CHD9. The percentage of patients with CHD with a record in the last 15 months that aspirin, an alternative antiplatelet, or an anticoagulant is being taken (unless contraindicated or a side-effect recorded).	7	90%
CHD10. The percentage of patients with CHD who are currently treated with a b-blocker (unless contraindicated or a side-effect recorded).	7	50%
CHD11. The percentage of patients with a history of myocardial infarction CHD (after 1/4/03) who are currently treated with an ACE inhibitor.	7	70%
CHD12. The percentage of patients with CHD who have a record of influenza vaccination (1st September–31 March).	7	85%

lifestyle and secondary prevention measures. Whilst the audit standards based on the SIGN guidelines are reasonable and evidence based, the extra workload in primary care will be significant.

Performance audit

The new GMS contract will put angina and CHD management on a robust systematic basis. The link of performance to financial reward should provide the resources necessary for this process and ensure that practices do get some return on their efforts. As a population, patients with stable angina can expect to experience improved uniformity of lifestyle advice and preventive therapy, whilst new cases will be better diagnosed and risk assessed and where appropriate, invasively treated.

The whole process requires effective data recording on practice computers, using specific diagnostic and process codes. Practices will be supported to improve their information technology quality and capacity, whilst specific support staff will be required to supplement the clinical input from nursing and medical team members.

Conclusion

The future management of patients with angina will be largely driven by new funding arrangements and incentives in primary care. The evidence base for patient care is substantial. If implemented fully, this will be likely to decrease the mortality associated with angina but will increase the need for expert primary care. The real challenge that remains is to retain individual clinical relationships with patients who are not naturally concerned with population medical issues. Many patients still rely entirely on primary-care teams to provide support and treatment. They can reasonably expect advice on appropriate lifestyle and therapies, and reasons for referral.

> The evidence base for patient care is substantial. If implemented fully, this will be likely to decrease the mortality associated with angina but will increase the need for expert primary care.

Key points

- Angina is a common symptomatic condition that will present in primary care, generally without the need for active case finding.

- A primary-care practice with a total of 2000 patients can expect to see about 5–10 new cases of angina each year, with chronic cases totalling ten-times this number.

- The size of the practice is a major determinant in the system of care employed when managing patients with angina and may involve nurse-led clinics working with GPs who have a special interest in the field.

- The main objectives of treatment are to reduce the symptoms of angina and the risk of future thrombotic vascular occlusion.

- The GMS contract requires the following details to be recorded when managing angina cases: smoking status and the support offered for smoking cessation, the use of lipid-lowering agents, antithrombotics, blood pressure management, β-blockers and ACE inhibitors. This requires effective data recording on practice computers.

- Developments in care will allow existing patients with angina to receive consistent lifestyle advice and preventive therapy, whilst new cases of angina will be more effectively diagnosed, assessed and treated.

4. Asthma

Kevin Gruffydd-Jones MA (Oxon) BM BCh MRCGP DRCOG Dip Sports Med Dip Occ
Health, General Practitioner, Box, Wiltshire
Honorary Lecturer, University of Bath and University of Aberdee
Member of the General Practice Airways Group

Summary

Despite recent improvements in structured care and the treatment of asthma within the primary-care sector, the condition remains a major burden on limited healthcare resources. Much remains to be done to address misconceptions amongst many clinicians that we have all but conquered this debilitating condition. With asthma not recognised as one of the main clinical priorities in the new NHS plan, making further improvements to its clinical management poses a significant challenge to GPs. There are also other significant barriers to its effective management, including confusion over appropriate diagnostic techniques and patient adherence to treatment. Here, practical solutions relating to improved education, diagnosis, patient communication and clinical audit are proposed to help overcome some of these barriers.

The burden of asthma in general practice

There have been huge improvements in the organisation of asthma care in general practice and in the treatment of asthma over the past two decades. In particular, there has been a significant reduction in asthma mortality – principally due to the widespread use of inhaled steroids – despite a significant rise in the prevalence of the disease during this period. However, asthma continues to represent a huge burden to primary care. For example, an average Primary Care Organisation (PCO) with a population of a third of a million patients can expect to include:

- 45,000 patients with diagnosed asthma
- more than 400 asthma-related emergency admissions to hospital per annum
- eight deaths from asthma per annum.

In addition, there is significant unmet need amongst asthmatics relating to successful treatment, with large surveys indicating that 20–40% of patients still have limitations in their everyday lives as a consequence of their condition, despite receiving active treatment.

What are the barriers to effective asthma management?

1. Professional complacency and lack of government prioritisation

There is a perception amongst health clinicians and administrators that asthma is essentially 'done and dusted'. However, the extent of the problem, as illustrated in the previous section, shows that this is far from true. The antipathy towards organised management of the condition is further reinforced by the fact that asthma is not one of the main priorities identified in the NHS plan. As a result, PCO and practice resources are inevitably diverted towards areas such as cardiovascular disease and diabetes which are the current government priorities.

2. Diagnostic confusion

Asthma continues to be misdiagnosed. In particular, there are significant diagnostic problems at both ends of the age spectrum. For example, the wheezing infant may too readily be given a diagnosis of asthma or inappropriately given antibiotics. Many of our 'asthmatics' over the age of 40 in fact have chronic obstructive pulmonary disease. A recent audit in our practice, which has a strong interest in respiratory disease, showed that fewer than 50% of adult asthmatics had objective evidence of asthma in their records.

3. Poor patient adherence

Non-adherence to treatment is a significant problem in this area, and manifests in two distinct ways:
- poor compliance with preventative medication
- poor compliance with regular review in the surgery.

There is evidence that 50–60% of patients do not fully comply in both of these areas, and this in turn is linked to increased asthma morbidity. The common thread underlying this non-adherence appears to be patients' misconceptions about their asthma. For example, it is common to hear statements from our patients such as: "I'm not bad enough to keep taking my preventer or to need a check-up" or "I've only got asthma when I'm breathless. I don't need to take my preventer all the time".

4. Lack of awareness of current management guidelines

It is perhaps inevitable that general health professionals who are faced with a multitude of disease entities, each with their own clinical guidelines, may not be up to date with them all. To refresh the reader's memory, the management strategies described in this article are based on the 2003 British Guideline on the Management of Asthma (available via *www.brit-thoracic.org.uk*).

What should a practice do to overcome these barriers?

1. Overcoming complacency and improving compliance with review visits

Effective asthma management can be very rewarding for a GP! Asthma is a condition where effective treatment given within primary care can transform people's lives within just a few days. However, organising efficient asthma care within a practice requires more than enthusiasm and demands time and resources. Achieving the quality standards for asthma outlined in the 2003 General Medical Services (GMS) GP contract can partially help this. These indicators are illustrated in Table 1.

Organised asthma care can be established either by dedicated asthma appointments or by an asthma clinic. Increasingly, nurses have taken over this role, but there is evidence that their acquisition of a higher qualification such as an asthma diploma can further reduce asthma morbidity. However, it is equally important that a designated GP works in conjunction with the asthma nurse to reduce the chance of complacency ("we leave asthma management to the nurse") and to avoid 'de-skilling' the GP.

According to diagnostic criteria one of the most difficult quality markers is arranging regular review of our patients. This is perhaps best exemplified by surveys which estimate current non-attendance rates of 50–60% in asthma clinics. There are, however, a number of effective strategies that we can employ to encourage greater attendance. These include:

- reminders on repeat prescriptions
- written reminders (the GMS contract allows a non-attendee to be counted if three written reminders have been sent)
- telephone review (recent and on-going studies are looking at the effectiveness of this system – one criticism though is that it does not allow inhaler technique to be reviewed).

Table 1. Indicators from the 2003 General Medical Services GP contract for asthma management.

Indicator	Points	Maximum threshold
Records		
ASTHMA 1. The practice can produce a register of patients with asthma excluding patients with asthma who have been prescribed no asthma treatment in the last 12 months	7	N/A
Initial management		
ASTHMA 2. The percentage of patients aged 8 years and over diagnosed as having asthma from April 2003 where the diagnosis has been confirmed by spirometry or peak flow measurement	15	70%
Ongoing management		
ASTHMA 3. The percentage of patients with asthma between the ages of 14 and 19 in whom there is a record of smoking status within the previous 15 months.	6	70%
ASTHMA 4. The percentage of patients aged 20 years and over with asthma whose notes record smoking status in the previous 15 months, except those who have never smoked where smoking status should be recorded at least once.	6	70%
ASTHMA 5. The percentage of patients with asthma who smoke and whose notes contain a record that smoking cessation advice has been offered within the last 15 months.	6	70%
ASTHMA 6. The percentage of patients with asthma who have had an asthma review in the last 15 months.	20	70%
ASTHMA 7. The percentage of patients aged 16 years and over with asthma who have had influenza immunisation in the preceding 1 September to 31 March.	12	70%

2. Improving diagnosis

Asthma diagnosis in older children and adults is largely based on a characteristic history and on objective lung function testing. Asthmatics usually present with one or more of cough, chest tightness, shortness of breath or wheeze. Characteristically these symptoms are variable and intermittent, being worse at night and provoked by trigger factors such as exercise or pollen. Although the results of the examination may be normal, it is important to exclude other causes of wheeze, for example, heart failure in the older patient.

Objective tests

The British Thoracic Society/Scottish Intercollegiate Guideline Network (BTS/SIGN) criteria for the objective diagnosis of asthma using peak flow

> **Table 2.** Objective diagnosis of asthma using peak flow/spirometry.
>
> - 20% or greater variability in peak flow (highest − lowest/highest × 100).
> - Persists ideally for 3 days a week over 2 weeks.
> - An increase in FEV_1/PEFR following inhalation of a short-acting β_2-agonist such as 5 mg nebulised salbutamol or 400 mg salbutamol given via a metered-dose inhaler plus spacer.
> - A decrease in FEV_1/PEFR monitored every 10 minutes for 30 minutes after 6–8 minutes of exercise.
> - An increase in FEV_1/PEFR following a trial of oral prednisolone, 30 mg/day for 14 days.[a]
> - With each of the above methods a change of ≥20% PEFR and 60 L/minute or ≥15% FEV_1 and 200 mL provides objective evidence of asthma.
>
> [a]Seldom used in primary care except in cases of uncertainty or where the presenting symptoms are in the form of acute asthma.
> FEV_1, forced expiratory volume in 1 second; PEFR, peak expiratory flow rate.

or spirometry is illustrated in Table 2. In practice, it is often more convenient to carry out β_2-agonist reversibility testing when a patient first presents with asthma-like symptoms. This can provide a rapid diagnosis in addition to therapeutic relief for the patient. Peak flow charts are particularly useful in detecting occupational asthma and demonstrating 'before and after' benefits of preventative therapy. Exercise testing can be carried out by asking the patient to step up and down on an 18-inch high couch step for 6–8 minutes.

Other tests may be of help where doubt persists over the diagnosis. For example, a chest X-ray is advisable in patients presenting for the first time after the age of 45 (especially in smokers) or in areas where there is a high prevalence of TB. Referral to a chest physician is indicated where significant diagnostic doubt persists (where histamine or methacholine challenge test may be carried out) or where occupational asthma is present.

A chest X-ray is advisable in patients presenting for the first time after the age of 45 (especially in smokers) or in areas where there is a high prevalence of TB.

Diagnosing asthma in young children

The diagnosis of asthma in young children is often problematic due to difficulties in performing objective testing in this patient population. Consequently, the diagnosis of asthma in pre-school children is principally based on:

- a suggestive history and high index of suspicion of alternative diagnoses
- assessment of the response to a trial of adequate asthma therapy.

The principal features suggestive of asthma in young children are:
- a recurrent and episodic cough or wheeze

- symptoms triggered by exercise or exposure to animal allergens etc.
- diurnal variation of symptoms
- family history of allergic disease (especially maternal; e.g. asthma, allergic rhinitis or eczema)
- history of atopic eczema in the child
- failure to 'thrive'.

A physical examination is absolutely vital in establishing a diagnosis in young children, as a child with bronchiliolitis or pneumonia can often present with wheeze. An 'adequate trial of therapy' usually involves giving an anti-inflammatory agent for an appropriate length of time. The response to inhaled β_2-agonists at this age can be highly variable and is therefore not used as a diagnostic test.

Inhaled steroids should be given via a large volume spacer with a mask for at least 4 weeks and the symptomatic response assessed. If there is improvement the steroid dose can be reduced to an appropriate level to maintain control (usually 50 µg twice daily). An alternative is to give a 4-week course of montelukast, 4 mg/day. Oral steroids (prednisolone, 20 mg/day, for 3 days) can produce a dramatic improvement in symptoms, but have low specificity for asthma and should not be relied on as a diagnostic test. It is vital that the child is closely followed up and a high index of suspicion held for alternative diagnoses. For example, at one end of the spectrum a child from a non-atopic background who wheezes only when a viral infection is present and is otherwise well is likely to have 'viral-induced wheeze' and thus requires symptomatic treatment only.

3. Improving management

Table 3 shows a scheme for the management of asthma in primary care, from initial presentation to regular review. Management of patients within this scheme occurs over several consultations and should involve both the doctor and the practice nurse.

In pre-school children, as described above, objective testing is unhelpful. A therapeutic trial of inhaled steroids or montelukast should be given. It is likely that more frequent initial visits will be necessary to assess response than with an adult patient.

> In pre-school children, objective testing is unhelpful.

Pharmacological management

Figure 1 illustrates the classic SIGN/BTS step-up approach to asthma management in adults and pre-school children.

The initial pharmacological management of asthma in primary care depends very much on the nature of the initial presentation. All patients

Table 3. Scheme for the management of asthma for adults and older children in primary care.

Visit	
Visit 1	• Initial presentation
	• Provisional diagnosis of asthma on the basis of symptoms and examination
	• Explanation given with appropriate support materials
	• Patient issued with peak flow chart and/or reversibility testing carried out or arranged
	• Additional tests (e.g. chest X-ray if there is doubt over diagnosis)
	• Short-acting β_2-agonist prescribed (or for those with more severe asthma, oral steroids or inhaled steroids may need to be given to obtain control)
Visit 2 (allow 20–30 minutes)	• Confirmation of diagnosis by peak flow chart or reversibility testing
	• Establish severity of asthma and identify possible trigger factors (including smoking)
	• Reiterate explanation, deal with patient concerns and reinforce with self-help information.
	• Establish control of asthma using appropriate pharmacotherapy (see text)
Visit 3	• Review asthma control and adjust medication
	• Check inhaler technique and compliance
	• Discuss non-pharmacological management (e.g. smoking cessation, influenza immunisation, avoidance of trigger factors)
	• Issue asthma action plan
	• Discuss outstanding patient concerns
	• Arrange regular review

will require a short-acting β_2-agonist for relief of symptoms. Inhaled steroids will be needed for patients with persistent night-time and daily symptoms. The majority of patients will show improvements in lung function and symptoms with beclomethasone, 400 μg/day, or equivalent for adults, and 200 μg/day for children.[a] However, if there are problems with drug delivery, a 400 μg dose may be necessary in children under 5 years. Improvements are usually apparent within 48 hours, and then plateau after 4–6 weeks.

Oral steroids may be necessary to obtain control in patients who present with acute severe asthma.

Assessment of asthma control

Asthma control has traditionally been assessed in primary care by looking at changes in lung function or improvements in symptoms. Whilst these

---

[a] Mometasone is not currently recommended for use in children in the UK.

Figure 1. Step-wise pharmacological management of (A) adults and (B) pre-school children with asthma. Adapted from the Scottish Intercollegiate Guidelines Network and the British Thoracic Society British Guideline on the Management of Asthma (*www.brit-thoracic.org.uk/sign/pdf/SIGN63.PDF*).

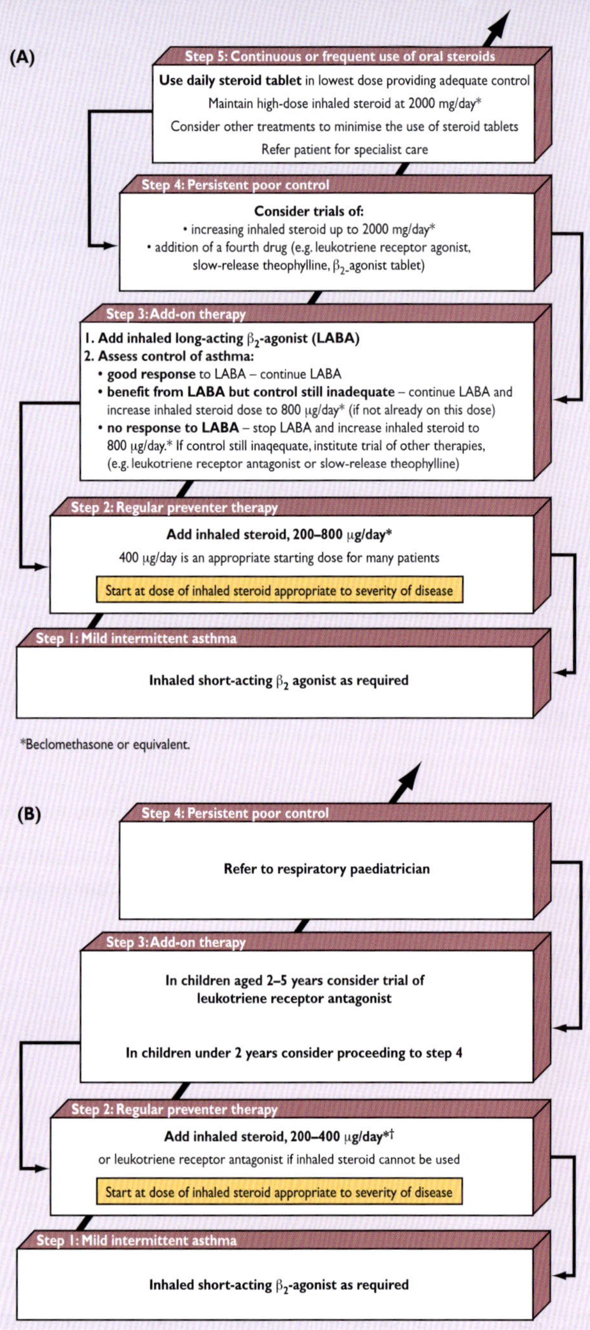

*Beclomethasone or equivalent.
†Higher nominal doses may be necessary in cases where drug delivery is difficult.

remain useful tools, it should be remembered that patients may present with few symptoms because they avoid activities which trigger their asthma. Similarly, patients may experience significant restrictions in their lives as a result of asthma, but have little change in lung function. One useful measure of asthma control is the Royal College of Physicians' Asthma Morbidity Index. At review patients are asked three questions relating to their symptoms in the last week or month.

- Have you had difficulty in sleeping because of your asthma symptoms (including cough)?
- Have you had your usual asthma symptoms in the day?
- Has your asthma interfered with your usual activities (e.g. work, school, housework)?

If there is an affirmative response to any of these questions then the management of the patient should be adjusted. However, before medication is increased the following factors should also be checked:

- inhaler technique
- compliance with medication
- alteration in trigger factors.

The roles of various controller therapies are considered in the following sections.

Inhaled steroids

Inhaled steroid therapy is the cornerstone of asthma management and has been shown to improve lung function, symptoms and quality of life, and reduce exacerbations. For the majority of patients seen in general practice, inhaled steroids are generally safe and effective below the maximum daily dosage recommendations.

The choice of inhaled steroid largely depends on the choice of inhaler device and cost. There is some evidence that beclomethasone may exhibit more short-term growth suppression in young children than low-dose budesonide or fluticasone.

Long-acting inhaled β_2 agonists/combination inhaled steroid therapy

The 2003 British Asthma Guidelines recommend that long-acting β_2-agonists should be added to the treatment of patients who are poorly controlled on low-dose inhaled steroids. This may be given in combination form, providing rapid improvement in control and probably improving compliance with controller therapy.

> Asthma control has traditionally been assessed in primary care by looking at changes in lung function or improvements in symptoms.

Leukotriene receptor antagonists

Leukotriene receptor antagonists are considered as second-line controller therapy in the British Asthma Guidelines, but may be of particular help in the following groups:

- children under 5 years of age
- patients with exercise-induced asthma
- patients with allergen-induced asthma, especially when associated with allergic rhinitis
- patients with poor adherence with inhaled medication

Referral to a specialist chest physician or paediatrician should be considered when a patient is still poorly controlled with inhaled steroids above 2000 µg per day in adults (800 µg in older children) and add-on therapy.

Once control has been obtained, step down of the dose of inhaled steroids to the lowest effective dose should be initiated in order to minimise the chance of side-effects. Bone densitometry should be performed in all patients on inhaled steroids above
800 µg/day for more than a few months. Growth should be checked regularly in all children with asthma.

Non-pharmacological management

Smoking cessation and influenza vaccination should be encouraged and are integral components of the quality markers for asthma in the GMS GP contract. Avoidance of trigger factors by the patient can be helpful, but radical avoidance measures (e.g. house dust eradication and pet avoidance) may be impractical and can cause huge distress. Exercise should be positively encouraged whilst breathing retraining may help patients with dysfunctional breathing.

Personalised asthma action plans

Personalised action plans as part of structured asthma care have been shown to improve asthma morbidity, yet a recent survey showed that only 6% patients were given a written action plan. There is no evidence regarding the exact style of plan, but it is generally agreed that it should be individually tailored to the patient. An example of an appropriate asthma management plan is given in Table 4.

Smoking cessation and influenza vaccination should be encouraged and are integral parts of the asthma quality markers in the GMS GP contract.

Personalised action plans as part of structured asthma care have been shown to improve asthma morbidity.

Table 4. Example of an asthma action plan.

Good control	• No limits on daily activity • No night waking • Using reliever less than twice per week • Peak expiratory flow rate at highest recorded level
Worsening control	• If you need to wake at night because of asthma • Require reliever more than once per day • Daily activities restricted by asthma • **Increase preventer medication** • **Increase reliever medication**
Poor control	• If you need reliever more than 4 times in 24 hours • If peak flow is less than 60% of predicted value • **See doctor or asthma nurse**
Danger signs	• If reliever only lasts 1 hour • Unable to speak in sentences because of breathing trouble • **Call doctor immediately**

Clinical audit

Audit still fills many primary care professionals with dread. However, there is clear evidence to suggest that appropriately audited organised asthma care markedly improves asthma morbidity. The new GMS GP contract has undoubtedly encouraged audit of certain 'process' markers. However, additional factors amenable to clinical audit could include the use of personalised action plans or the number of asthma exacerbations experienced by patients. The General Practice Airways Group website offers some further ideas and help for audit (*www.gpiag.org.uk*).

Conclusion

Asthma still provides a great challenge for primary care, with a large unmet need amongst asthmatics. However, treating asthma is rewarding for the physician and can produce huge improvements in sufferers' lives.

Key points

- Whilst significant advances have been made in the management and treatment of asthma in the past 20 years, it continues to represent a major clinical burden for primary care.

- Many of the practical issues that remain relate to complacency and a lack of government prioritisation towards the condition. In addition, diagnosis continues to be an issue, with a significant number of asthmatics misdiagnosed, and consequently not optimally managed.

- There are also significant issues relating to treatment adherence, and a lack of awareness of the latest clinical guidelines.

- Improving structured care should involve the whole primary healthcare team in the management of the condition. Practice nurses have a critical role to play, whilst establishing dedicated asthma clinics will also serve to improve care.

- The latest clinical guidelines offer useful advice in terms of diagnosis and treatment. Non-pharmacological interventions should be implemented to maximise the care of our patients. Personalised asthma plans are useful tools in improving care, and also open up lines of communication between doctors and their patients.

5. Atherothrombosis

Dr Alan Begg MB ChB FRCGP DA D.Ch. DRCOG FPCERT
General Practitioner, Montrose, Scotland

Summary

The burden of morbidity and mortality associated with cardiovascular disease (CVD) continues to exert a significant impact on the day-to-day workload of GPs. Atherothrombosis is the underlying pathophysiological state that ultimately leads to the clinical manifestations of CVD. The management of patients with CVD should focus on reducing the risk of index events and prevention of recurrent events via a combination of lifestyle interventions and drug treatment, in particular antiplatelet therapy. As with all chronic conditions, effective management requires a correct initial diagnosis to be established. Identifying appropriate patients who may be at risk, and thus in need of intervention, together with their management after discharge from secondary care is an essential part of overall management, and critical roles exist for all members of the primary-care team, utilising their individual skills in a coordinated manner.

Vascular disease burden in general practice

CVD is the principal cause of death not only in the UK but also worldwide. In the UK, about a half of all CVD-related deaths are due to coronary heart disease (CHD), with about one-quarter due to stroke. Whilst death rates from CVD in the UK have fallen by up to 40% over the past 30 years, this fall has not been as dramatic as in other countries. In addition, the morbidity associated with CVD continues to increase, with the majority of this growing burden falling on general practice. For example:

- 135,000 patients survive a myocardial infarction (MI) each year in the UK
- 2 million people suffer from angina
- 650,000 individuals have diagnosed heart failure, mostly due to CHD.

Regional differences in the incidence of CVD also prevail within the UK, with the west of Scotland and north of England having the highest

> The morbidity associated with CVD continues to increase, with the majority of this growing burden falling on general practice.

incidences of the disease. Both male and female manual workers and south Asians also have higher rates of CVD throughout the country.

Up to 120,000 people in the UK will have a stroke each year, and of the half who survive for more than a year, a third will remain significantly disabled and as many as 5% will require long-term residential care.

Finally, it is estimated that up to 20% of patients in the UK aged between 65 and 75 years have peripheral artery disease (PAD), though only a quarter of these have presented clinically.

Atherothrombosis: one disease process, three disease categories

The underlying pathophysiology of CVD involves the progressive development of atherosclerosis, which can affect the whole arterial tree. Early atheroma is usually evident from the third decade of life, whilst from the fourth decade onwards mature atherosclerotic plaques develop, which comprise a lipid core surrounded by a connective tissue matrix. Coronary artery disease in its various forms arises when the coronary arteries are involved. Similarly, stroke and transient ischaemic attacks (TIAs) occur when the atherosclerotic burden affects the arteries of the head and neck. PAD, the third disease category arising from the same underlying process, develops when the arteries in the legs are affected.

Recruitment of patients with vascular disease into clinical trials has revealed a considerable degree of overlap of these three disease categories in patients at high risk of vascular events. A similar pattern of overlap of the different categories of atherosclerotic disease is also observed in UK general practice (Figure 1). Although significant regional variations exist in the prevalence of CVD, the number of patients expected in each category can be estimated from a notional general practice list of 10,000 patients taken from an area where the disease incidence is close to the national average (Table 1).

A similar pattern of overlap of the different categories of atherosclerotic disease is observed in UK general practice.

Establishing a diagnosis

Confirming an accurate diagnosis is clearly essential before a clinical condition can be effectively managed, and further events arising from the primary condition can be prevented. This is especially true for vascular disease since patients without a correct diagnosis may be denied effective preventative therapy.

Angina

The National Service Framework (NSF) for CHD encouraged the establishment of nationwide chest pain clinics as part of a strategy for rapid

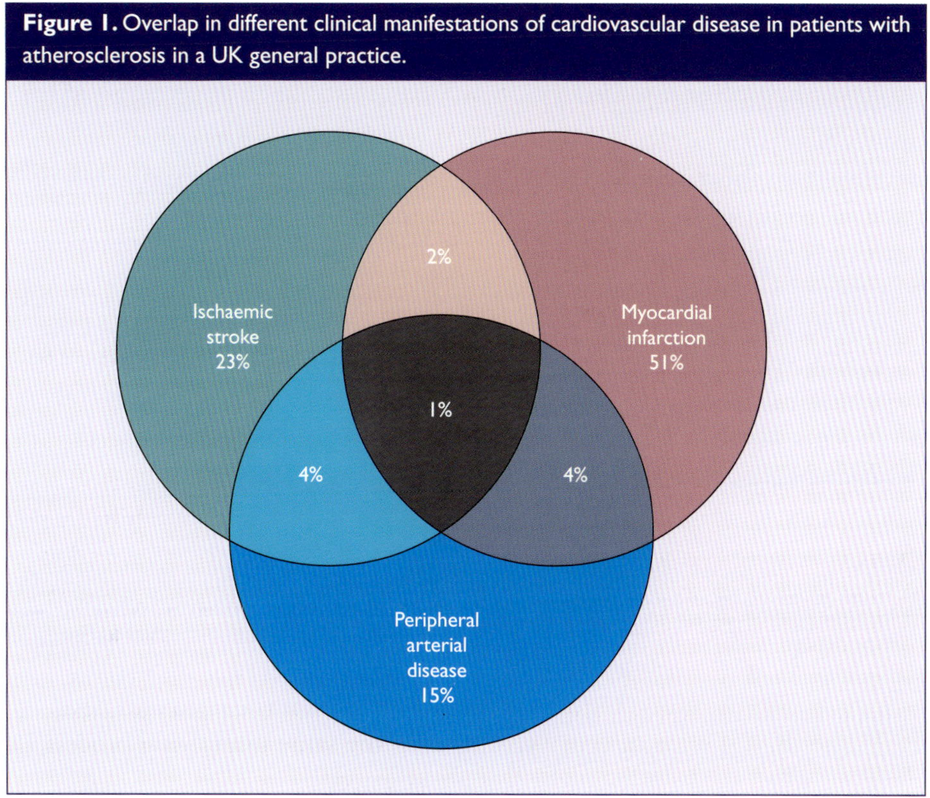

Figure 1. Overlap in different clinical manifestations of cardiovascular disease in patients with atherosclerosis in a UK general practice.

Table 1. Incidence of cardiovascular disease (CVD) in a notional UK general practice population of 10,000 patients with an average incidence of CVD.

Disease	Incidence (per 10,000 patients)
Myocardial infarction	191
Chronic angina (no previous myocardial infarction)	168
All strokes	121
Transient ischaemic attack	59
Peripheral arterial disease	77

identification of patients with suspected CHD, thereby ensuring optimal management. When an atheromatous plaque produces a stenosis of greater than 50% of arterial diameter, or reduces the cross-sectional area by 75% or more, the reduced blood flow that results during exertion can lead to the pain of angina. Most regions of England now have a chest pain assessment clinic to which patients presenting with exertional chest pain for the first time can be referred.

Acute coronary syndromes (ACS)

Acute coronary events arise when an atherosclerotic plaque ruptures or erodes, with differing degrees of superimposed thrombus formation and distal embolisation (atherothrombosis). Evolving MI and unstable angina develop from this common underlying pathophysiology. Two categories of patients, requiring different management approaches, are seen in clinical practice (Figure 2):

- patients with acute total occlusion (ST-segment elevation MI), in whom immediate management involves reopening the occluded artery via the administration of a thrombolytic agent or primary percutaneous transluminal coronary angioplasty (PTCA)
- patients with biochemical evidence of myocardial necrosis (non-ST-segment elevation MI) or without such evidence (unstable angina).

Stroke

All patients suspected of an acute stroke should undergo a computed tomography (CT) scan, ideally within 48 hours, by referral either to an acute admissions unit or a neurovascular clinic. This will enable the clinician to differentiate between haemorrhagic and ischaemic stroke, thereby ensuring appropriate management (Table 2).

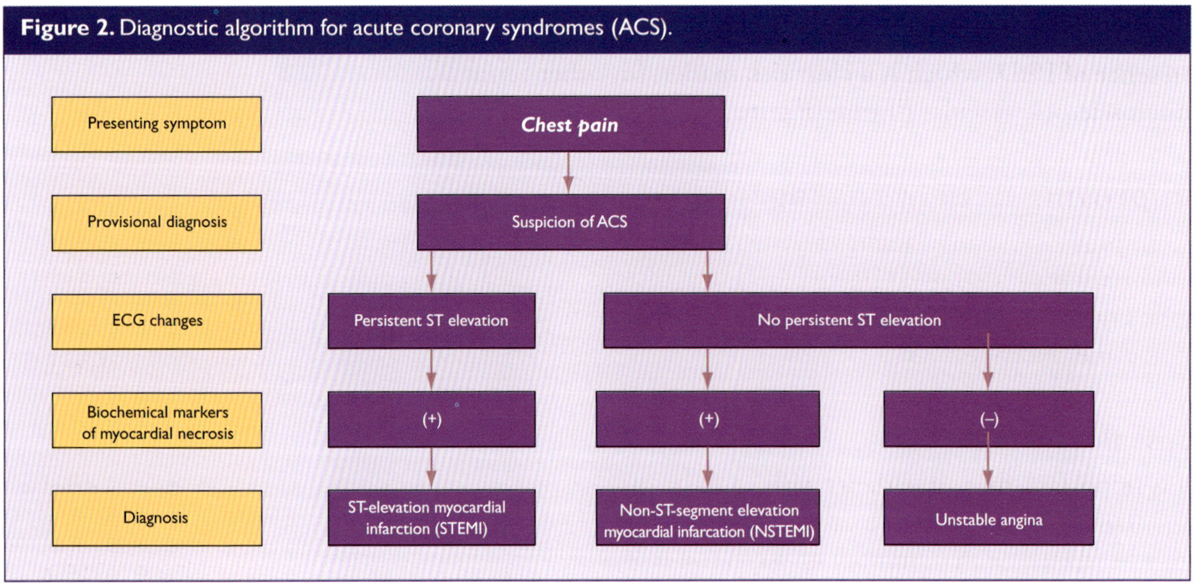

Figure 2. Diagnostic algorithm for acute coronary syndromes (ACS).

Table 2. Different types of stroke seen in clinical practice.

Type of stroke	Incidence and cause
Ischaemic	• 50% arise as a result of a thromboembolus from the heart or proximal vessels • 25% are lacunar infarcts due to occlusion of small deep penetrating arteries • 25% are due to atherothrombotic disease of the intracranial arteries or one of a number of rarer causes
Haemorrhagic	• 15% of all strokes are due to a primary intracerebral haemorrhage • 5% of all strokes are due to a subarachnoid haemorrhage

PAD

Narrowing of the leg arteries can result in muscle pain in the lower limbs on exercise (intermittent claudication). If this history is present together with absent pulses on physical examination, along with a reduced ankle brachial pressure index (ABPI) measurement of less than 0.9%, a diagnosis of PAD can be confimed thereby allowing optimised medical treatment (Table 3).

Primary care is very much dependent on the specialist sector to fully confirm the presence of CHD and the different categories of ACS and stroke. Nevertheless, the primary-care team, with the minimum of equipment and expertise, can still play a significant role in establishing the presence of PAD, which is a clear risk marker for other forms of atherosclerotic vascular disease (Figure 3).

Improving patient management

To improve the management of patients with CHD in primary care, it is important for individual GPs to commit to improving their practice in this area. Given below are a few practical pointers as to how this can be achieved in routine, everyday care.

Case finding

It is important that all patients with vascular disease are readily identified, and that the specific disease category is appropriately coded. Such patients may be identified in a number of ways, some of which are outlined below.

● By searching the practice's existing computer systems. In this undertaking, it is important that the whole range of codes that are likely to have been used over a number of years are also searched. For example,

It is important that all patients with vascular disease are readily identified, and that the specific disease category is appropriately coded.

Table 3. Measurement of the ankle/brachial pressure index (ABPI) using the Doppler method.

Preliminary procedure
- Explain the procedure to the patient and encourage relaxation.
- Lie the patient flat and ensure that they are comfortable, rested, and with no pressure on the proximal vessels.

Measurement of the brachial systolic blood pressure
- Place an appropriately sized cuff around the upper arm.
- Locate the brachial pulse.
- Apply contact gel to a hand-held continuous wave Doppler ultrasound probe.
- Hold the probe between forefinger and thumb at a 45° angle over the pulse and obtain the best signal.
- Keeping the probe still, inflate the cuff until the signal disappears. Slowly deflate the cuff and record the pressure when the signal returns.
- Repeat on the opposite arm and record the highest of the two values.

Measurement of the ankle systolic blood pressure
- Place an appropriately sized cuff around the ankle, just above the malleolus.
- Apply contact gel and obtain the best signal from the dorsalis pedis pulse.
- Inflate the cuff until the signal disappears. Record ankle systolic pressure on deflating the cuff, when the signal reappears.
- Repeat the measurement on the posterior tibial pulse and record the highest of the two values.

Calculation of the ABPI
- To calculate the ABPI, divide the ankle pressure reading by the brachial pressure reading.

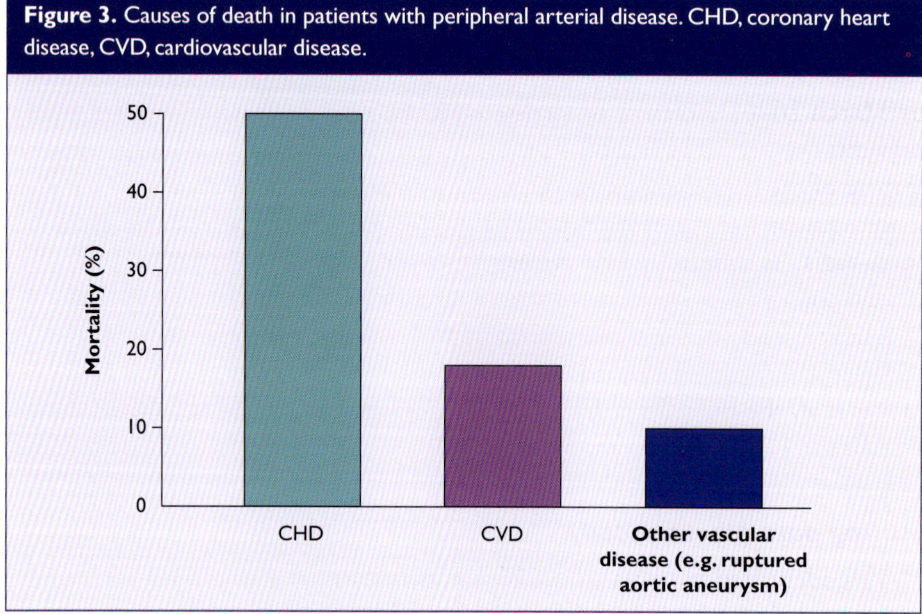

Figure 3. Causes of death in patients with peripheral arterial disease. CHD, coronary heart disease, CVD, cardiovascular disease.

history of stroke (14AZ), hemiplegia (F22), unspecified stroke (G66), or personal history of stroke (ZV125).

- By identifying patients who are receiving particular medications associated with vascular disease management and prevention. For example, antithrombotics, statins, β-blockers or angiotensin-converting enzyme inhibitors. Again, this can be done through a computer search of repeat or acute prescriptions, or can be triggered when requests are made for repeat prescriptions.
- By identifying patients in specific risk categories from those attending existing clinics for diabetes, hypertension, lipid management, weight control or smoking cessation.
- Opportunistic identification through surgery attendances or via new patient registration.
- Identification from non-electronic practice registers and local audit or research databases.
- By checking with other members of the community health team (e.g. district nurses) who may have a list of patients they are attending (e.g. patients with stroke).
- By identification of patients experiencing new events from the out-of-hours log or from comprehensive discharge information.
- Via local hospital codes of discharge diagnoses. This information may be available for a defined period, either electronically or as a print-out.

Practice-based registers

The NSFs have set specific target dates for practices to have systematically developed and appropriately maintained practice-based registers for CHD, stroke and diabetes. It is intended that that these systems should be in place by March 2006, and that the registers will be used to provide structured preventative care. The establishment of disease registers is also an important feature of the new General Medical Services (GMS) contract, and is seen as a prerequisite for monitoring patients in a specific disease category. Ideally these registers should be as accurate as possible, with it being the responsibility of the practice to demonstrate both the quality of the data and how the registers are maintained. Comparisons can then be made between the reported and expected prevalences of these diseases, which makes it all the more important that accurate diagnoses are made and that disease categories are accurately recorded.

Storing data electronically

Having identified patients with CVD, it is important that all the necessary data is stored in such a way that it can be easily retrieved and made available for day-to-day clinical management. The increasing trend towards the use of electronic patient records is certain to continue. Although practices that continue to use manual records will not be disadvantaged by the new contract, these practices will be encouraged to transfer their audit data into an electronic format, thereby encouraging the development of practice-based registers and other systems and processes that have been initiated to meet the requirements of the NSF. Plans are also underway to develop an integrated care records system, which will centralise electronic patient records. Patient data will then be uploaded into a central record repository held at the level of the Primary Care Organisation (PCO), which can then be accessed by a variety of healthcare professionals with the appropriate permissions and authority. However, it is possible that this development will be slowed by the continuing push to develop effective, non-web based, stand-alone practice systems.

Read codes

Read codes are the recommended national standard coding system currently in use in primary care. Essentially, they represent a thesaurus of clinical terms. The codes are arranged hierarchically, with the level of detail increasing downwards on the hierarchy. The system allows users to find related terms and decide on the appropriate level of detail they wish to use. A set of preferred Read codes for the new contract has been published in order to facilitate the electronic transfer of patient data and records, and allow comparisons of clinical activity (Table 4). Again the use of other codes than these should not disadvantage practices. Work is also underway by the NHS Information Authority to align Read codes with those used by the College of American Pathology. This new system (Systematized Nomenclature of Medicine [SNOMED] Clinical Terms) will create the essential building blocks of a common computerised language for worldwide use.

It is important that all the necessary data is stored in such a way that it can be easily retrieved and made available for day-to-day clinical management.

Read codes are the recommended national standard coding system currently in use in primary care.

Table 4. Preferred NHS Read codes for cardiovascular disease.

Coronary heart disease	G 3%
Myocardial infarction	G 30%
Haemorrhagic stroke	G 61%
Ischaemic stroke	G 64%
Transient ischaemic attack	G 65%
Peripheral arterial disease	G 73%

Assessing risk

The absolute global risk of a patient who has not experienced a vascular event or presented with any clinical symptoms can be assessed on the basis of a variety of individual risk factors using one of the currently available risk calculation tools. These are predominantly based on the Framingham risk function. The Joint British Societies recommendation charts, which are the most commonly used risk calculators in the UK, measure coronary event risk, but this equates directly with total cardiovascular risk. More recent European charts (e.g. The Score Project – Systematic Coronary Risk Evaluation) provide a measure of risk based on total cardiovascular mortality. Patients with established CVD or a previous cardiovascular event are at much higher risk of future events, and this increased risk does not need to be specifically quantified before the institution of preventative measures (Table 5). However, there is a wealth of evidence that the uptake of secondary preventative measures, which could help prevent a further event, is not as high as it should be in patients who have suffered MI. In patients who have had a TIA and not received appropriate treatment, there is a 10% risk of major stroke within the first year, and an approximate 5% risk for each year thereafter. The risk of a patient who presents with intermittent claudication progressing to critical limb ischaemia and amputation is less than 1%. However, the risk of death from coronary or cerebrovascular events in such a patient could be as high as 10% per year – up to four-times greater than that for the general population matched for age and gender.

> There is a wealth of evidence that the uptake of secondary preventative measures is not as high as it should be in patients who have suffered MI.

Structured care in general practice

Preventative care can be provided as part of a routine consultation in general practice or, alternatively, structured into specific prevention clinics. Such clinics are invariably nurse-led, but supported and complemented by

Table 5. Increased risk of a second vascular event vs background risk in the general population.

Original event	Risk of second event compared with general population	
	Myocardial infarction	Stroke and transient ischaemic attack
Myocardial infarction	× 5	× 3
Stroke	× 2	× 9
Peripheral arterial disease	× 4	× 2

other members of the practice team to provide the necessary range and mix of skills. Multi-practice clinics can also be organised under the umbrella of a primary-care organisation. As the new GMS contract is implemented, a comparison between these two approaches will determine whether providing a direct financial incentive to practices can achieve the expected higher level of clinical indicators.

Programmes for disease management can improve the process of care, reduce admissions to hospital, and enhance health-related quality of life. Nurse-led secondary prevention clinics have been shown to improve therapeutic provision, and most of the lifestyle components of secondary prevention, together with health-related quality of life. These improvements can ultimately translate into reduced rates of death and vascular events.

Components of structured care in general practice

- Accurate and up-to-date register.
- Effective and comprehensive call–recall system.
- Effective patient education (which includes dealing with misconceptions).
- Ensuring that patients fully understand their condition and its symptoms.
- Information gathering as appropriate.
- Use of dietary assessment questionnaires.
- Use of symptom control questionnaire (e.g. Cardiovascular Limitations And Symptoms Profile – CLASP).
- Risk factor assessment and monitoring.
- Lifestyle and behaviour change with modification of risk.
- Drug therapy to ensure adequate symptom control and vascular protection.
- Monitoring of compliance with treatment.
- Identification and recording of any side-effects.
- Feedback to include written agreement of specific action plans.
- Provision of drug leaflets and patient information leaflets.
- Follow-up plans.

Quality standards

The NSFs for CHD and for older people have established a 10-year programme for improving care, which sets initial milestones for each quality standard so that progress can be effectively monitored. The quality and outcomes framework of the new GMS contract defines a series of clinical indicators organised by disease category, with contract-related payments

Table 6. Clinical indicators for cardiovascular disease in primary care recorded or measured in a UK general practice over 15 months to June 2003.

	Established coronary heart disease	Stroke and transient ischaemic attack	Peripheral arterial disease
Included in new GMS contract	X	X	–
Practice register	X	X	X
Diagnosis confirmed by CT or MRI scan	–	X	–
Diagnosis confirmed by ABPI	–	–	X
Smoking status	X	X	X
Smoking cessation	X	X	X
BMI recorded	X		
BP recorded	X	X	X
BP target set (≤150/90 mmHg)	X	X	X
Cholesterol measured	X	X	X
Cholesterol target set (<5 mmol/L)	X	X	X
Anti-thrombotic drugs	X	X	X
β-blockers (unless contraindicated)	X	–	–
ACE inhibitors	X (if MI)	–	Consider
Influenza vaccination	X	X	X

ABPI, ankle–brachial pressure index; ACE, angiotensin-converting enzyme; BMI, body mass index; BP, blood pressure; CT, computed tomography; MRI, magnetic resonance imaging.

being based on the level reached for each indicator (Table 6). This framework does not cover every precise detail of the structured care of patients with chronic diseases, but rather is designed to encourage the process. By collating the percentage of indicators achieved within the primary-care organisation, this comparative benchmarking process can also be used to encourage a steady improvement in the standards of care.

It is intended that this should not be a data collection exercise, but that the data required should be captured as part of routine clinical care. The standardised report for verification and payment, ideally electronic, should be automatically extractable from the data. Fortunately, practices will not be penalised if achieving quality improvement is outside their control, as long as it is within given parameters (Table 7).

Some of the other features and limitations of the quality and outcomes framework are outlined below.

- PAD is not included in the current list. However, its importance as a risk marker for CHD and stroke needs to be emphasised.
- Meeting blood pressure targets in clinical practice is not easy, though it is something we should aim to achieve. An interim step may be to achieve

> **Table 7.** Exception reporting for GMS contract quality and outcomes framework.
>
> - Patient refuses to attend for review who has been invited on at least three occasions during the preceding 12 months.
> - Disease management review inappropriate due to patient circumstances (e.g. terminal illness, extreme frailty).
> - New patient, where lack of time precludes reaching the clinical standard.
> - Patient on maximum tolerated level of medication.
> - Medication not clinically appropriate (e.g. allergy, adverse reaction or contraindication to medication).
> - Medication intolerance.
> - Informed dissent recorded.
> - Local investigative or secondary care service not available.
> - Patient has a supervening condition making treatment inappropriate (e.g. cholesterol reduction in the presence of liver disease).

the audit standards of the British Hypertension Society (BHS) guidelines rather than the suggested targets of the quality and outcomes framework. Once these have been achieved we may then move on and attempt to achieve the more stringent targets.

- Lower cholesterol levels translate into lower event rates, and therefore the case could be made for every patient with established atherosclerotic vascular disease to be prescribed a lipid-lowering agent.
- Unnecessarily frequent updates to reflect the changing evidence base may have a demotivating effect on practice programmes.
- Only one lifestyle indicator has been selected, though it is important that appropriate lifestyle advice should be available for all patients with vascular disease.

Workload implications for general practice

Attempts have been made to quantify and cost the work involved in the identification and management of patients at risk of vascular events, in line with the requirements of the NSFs. Achieving as high a level as possible of the clinical indicators will undoubtedly become the main priority for primary care. The overlap of disease categories and associated comorbidities in patients with vascular disease offers primary-care practices a clear opportunity to take a patient-centred approach to clinical and preventative care. Using appropriate information technology, the potential for fragmentation of care based on disease categories can therefore be avoided.

By offering an integrated and coordinated service for patients with vascular disease, diabetes and hypertension, which overlap considerably, the doctor's workload can be reduced and indeed more can be achieved with available resources.

Competency and training

Managing vascular disease within primary care involves multidisciplinary working that fully utilises the skills mix. Appropriate delegation and good management support are essential to the process.

Staff should be competent and confident to carry out the roles expected of them, and appropriate training and education should be part of their continuing professional development. Statements of competency for the activity expected of staff need to be accompanied by examples of the evidence required to meet that competency and descriptions of how achievement will be recognised and documented.

Training and education can be arranged at practice level or at the level of the primary-care organisation, with appropriate funding being made available for those intending to enrol in national residential or distance-learning courses (Table 8).

Table 8. Training courses for cardiovascular disease.

Developments in cardiovascular education
www.gla.ac.uk/schools/nursing/distanceedu.html

Heart manual
www.cardiacrehabilitation.org.uk/heart_manual/HeartManual.htm

National CHD training programme
www.heartsave.org.uk

CHD training in primary care
www.primarycaretraining.co.uk

Key points

- Atherothrombosis is the disease process underlying the pathophysiology of CVD, and it manifests clinically in three distinct and specific disease categories.

- Appropriate management and prevention of CVD depends on ensuring that the correct diagnosis is made.

- Critical roles exist for all members of the primary-care team, utilising their individual skills in a coordinated manner.

- The provision of a one-stop, patient-centred service can minimise the impact of the increased workload in primary care.

- Data collection should be part of routine clinical care, with single data entry.

- Different practices will evolve their own approaches, with external help being complementary to that process.

6. Atopic eczema

Dr Stephen Kownacki MB BS MRCGP
General Practitioner, Wellingborough, Northamptonshire
Hospital Practitioner in Dermatology, Northampton General Hospital Trust
Chairman, Primary Care Dermatology Society

Summary

Atopic eczema has a profound impact on individual patients and their carers, and is also a major burden on primary healthcare resources. For example, as GPs in the UK we can expect to see, on average, about one patient during every surgery we hold. Thus, a thorough appreciation and understanding of the burden of this major condition is essential for its effective management. By examining how we currently deal with the problem of atopic eczema, we can formulate effective management plans. The involvement of the entire primary-care team and the adoption of an education and awareness campaign will also help in managing the condition. Patient education and support is also widely available. Effective diagnosis, of course, lies at the heart of successful clinical management, and whilst this is usually straightforward for atopic eczema, there are a number of other complicating factors. Lifestyle changes can help minimise disease flares and improve overall control of their condition, but, as we have seen in the preceding sections, a variety of pharmacological approaches are available to manage the disease.

Introduction

Atopic eczema is a significant and growing problem for healthcare services, and profoundly impacts on the individual patient. Over recent years, we have seen a three-fold increase in the prevalence of atopic eczema, and in the developed world up to 20% of all children are likely to develop the condition. From these data, we can predict that an average UK GP will see one dermatological problem for every six or seven consultations and, of these, about one-third will be cases of atopic eczema. This equates to approximately one patient presenting during each surgery. Consequently, in primary care we must have strategies to cope with this demand, with facilities and resources to match. It is no longer an option to remain

It is no longer an option to remain ignorant or dismissive of such a major disease.

ignorant or dismissive of such a major disease even if the medical schools still relegate dermatology to a minor section of education!

Management not just treatment

Like so many diseases managed in primary care, atopic eczema should be regarded as a management problem rather than a simple treatment choice. Knowing what to write on a prescription is only a small part of the process. So what else do we need to consider? Are there special circumstances that make atopic eczema different from all the other chronic diseases we have to deal with?

Organisation

As dermatology has not been awarded special funding status like for example asthma, we do need to take a fresh look at our approach. For example:

- how do we greet our patients with atopic eczema?
- can patients get to see the right person easily and in an appropriate time frame?
- does your practice have partners and health visitors or, if you are especially lucky, a specialist nurse with dermatology expertise?
- are your reception/telephone/prescription staff sympathetic to signs of itch and distress, as well as the more dramatic disease presentations?

A prompt repeat prescription perhaps asked for at an early stage or a new antibiotic prescribed for a secondary infection may prevent family disruption, missed school days or even avoid a hospital admission. For this reason, I strongly recommend awareness education for all the practice staff to complement the specific expertise within the nursing team along the same lines as asthma management.

Equipment

Fortunately this section is mercifully small. There is a need for good, light, warm and private surroundings in which to examine the undressed patient (as the whole patient needs to be assessed) and perhaps a magnifying glass for us older practitioners! The facility to take swabs for bacteria and viruses and to take mycological scrapings to exclude alternative or coexistent fungal disease is also required (for example a scalpel blade and some coloured paper or a universal specimen pot for nail clippings.) A bath in which to soak a child before wet wrapping is a luxury rarely needed and probably leads us into the realms of intermediate or secondary care.

I find it very useful to have a selection of emollients in sample sizes, both of bath additives and topical applications, which can be sampled by the patient and/or their carer. The best emollient for any patient is the one the patient will use and cannot be dictated by the experts and certainly not by prescribing advisers. The Skin Care Campaign (*www.skincarecampaign.org*) recently fought an attempted imposition of aqueous cream as the only permitted emollient! Whilst it may be a useful soap substitute, it contains far too much water and has a significant allergenic potential as well. A choice of emollient is vital to our patients since different skin types require different levels of grease with, for example, black skin often requiring the more greasy applications.

Assessment

Effective and accurate diagnosis is a prerequisite for successful management and although usually obvious, the consequences of mistakes can, at the very least, be distressing for the patient and embarrassing for the doctor!

Other forms of eczema should be considered when establishing a diagnosis:

- discoid eczema which requires a higher potency corticosteroid and is more resistant to treatment
- allergic or contact eczema which may require patch testing and allergen avoidance
- asteototic eczema in the elderly where one should avoid potent steroids on the thinned and cracked skin
- varicose eczema often with auto-sensitisation to the trunk and upper limbs which will not settle until the primary lower leg eczema is effectively treated.

Seborrheic dermatitis in the infant may also confuse the diagnosis. However, it is not itchy and often involves the scalp (cradle cap) and the nappy area, unlike atopic eczema. It is likely to settle with the minimum of treatment using emollients and perhaps a weak corticosteroid. Remember, "if it does not itch, it is not eczema". But remember to beware of scabies since we can all miss it sometimes!

A typical assessment and management plan may include the features outlined below.

- Record the age, type of onset, extent of disease, evidence of infection or lichenification, exacerbating factors, previous management and the patient or carer's view of the success, or otherwise, of the treatment.

Remember, "if it does not itch, it is not eczema".

- Listen to the fears and sometimes the misunderstandings of disease and its treatments (e.g. equating steroids with bodybuilder anabolics), as the degree of distress will also affect your approach.
- Offer empathy and education relating to the disease and its management, alternative treatments and advice as to "what to do and when".
- Provide written information using leaflets or booklets, but also, for example, personally tailored body maps. Alert your patient to other sources of support and information, in particular the National Eczema Society (*www.eczema.org*), which can reinforce your advice and has many leaflets of its own which are most useful.
- Patient follow up is vital to fine tune treatment. In particular, it especially allows you to show your continued support or better still the support of the whole primary-care team. Advice as to how and when they should seek urgent help and from whom is also important.

Lifestyle

Atopic eczema is a chronic relapsing incurable disease, which inevitably has attracted many "old wives tales" often as a consequence of the failure of traditional medicine. Moreover, research has not yet taught us all we need to know. For example, breast-feeding has been thought to be protective. However, a recent study has shown that the effect may indeed be the opposite! One of the latest suggestions with positive evidence is the ingestion of probiotics during the latter stages of pregnancy to reduce the likelihood of atopic eczema in the new baby. Despite the imperfection of our knowledge we should not let it prevent us sharing what we have learnt from studies and our experience as long as we are clear where this comes from.

Avoidance of irritants and allergens is of major benefit and may preclude certain occupations such as nursing or hairdressing, where contact with such chemicals is inevitable. As such, early career advice may save later disappointment! Dust mite allergy is common but avoidance is difficult but worth trying if the eczema is severe. Simple advice regarding soft toys, furnishings and carpets along with wet dusting and washing of pillows may be helpful but can be very complex! Pets, especially cats, are a common allergen but their dander can persist for many years after the cat has gone. In addition, children can still be exposed to dander from their cat-owning school friends; and once a cat is installed in a family home, "catricide" is not a major recommendation!

Stress is another identifiable factor in the development of eczema flares, which of course is easier to spot than cure. It can both be a cause and a consequence of a flare and in children can be a useful parental control technique!

Food additives and allergens provoke significant debate and are often the cause of secondary care referral. In the very young (less than 1 year) dietary measures (particularly cow's milk exclusion) have a much better chance of helping atopic eczema. However, great care must be taken to ensure an adequate intake of nutrients, and thus professional dietary advice is strongly recommended. In older children and adults, the benefits are much less obvious unless the cause is clear (e.g. sudden flare of the face after eating tomatoes), and here the advice is pretty obvious. Avoiding the colourings in foodstuffs may also be worth trying and is not quite so hard as avoiding a major foodstuff.

In real life, however, most patients are controlled by fairly simple and safe treatment regimens, which preclude the need for significant changes in family life that major dietary manipulation requires. Indeed, the best benefit–effort ratios are achieved only by those with severe disease.

Clinical management

Patients usually present in an acute flare situation looking for relief. However, before prescribing it is important to establish the cause of the flare. The most common causes are increased scratching due to irritants such as raised environmental temperature, clothing, stress and/or concurrent skin infection. Infection is usually staphylococcal in origin but may start as molluscum contagiosum. Alternatives to look for include infestations with scabies or lice.

Therefore, the first drugs on any prescription usually deal with the cause of the flare, for example antibiotics such as flucloxacillin or erythromycin to deal with an infection, and perhaps something to suppress the itch especially if sleep is disturbed (e.g. sedative antihistamines such as chlorpheniramine or trimeprazine).

Atopic eczema is a dry skin condition, and therefore the central element of all management algorithms (albeit with minimal experimental proof) is the copious use of emollients. These act by sealing the leaky skin surface to prevent the penetration of irritants and allergens and to keep the skin hydrated which, in itself, may reduce the associated itching. Emollient therapy is perhaps best delivered by oil in the daily bath, a soap substitute for washing and then stroking on the preferred emollient cream or ointment whilst the skin is damp, without vigorous rubbing and allowing it to soak in. The emollient should be re-applied as often as the skin feels dry – perhaps several times a day.

> Most patients are controlled by fairly simple and safe treatment regimens, which preclude the need for significant changes in family life.

> Atopic eczema is a dry skin condition, and therefore the central element of all management algorithms (albeit with minimal experimental proof) is the copious use of emollients.

Emollients, however, do not suppress inflammation. In that case, what should we use to treat inflammatory flares? Here we come to the essence of this discussion. Do we use topical corticosteroids or one of the new calcineurin inhibitors (pimecrolimus and tacrolimus) and if so which one and where?

Corticosteroid therapy has been the mainstay of treatment in atopic eczema for more than 40 years and if used properly is usually safe and effective. Thus, for mild atopic eczema on a thick skin area, a weak corticosteroid such as 1% hydrocortisone is a safe and effective treatment, even in infants. Often, however, it is not sufficient and a stronger grade 2 or even grade 3 (moderately potent/potent) agent has to be used for a few days (less than 7 days is the current recommendation). For the face, which is more susceptible to the adverse effects of corticosteroids (e.g. skin thinning, teliangectasia), especially in children, potent steroids are a worry not only for the prescribing doctor, but also for patients/carers and other health workers such as health visitors and pharmacists who have had the exaggerated fears of steroids communicated to them. This irrational fear of steroids has been coined 'steroid phobia'. Working in a district general dermatological department, I am fully aware that we spend much more time encouraging patients to adequately use steroids than we ever have to curb their overuse. The skin flexures are another area of concern. A useful rule of thumb here is that the potency of the steroid used will be as effective as a grade higher because of increased absorption in these areas.

Calcineurin inhibitors are possible alternatives, and are useful at the very least to treat problem areas (i.e. the face, the flexures) and also for steroid phobics. They appear to have no skin thinning potential and do not affect the blood vessels. As with all new products, there is a natural reluctance to use them widely until we gain more experience. However, with the likelihood that the number of indications for these agents will increase in the future, both with regard to age limits and the types of eczema, further experience will be gained and more extensive use is likely to develop.

If we think back to our patient whose acute presentation has been dealt with, do we now send them away and wait for their next exacerbation before treating them again? Historically, the answer has been a resounding yes! However, there are a number of good studies, outlined in detail in the previous section, which demonstrate that pimecrolimus, when applied at the first signs of a flare when the skin becomes sore, itchy or red, can abort the flare. When pimecrolimus application is repeated, the number of flares is also significantly reduced. Having taken part in some of this clinical research, I have seen patients who have been transformed by this technique. It does, however, take time and effort initially to educate the patient/parent, which is much more difficult in everyday practice than in a clinical trial setting. This is where trained nurses can be very helpful, especially because support and reinforcement is so necessary. The concept of emollient therapy to keep the skin healthy and having a tube of prevention cream to use when necessary (e.g. pimecrolimus) and only resorting to a potent corticosteroid if it becomes too severe, will take time to be fully understood and accepted.

Which agent should we use?

I have referred to pimecrolimus specifically because I have had extensive experience with this agent. It is indicated for use in primary care and for mild-to-moderate atopic eczema which constitutes the vast majority of patients we see in primary care. Tacrolimus may be more effective, certainly in severe eczema, and has been used more as an alternative to a potent steroid in secondary or perhaps intermediate care, for example by GPs with a special interest in dermatology. It is probably a little more irritant for some patients, certainly in the first week of treatment, which can be a crucial period when treating small children, and apparently has increased absorption and potential systemic immunomodulatory effect. This suggests to me that in practice we should use the weakest, safest effective treatment, increasing the potency only if required, as we do with corticosteroids.

Constraints

The cost of calcineurin inhibitors (both are approximately equivalent) is the major restrictive factor and may explain some of the reports from advisory boards and prescribing advisers at Primary Care Trust (PCT) level. There is an understandable reluctance to permit prescribing by GPs for fear of rapidly escalating costs, particularly since the gram-for-gram cost ratio of calcineurin inhibitors to corticosteroids is of the order of 18:1. However, the morbidity saved and its effectiveness for most patients, makes its sensible use, in the way I have indicated, a cost-effective option. Lost school/work time and family tensions are hard to financially quantify and, whilst they do not impinge on the PCT budgets, they make a big difference to quality of life. Those of us who look after sufferers of atopic eczema fully understand the need for effective and acceptable treatment.

Clinical audit

The collection of data regarding the number of repeat prescriptions of topical corticosteroids can be a useful, if horrifying, undertaking. Currently, clinical audit has particular relevance regarding the overuse of antibiotic/steroid combination topicals which appear to be producing increased resistance figures. A useful assessment of patient education is the simple ratio between emollient and corticosteroid quantities with the ideal ratio being 10:1 or greater.

A study questionnaire, distributed to all members of the primary healthcare team regarding attitudes to atopic eczema, or indeed skin disease in general, and its treatment may lead to a productive discussion so that the patient receives the same message from all, and not conflicting advice which confuses.

Support

Support is vital for patients and their families with this chronic relapsing incurable condition, which has the ability to ruin lives and families, but can nearly always be controlled. The National Eczema Society help line (0870 241 3604) is a useful source of this support.

In terms of professional support, GPs can access information from the Primary Care Dermatology Society (PCDS), and the joint PCDS and British Association of Dermatologists atopic eczema guidelines (due for revision shortly) are available at *www.pcds.org.uk*.

Conclusion

The addition of calcineurin inhibitors has made a significant contribution to our armament in the management of atopic eczema and promises much if only we are allowed and encouraged to use them. Then we can change the traditional pattern of fire-fighting acute exacerbations into a scenario where patients avoid such distress by effective prevention. Not only are there new and effective ways of treating atopic eczema at early signs and symptoms of a flare, but treating atopic dermatitis earlier in life and more effectively holds the intriguing possibility that fewer children would go on to develop asthma and allergic rhinitis, a frequently observed phenomenon called the atopic march. The pathophysiological link between atopic dermatitis and other atopic diseases is currently being investigated with potentially exciting implications for the future management of atopic disease. If this hypothesis is confirmed in subsequent studies, it will give even greater impetus to the compelling arguments in favour of the pro-active management of atopic dermatitis.

Key points

- Atopic eczema is a highly prevalent condition, particularly in childhood, with the average UK GP seeing about one patient with the condition during each surgery.

- Organised care, for example by establishing a repeat prescription service, may go a long way towards improving patient management.

- Whilst accurate diagnosis of atopic eczema is relatively straightforward, there are a number of other diagnoses that should be considered, which may impact on patient management.

- Clinical assessment and management plans are a recommended tool to record patients' progress and also provide a means of education and support.

- Lifestyle modification can control exacerbations of the condition, but pharmacological intervention is often required to maintain control of the disease. This takes the form of emollients and topical corticosteroids, although the availability of novel calcineurin inhibitors offer the promise of good efficacy and superior tolerability.

7. Benign prostatic hyperplasia

Dr Chris Barclay MB ChB MRCOG
General Practitioner, Sheffield, South Yorkshire

Mr Christopher Chapple,
Consultant Urologist, The Royal Hallamshire Hospital, Sheffield

Summary

The management of men's health issues has been relatively neglected over the years. However, given the holistic nature of primary care, it is ideally placed to assist in improving male health. The management of benign prostatic hyperplasia (BPH) is now firmly routed in general practice. This has arisen principally from the availability of effective treatments for the condition, meaning that GPs now manage the major share of this disease, and only refer patients to urology specialists in particular scenarios. By adopting a proactive approach to identifying and treating patients with BPH, we can expect to improve the management of the condition even further in the future.

A GP's perspective

Introduction

In recent years there has been an increasing awareness within the NHS in general, and within primary care in particular, of our relative 'neglect' of men's health issues. Men generally die 5 to 10 years earlier than women and, moreover, they can expect to be chronically ill for at least 15 years of their lives. Management of their health problems should therefore be a major priority for practitioners in primary care.

Women are, by nature, far more disposed to talk about their health problems than men, so they become much more accustomed to the array of services that healthcare professionals offer from their teenage years onwards. Women will visit their GPs repeatedly throughout their lives, not just for illnesses, but also for family planning advice, cervical smears, ante- and post-natal care, and children's immunisations. Furthermore, health services are often provided by women, and usually staffed by women, making the average, independent-minded male even less likely than his mother, wife or

> There has been an increasing awareness within the NHS in general, and within primary care in particular, of our relative 'neglect' of men's health issues.

sister to avail himself of the array of services on offer. Quite often, when a male patient walks into surgery the first thing he does is to apologise that he feels he is wasting the GP's time! It is not uncommon for us then to hear that it was 'the wife' or another family member that sent him. This is a pity, as statistics on such diverse conditions as male suicide and deaths from malignant melanoma show that much morbidity and mortality could have been avoided had an earlier approach been made to utilise the health services available in primary care. However, if men are reluctant to seek help and advice about potentially deadly lesions on their skin, for example, how much less likely are they to discuss 'waterworks' problems with their GP?

The science behind BPH and the evidence relating to the use of various drug therapies to treat is beyond the scope of this article. However, what remains critical is how we can incorporate our knowledge of BPH and the variety of treatments for it into our daily working practices, thereby making a real difference to our patients. This section will provide further practical suggestions as to how GPs might set about improving clinical practice as regards treating BPH.

Nomenclature

The nomenclature relating to prostate-related problems has become significantly more refined and precise in recent years. BPH is a histological term, and thus its use implies that a biopsy has already been performed. In practice, however, prostate biopsy is infrequently performed, and thus the term is alternatively used to describe a constellation of symptoms that imply the presence of BPH. The label is usually applied to symptomatic men in whom a diagnosis of carcinoma of the prostate has been either excluded or appears unlikely. In practice, the descriptive phrase, lower urinary tract symptoms (LUTS), is far more appropriate for such patients.

Urinary tract symptoms are now clustered under two headings: voiding symptoms and storage symptoms. These terms have replaced the older and much less precise symptomatic labels, obstructive and irritative, respectively. For many men with LUTS, clinical examination may reveal benign prostatic enlargement (BPE) alongside their storage or voiding symptoms. After clinical examination we may conclude that the cause of their symptoms is BPE and the underlying pathology is likely to be BPH.

Burden of prostate disease

Every year in Britain, about half a million men are diagnosed with BPH, though this is the tip of the iceberg. Realistically, as many as 2.5–3.5 million men may be suffering from BPH-associated LUTS. The most important predictor for BPH and LUTS is age. The older a man is, the more likely he is to have difficulties with his prostate. By the age of 70 years, 70% of men will have an enlarged prostate, whilst 40% will have LUTS. Although symptoms may regress, the natural history of BPH is for the condition to progress slowlybut steadily. In men with BPH, prostate size will increase and urinary flow rates decrease by almost 2% per annum. The likelihood of the development of acute retention of urine in subjects with LUTS is also around 2% per year.

> Realistically, as many as 2.5–3.5 million men may be suffering from BPH-associated LUTS.

Although many men tolerate LUTS and accept them as a natural consequence of ageing, a small proportion do seek help. For example, in 2001 the NHS treated over 40,000 men with a primary diagnosis of BPH, and more than 30,000 underwent transurethral resection of the prostate (TURP). This does not mean that three-quarters of men admitted to hospital with BPH will undergo TURP; these statistics come from different studies and hence are not directly comparable. An even greater number of men will have either ignored their symptoms and not sought care, or found some other way of coping with their condition. These figures illuminate the magnitude of the problem confronting the NHS. In 1995, the cost to the NHS of TURP alone was almost £1.5 billion, whilst a significantly greater proportion of patients had treatment with drugs. The situation is analogous to that with osteoporosis, another silent epidemic, where annual expenditure in the NHS reaches about £1.7 billion, much of this spent on repairing preventably fractured bones and lives.

> Make it a practice to enquire about urinary function when reviewing an elderly patient's medication.

Improving practice

Identifying patients

The current default policy in primary care is to wait for men to come to us with LUTS and then to treat or refer them to specialist care accordingly. Treatment in primary care may include so-called watchful waiting. But is the default approach for treating men with LUTS good enough? Should we not be actively seeking out cases? Should we not, at the very least, be making an effort to increase awareness of the services we can offer to individuals? In my opinion, the answer to these questions is that simply treating on request is no longer acceptable when it comes to LUTS. There may be no reliable figure for the numbers of men tolerating what must often be significant LUTS in the community. Nevertheless, these must surely be considerable and almost certainly more prevalent in less health-conscious, more deprived communities.

Although health screening in primary care is a requirement only for newly registering patients, many practices do offer well-person screening appointments. Traditionally these have been taken up mainly by women

having cervical cytological tests or at around the time of the menopause. Increasingly, however, men are coming to realise that conditions that often come with age, such as type 2 diabetes, hypertension, and coronary heart disease are identifiable at an early stage and amenable to therapy. Urological enquiry does not usually constitute part of a standard well-man check. However, I believe that we should include active enquiry about LUTS when we see all men aged 50 years and older for well-person checks.

Men who tolerate LUTS are known to be generally less well in themselves. They are more prone to anxiety and their quality of life is compromised, whether or not they realise or acknowledge it. Simply reducing the symptoms can improve their general health and well-being in addition to relieving the physical nuisance. Moreover, well-person checks for men in middle age and beyond can be performed very effectively by practice nurses as well as GPs. For this reason, my first suggested objective for improving practice is to include active enquiry about LUTS in our well-man checks in the over 50s.

The new General Medical Services (GMS) contract requires us to screen patients over 45 years of age for cardiovascular risk, especially hypertension. This represents an excellent opportunity for GPs to talk to their male patients about any genitourinary problems they may have. To reach those patients who will not come to surgery, GPs need to form an alliance with local community pharmacists, who often serve men with antacids and other over-the-counter remedies. Another option may be to enlist the help of the occupational health departments of local industries. Such strategies can play a crucial role in identifying men with problems and directing them to their GP.

The National Service Framework (NSF) for older people requires that patients over 75 years of age should have an annual review of medication (increasing to six-monthly if they are on four or more agents). This regular review represents yet another opportunity for GPs to spot problems and promote health initiatives (e.g. influenza vaccination and smoking cessation). It also provides an excellent platform to make general enquiries about urinary function. Even if an enquiry reveals that there are no apparent difficulties, it has at least given the patient the subliminal message that LUTS are important and that there is something that we can do about them should they develop or deteriorate. The International Prostate Symptom Score (IPSS) questionnaire, American Urological Association (AUA) symptom score questionnaire and the BPH impact score questionnaire are very useful in both identifying and quantifying LUTS. They are also of use in tracking deterioration and indeed the response to treatment over time. Therefore, my second suggested objective for improving practice is to make it a practice, or at the very least a personal policy, always to enquire about urinary function when reviewing an elderly patient's medication.

Managing patients

In men identified with LUTS it is important to distinguish those who are suitable for treatment within the primary-care setting from those for whom a specialist urological opinion is required. Where carcinoma of the prostate gland is suspected, patients should be referred to a urologist urgently.

The prime risk factors for developing carcinoma of the prostate are male gender, getting older, and having hormonally functional testes – factors that are of little practical help in screening for higher risk patients! Often, the diagnosis of prostate cancer is based purely on suspicion, as it often does not cause symptoms, particularly in early disease. When symptoms do occur, most men with carcinoma will present with symptoms related either to their primary disease (e.g. pain, voiding difficulty, haematuria) or to secondary growths (e.g. pathological fracture, bone pain in the spine, pelvis or loins). Weight loss is another alarm symptom. The principal diagnostic sign is the detection of an irregular hard mass in the prostate gland. Other signs may be identifiable if there is obstruction to the free flow of urine, above or below the bladder, and if there is metastatic disease.

In addition to suspected prostate cancer, a urological opinion should be sought in the presence of any of the following:

- recurrent urinary tract infection
- suspected calculus
- haematuria
- haematospermia
- incontinence
- acute or chronic retention of urine.

Screening asymptomatic men for prostate cancer via prostate-specific antigen (PSA) testing is both topical and controversial. The World Health Organization defines a good screening test as one that reliably identifies a condition where an intervention exists that has been shown to make a difference. The problem with PSA screening is two-fold. First, many of the 'worried well' who undergo PSA testing may ultimately be identified as false positives (i.e. their PSA levels were raised but they did not have cancer). PSA can be falsely elevated because of urinary tract infection, prostatitis, ejaculation within 72 hours of the test, acute urinary retention or as a consequence of prostatic surgery or biopsy.

Unfortunately many patients will have had very uncomfortable multiple transrectal prostate biopsies in order to gain reassurance about the absence of cancer. In addition, and more important, those identified with asymptomatic prostate cancer are faced with a choice of surgical or radiotherapy procedures that can not only render them incontinent and impotent, but also have not been shown to prolong life. We must therefore accept that PSA is just a protein specific to the prostate, and that increased serum levels, though associated with an increased risk of cancer, are not necessarily cancer specific. The PSA cut-off values given by the Department of Health, Prostate Cancer Risk Management Programme are shown in Table 1.

Primum non nocere is a cardinal tenet of medicine. Anecdotal reports do not constitute persuasive evidence and so my personal position is to counsel against screening in the asymptomatic, but to readdress the question every year or two to allow for medical progress. GPs are of course obliged to offer the test if a patient still wishes it done.

Watchful waiting is a perfectly reasonable policy that can be adopted in situations where symptoms are mild and tolerable. It should be emphasised that watchful waiting is not the same as doing nothing. Review should be performed annually and can be facilitated by using the symptom score questionnaires discussed earlier, which give a semi-objective numerical score. An annual digital rectal examination (DRE) of the prostate should also be considered in such cases. Watchful waiting also encompasses advice that can reduce the significant impact of mild LUTS on an individual's everyday life. This may include, for example, cautioning against drinking fluids, particularly coffee, later in the evening before retiring. Such simple advice can greatly reduce the impact of symptoms in some patients. It also empowers them by giving them a degree of control over their problem.

The introduction of the α-blockers and 5α- reductase inhibitors has had a major impact on our ability to treat men with LUTS due to BPH. Firstly, they have reduced the number of men who need referral for surgical intervention. Secondly, they have made the medical treatment of the condition one that can be initiated and continuingly managed in primary

Table 1. Prostate-specific antigen (PSA) cut-off values given by the Department of Health, Prostate Cancer Risk Management Programme. *www.cancerscreening.nhs.uk/prostate/ prostate-booklet-text.pdf*

Age range (years)	PSA cut-off (ng/mL)
50–59	≥3.0
60–69	≥4.0
70 and over	≥5.0

care. Both agents are generally well tolerated, but vary in their treatment outcomes. Thus, whilst α-blockers have a rapid onset of acton, they do not alter the size of an enlarged prostate – an effect which is associated with 5α- reductase use. Hypotension is something that must be monitored with α-blocking drugs, particularly in the elderly, the very people most in need of treatment for LUTS. On the other hand, their hypotensive effects can be employed to advantage in men who have concomitant hypertension. Here again the use of symptom questionnaires allows the impact of the therapy to be monitored more objectively.

In practice, before I initiate treatment with these agents in men with LUTS I have to convince myself that the risk of an underlying cancer is low. Where there is any doubt in my mind, I obtain a urological opinion, knowing that I will be comfortable to maintain any therapy they might wish to initiate. In any event, an annual review of medication is essential to monitor efficacy and side-effects, to evaluate blood pressure changes, to exclude the development of chronic retention and to monitor renal function.

A urological opinion should be obtained in cases where the warning signs or symptoms mentioned above are present, as well as for those who do not respond to, or tolerate, medical treatment. For many of those referred, TURP is one of the options considered. This procedure has become an industry standard against which other treatments are now compared.

Clinical audit

As primary care physicians we have a much more holistic remit for our patients than do our colleagues in secondary care. In my practice, we are increasingly working in partnership with our patients. Indeed, to a certain extent we are our patients' advocates. However, our holistic approach must also extend beyond individual patients who consult us, and should involve us, as physicians, delivering scarce resources to a whole community of patients. As such, I believe that we have to be strategic in our approach to many disease and lifestyle issues. This is no less true with LUTS than, for example, heart failure or asthma. One of the paradoxes of preventative medicine is that those least in need are frequently the ones at the head of the queue for our time and help. Conversely, those less vocal and confident in communicating with their GP may be the ones in greatest need of our attention. Thus, it can be extremely difficult to find a way to ensure that they are not excluded from accessing the healthcare options on offer. Tempting though it may be to 'let sleeping dogs lie', we need to be proactive when offering advice and services to those who are least likely to ask and most likely to tolerate their LUTS in silence.

We have to be strategic in our approach to many disease and lifestyle issues. This is no less true with LUTS than, for example, heart failure or asthma.

LUTS is not a condition with an NHS Read code, but it is one where clinical audit can be usefully applied. Men may be identifiable from computerised records of prescriptions for specific BPH therapies. Representative samples can be collected by offering questionnaires. The annual influenza vaccination programme is one in which large numbers of middle-aged and elderly men attend their GPs' surgeries, and which could serve as a useful platform from which to gather data.

The primary aim may be to determine how well we identify and manage our community of men with overt or covert LUTS. This can be performed by identifying men who are receiving medication and enquiring about the benefits and side-effects. Formal clinical audit can be performed by administering a one-off, standard symptom questionnaire before the initiation of treatment,and later during the course of treatment. This can be undertaken by either a doctor or a nurse. Auditing clinical data for men with LUTS is a relatively straightforward procedure for GP registrars and medical students. The following are useful questions we should be asking:

- what proportion of men have LUTS?
- how many cases were previously known to the doctor or nurse?
- is any prescribed treatment giving benefit?
- are symptoms improving, deteriorating or static?
- are there any adverse effects with current treatment?

Repeating this audit allows us to identify trends and will answer the question: are we improving or deteriorating in the identification and treatment of men with LUTS?

Auditing the numbers and circumstances of men developing acute retention of urine is also theoretically straightforward. Whilst nationally this is a significant problem, fortunately it is a relatively uncommon event in day-to-day primary-care practice. However, acute urinary retention is suitable for critical-incident case analysis. For example:

- were there symptoms that might have predicted an enhanced risk of acute urinary retention?
- how was acute retention managed in the short-term?
- what was the long-term plan to prevent complications and recurrence?

Conclusion

With the greying of UK society, the already common condition of BPH is set to become one of the most important morbidities of older men in primary care. Men with LUTS, in whom prostate cancer has been excluded, are ideally placed to be investigated, diagnosed, treated and monitored in the primary-care setting. Prospectively promoting services and actively seeking cases is satisfyingly straightforward; and the good news is that for men with bothersome LUTS there are effective pharmacological interventions that can make a significant and gratifyingly rapid difference. I hope that after reading this article you will feel empowered to seek cases (they will not be difficult to find) and initiate effective therapy (which will not be difficult to do). For those of you wishing to perform audit, BPH and LUTS are eminently suitable subjects for practice-changing analysis.

BPH and LUTS are eminently suitable subjects for practice-changing analysis.

A specialist's perspective

Diagnosis

The diagnosis of LUTS related to BPH can readily be made in primary care and is based on a history, physical examination, rectal examination, simple investigations to exclude urinary tract infection and renal damage, and urinary flow measurement and ultrasound residuals (these latter two investigations may be available only in larger primary care units with a specialist interest). No specific symptoms reliably indicate bladder outflow obstruction (BOO), and there is no correlation between prostate size and LUTS, or between symptoms and objective data from urodynamics. Certainly, when it comes to assessing the efficacy of therapy, it is clearly established that better outcomes are associated with severe symptoms, low flow rates (<10 mL/second), and proven outlet obstruction. Some symptoms such as frequency, urgency and urge incontinence are associated with detrusor overactivity and a poor outcome after prostatectomy. Therefore, it is particularly important to be cautious when considering surgery in an elderly man with severe overactive bladder symptoms of this nature since this may be the primary problem rather than outflow obstruction. A measure of the severity of symptoms and, by inference, their impact on quality of life can be obtained by the judicious use of a sympton questionnaire such as the IPSS. A careful DRE can exclude locally advanced prostate cancer. However, irrespective of whether a GP or a urologist performs the DRE, it remains a wholly inadequate means of detecting early prostate cancer. Therefore, it is very much up to the individual doctors to use their clinical judgement effectively in order to identify patients most at risk of early disease and to decide whether the PSA level should be checked. Renal function should be assessed by measuring creatinine, but it is not recommended that the upper tracts should be routinely imaged unless there is a specific indication such as an upper tract obstruction or haematuria.

Many men with LUTS contact their GP because they are worried that they may have prostate cancer. In light of a negative DRE and in order to allay continued fears, PSA testing may be performed so long as the patient is fully counselled as to the implications and subsequent actions that may be required following such a test. PSA is also produced by benign prostatic epithelial cells, so many patients presenting with BPH and LUTS will have an elevated PSA. Serum PSA also increases with prostate size and age (by 3.2% per year). There is no doubt that a reliable tool to detect or rule out prostate cancer would be a major step forward. In the meantime we have to use our clinical judgement and employ the diagnostic tools we have, in consultation with our patients, to decide the best way forward. There is no evidence that BPH is associated with the development of prostate cancer.

Treatment

The non-operative treatment of LUTS includes watchful waiting and pharmacotherapy. Some men wish to avoid both medical and surgical therapy, and certainly conservative management (watchful waiting) is an acceptable alternative for some, particularly amongst those primarily seeking reassurance about the possibility of prostate cancer.

The last decade has seen a significant shift in practice, with an increase of over one-third in the numbers of men treated medically. This trend has been encouraged by increasing awareness on the part of both doctors and patients of the availability of drug treatment, and of the potential morbidity of surgical therapy.

It must not be forgotten that BPH can cause some serious complications. Surgical intervention is therefore recommended for complications of LUTS, such as acute urinary retention, gross haematuria secondary to BPH, renal failure or bladder calculi secondary to benign prostatic obstruction, and in patients with severe symptoms. In England and Wales, with the decline in prostatectomy in recent years, up to 30% or more of men undergoing prostatectomy do so because of acute urinary retention, which is associated with a doubling in the risk of death and morbidity compared with elective surgery. Moreover, chronic urinary retention may lead to renal failure and is responsible for 15% of prostatectomies in England and Wales. Referral to a urologist remains essential for any patient who has severe symptoms or is failing to respond to pharmacotherapy.

Key points

- Men's health is relatively neglected in the NHS particularly in comparison with the services available for women. This is in part due to the reluctance of men to discuss their health problems with their GP.

- BPH is a highly prevalent condition in the UK, and its treatment, either through medical or surgical interventions, represents a major cost to the NHS.

- By proactively identifying patients with BPH, we can expect to improve the care of patients with the condition. This can be done through active enquiry about urinary symptoms during routine 'well-man' checks and when reviewing an elderly patient's medication.

- The availability of two distinct classes of agent has meant that the treatment of most cases of BPH can be initiated and continuingly managed within primary care.

- Despite this, it is important to be aware of the criteria for specialist referral. Referral to a urologist is essential for any patient with severe symptoms and for those who fail to respond to pharmacotherapy.

- Clinical audit can be applied in the general practice setting to identify how well we manage patients with urinary symptoms.

8. Cholera

Dr George Kassianos MD (Hons) FRCGP DRCOG LRCPEdin. LRCSEdin. RCP&SGlasg. DFP DMedAcup. DMedHypn MILT
General Practitioner, Bracknell, Berkshire

Summary

Cholera is an important infectious disease globally, although it is infrequently encountered in developed countries. It is endemic in areas where water supplies, sanitation, food safety and hygiene practices are poor, and it imposes an enormous morbidity and mortality burden in these areas. The principal focus in this area from a primary-care perspective is providing appropriate education and vaccination for individuals at risk of developing the condition – namely travellers to endemic areas or individuals who are likely to spend prolonged periods of time in areas with a high risk of cholera infection. Education is vitally important and can encourage individuals to adopt appropriate preventive measures when abroad, such as ensuring that the water they drink and bathe in is taken from safe sources. Back home, GPs should be aware of how cholera presents. Whilst it is unlikely that a doctor will see a case of cholera in their surgery, it is important to rule out cholera infection in travellers returning home with diarrhoea. The availability of an effective oral cholera vaccine in the UK will ensure that individuals travelling to endemic areas of cholera infection minimise their risk of infection, although it is still important that vaccinated individuals remain aware of the preventive measures to take in order to minimise their exposure to the causative bacterium.

Introduction

In the history of mankind, two measures have saved more lives than anything else. They are the provision of safe and clean water and the provision of vaccines for controlling and eliminating infectious disease. We are lucky in the UK to have been provided with both of these measures for many years. However, the vast majority of people around the world are not so lucky.

Although rare in developed countries, cholera is still an important infection worldwide. It occurs as part of an epidemic, or sporadically, in

Although rare in developed countries, cholera is still an important infection worldwide.

many areas in the developing world. New outbreaks of cholera can be seen in regions where water supplies, sanitation, food safety and hygiene practices are inadequate. Therefore, overpopulated communities with poor sanitation and unsafe drinking water supplies are most at risk and the all too common mass refugee problems add considerably to the problem. In addition, cholera is also occasionally found in travellers returning from endemic countries.

The history of the disease

The Greeks thought of cholera as a bilious (khole=bile) disease of a virulent form. In the 19th Century it was thought to be due to 'miasma' or bad smells. During the epidemic of 1853–54, John Snow mapped all the cases in a severely affected area of London and found them clustering around a water pump in Broad Street, Soho. He later went on to discover that the sewage had been contaminating the well supplying this pump. The epidemic started declining soon after he removed the handle from the pump thus rendering it unusable. The last indigenous cholera infection in the UK was in 1893. Cholera became a notifiable disease in England and Wales in 1889 and it remains so under the 1984 Public Health (Control of Diseases) Act. It is also notifiable in Scotland and Northern Ireland.

Since 1961, cholera infection has spread from Indonesia through most of Asia, the Indian subcontinent, the Middle East into Eastern Europe and Africa, and from North Africa to the Iberian Peninsula and Italy where we saw epidemics as recently as the 1970s. In 1991, an extensive epidemic began in Peru and spread to neighbouring countries in South America. By 2001, 58 countries reported cholera infection to the World Health Organisation (WHO). At present, we are still experiencing this 'seventh pandemic' in countries in Africa, Asia, Middle East and South America.

The global challenge of cholera

It was not so long ago that the injectable cholera vaccine was available in the UK. At the time, as every GP or nurse that worked in primary care will remember, patients were asking for the cholera vaccine before discussing any other vaccine. This continued long after the parenteral vaccine was withdrawn, such was the fear of cholera.

Cholera is a rare disease in travellers who follow usual tourist itineraries and who observe food and water safety recommendations while travelling in endemic countries. However, cholera infection remains a challenge to those of our travellers who, during their travels, do not always have access to safe drinking and bathing water as well as adequate sanitation.

Although the risk of cholera infection in European and North American travellers has been estimated at 1 in 500,000 this may be an under-estimate. In Japan, where regular microbiological screening for cholera is carried out among returning travellers with diarrhoea, they have found the overall incidence to be 25 in 100,000, and more specifically, 65 in 100,000 in those returning from Bali. The WHO believes that 5–10% of the true overall cholera incidence is reported, and that even this might be optimistic for travellers.

Between 1995 and 2001, about 80 cases of cholera were imported into the UK. In 1998, 21 cases were reported, mostly imported from Asia, in particular the Indian subcontinent. This coincided with increased rainfall and flooding in these areas during that year.

The provision of safe drinking water and effective sanitation programmes have been a major challenge for many developing countries. Lack or misappropriation of funds, bureaucratic barriers in government offices, small allocations of funds to rural areas, and lack of qualified personnel can all hinder projects for delivering safe drinking water and the safe disposal of sewage.

Change and improvement in personal behaviour and hygiene practices are very important in breaking the cycle of water and food contamination via the faecal–oral route. However, health education is difficult in countries with low literacy rates.

The challenge for primary care

More than 8 million British people every year travel to developing countries. An appreciable number of these travellers visit friends and relatives and thus expose themselves even more to the local environment, including infections. According to data from the Public Health Laboratory, 90% of travellers to Pakistan tend to be indigenous to that country, compared to 60% of those visiting India. A large number of practices around the UK have considerable numbers of patients from the Indian subcontinent that frequently travel home to visit friends and relatives. Obviously, these patients are at particular risk.

Most of the UK's primary-care practices offer advice to their patient travellers and, where appropriate, vaccination against specific infectious diseases the traveller may encounter in the countries they are visiting. It is important to be able to give accurate advice on how a traveller should stay healthy abroad, how they can avoid accidents and how to prevent disease, especially infectious disease. Clinicians should also be able to recognise infectious disease in the returning traveller.

Recognition of cholera infection in the traveller

The incubation period for cholera is very short; from hours to 3 or 4 days. For this reason, the returning traveller may contract the disease and fully recover before returning to the UK. In 90% of cases cholera is mild and may present simply as 'gastroenteritis'. We should be alert to this possibility. Laboratory investigations (see below) should be undertaken to enable a firm microbiological diagnosis of gastroenteritis in a traveller to be made.

Although we are unlikely to see a case of cholera in our GP consulting rooms here in the UK, the possibility exists of us seeing such a case in a fellow passenger or in other people during travel abroad. It is important to remember the presentation of severe cholera. The volume of small intestine fluid reaching the colon in a patient with severe cholera far exceeds the maximum reabsorptive capacity of the colon (6 litres a day). This results in profuse diarrhoea. The dehydration can be sudden and fatal. The stools initially contain faecal matter (watery brown), but quickly change to pale fluid stools with a fishy odour, containing some mucous and cell debris ('rice-water stools'). Early in illness there can be vomiting too. Fever is not prominent.

If you are dealing with a case of severe cholera while abroad, the signs and symptoms to look for in addition to diarrhoea are hypotension, decrease in pulse volume and increase in rate, increase in respiratory rate, dry mucous membranes, sunken eyes and cheeks, lethargy, weakness, irritability, polydypsia, and oliguria or anuria. If the patient is a pregnant woman, the disease can be even more severe.

How to make a laboratory diagnosis

Treatment should not be delayed pending diagnosis. Examination of the diarrhoea stool will give an early indication as to the diagnosis. If we are abroad, we may or may not have access to a laboratory at the time.

If the patient is in the UK, freshly passed stools will need to be sent to a laboratory with minimum delay. In acute disease, *Vibrio cholerae* have characteristic darting motility in freshly passed stools examined under the microscope. However, to confirm the diagnosis the laboratory will need to demonstrate inhibition with specific antiserum.

It is my policy to send a stool specimen to the laboratory in every case where a returning traveller presents with diarrhoea. Other laboratory investigations should be carried out according to the case and suspicion.

It is my policy to send a stool specimen to the laboratory in every case where a returning traveller presents with diarrhoea.

Carriage of infection

The question of carriage will invariably arise when counselling the patient or their family. Asymptomatic carriage of Classic cholera strains is unusual.

On the other hand, the El Tor strains may be excreted by convalescent patients as well as asymptomatic carriers. A 5-day course of antibiotic therapy usually eradicates excretion in most cases. It is important to ensure such patients and their close contacts have follow-up stool examinations.

Treatment of infection

We must remember that in cholera, the mucosal cells are intact, therefore, their absorptive function is retained. Early rehydration can save the lives of nearly all patients with cholera. Oral rehydration is successful in 90% of cases. Intravenous fluids are only necessary in severely dehydrated patients, those that are exhausted, or in coma. When visiting developing countries, remember to take sachets of oral rehydration solution with you. If needed, they can save a life!

Antibiotics are only indicated in severe or prolonged disease. In such instances, they can reduce the length of the diarrhoea from about 4–6 days to about 2–3 days. In my opinion, the drug of choice is oxytetracycline, 500 mg, 6-hourly by mouth or via a nasogastric tube, for 3–5 days. An alternative therapy is ciprofloxacin, 500 mg by mouth or 200 mg intravenously, 12-hourly, for 3–5 days.

Preventing cholera infection in travellers

Water and food

It is important we remember how cholera infection is acquired in order to give the best advice to travellers on disease prevention. Drinking water that has been contaminated at its source or during storage, or taking ice or other products made of contaminated water, is the principal source of infection. Another major source of infection is ingestion of food contaminated during or after preparation (e.g. seafood, fruit and vegetables grown in soil contaminated with human waste or contaminated water). Tables 5 and 6 provide general advice that should be given to travellers with regards to water and food precautions.

Travellers to religious or other festivals or fairs, as well as those who are going to stay or work with locals in developing countries' need to take particular care and they need our personal attention.

Vaccination

In the UK, we no longer have the parenteral cholera vaccine available. Most of us will remember this vaccine as having a high incidence of side-effects, especially after intramuscular, or subcutaneous administration, resulting in

Table 5. General advice to travellers for safe water (adapted from Kassianos G. *Immunization Childhood and Travel Health,* 4th Edition (2001), Blackwell Science).

- Wash hands after using the toilet and before handling/eating food. Use paper towels or hot air to dry hands. Avoid used, damp, cloth towels – better to drip dry hands.
- Drink plenty, avoid tap water. Uncontaminated rain, spring or deep well water is usually safe.
- Unless confident about the safety of the local water do not use it. Make water safe by:
  - boiling at 100 °C for 10 minutes
  - chemical disinfection using iodine tablets etc.
  - filtration using commercially available water filters.
- Use bottled water from a reputable source. The seal must be intact and opened in your presence. Carbonated water is preferable – it is unlikely to have been filled from the tap.
- As a last resort use tap water that is uncomfortably hot to touch and allow to cool.
- Avoid ice in drinks as it may have been made using tap water.
- It is usually safe to drink wine, beer and minerals (cans and bottles) providing the seal is intact.
- Wipe clean surfaces that may come in contact with mouth. If possible use sterile, individually-wrapped straws. Avoid using straws unless they are individually wrapped.
- Hot coffee or tea is safe if water has been boiled for 5 minutes.
- Use 'safe' or preboiled water to clean teeth.
- Drink only pasteurised milk, or boil at 55°C for 30 minutes or 65°C for 1 minute.
- Always carry a 'safe' drink with you.
- Avoid excessive alcohol as it can exacerbate dehydration.
- Do not open your mouth while taking a shower or swimming. Prepare a bath with very hot water and allow it to cool before using.
- Do not swim in rivers or ponds. Seawater may also be contaminated with sewage.

In a meeting of the WHO in Geneva, it was recommended that the oral killed whole-cell/B subunit cholera vaccine be considered among the tools to prevent cholera in populations that may be at risk.

local pain, tenderness, erythema, induration, malaise, fever and headaches in most individuals.

Another vaccine we do not have available in the UK is the live, attenuated oral cholera vaccine (CVD 103-HgR strain of *Vibrio*). It is licensed in many European countries and Canada. Protection from this vaccine is short-lived. It is currently not recommended for children under the age of 2 years, and antibiotics as well as malaria chemoprophylaxis with proguanil-containing agents must be avoided from 1 week before until 1 week after administration of this live vaccine.

In a 1999 meeting of the WHO members in Geneva, it was recommended that the oral killed whole-cell/B subunit (WC-BS) cholera vaccine be considered among the tools to prevent cholera in populations that may be at risk of a cholera epidemic within 6 months, and not experiencing a current epidemic. This recommendation ensured cholera vaccination was not the sole measurement to prevent cholera outbreaks in emergency situations.

Table 6. General advice to travellers for safe food (adapted from Kassianos G. *Immunization Childhood and Travel Health*, 4th Edition (2001), Blackwell Science).

- Eat freshly prepared food that is roasting hot, thoroughly cooked. Pink meat should be avoided.
- All raw food is subject to contamination.
- Avoid cooked food that has been kept at room temperature.
- Avoid leftovers or reheated food.
- Soft cheeses may be a source of listeriosis or brucellosis.
- Ensure the yolk in an egg is cooked until solid.
- Avoid food, sauces, relishes etc. that have been left out and exposed to flies.
- Spicy foods do not have a lower risk of contamination.
- Avoid shellfish (e.g. clams, mussels, oysters, prawns etc.) or raw fish.
- Avoid cold cuts, salads, raw vegetables, watermelons (sometimes injected with water to increase their weight).
- Avoid dairy products (e.g. puddings and ice creams) unless pasteurised milk has been used.
- Only eat fruit that you can peel personally.
- Eat food from sealed packs or cans but not if package appears swollen.
- Avoid food from street vendors.
- Eat in busy, clean restaurants.
- Ensure the plates and cutlery have been washed with detergent and clean water and have been protected from flies.
- Wash hands before handling/eating food – dry under hand dryer or with disposable hand towels.
- Avoid nibbles at the bar – you cannot be sure of the personal hygiene of other customers.
- Never forget the golden rule :"Boil it, cook it, peel it…or forget it!"

The only vaccine that is currently licensed in the UK is the inactivated whole-cell *V. cholerae* strains (Classical and El Tor; Inaba and Ogawa) plus purified recombinant cholera toxin B subunit (WC-rBS). Dukoral™ vaccine is recommended for children over the age of 2 years and adults, including pregnant and breast-feeding mothers. It provides approximately 80–85% protection for 6 months against infection caused by *V. cholerae* O1 in young children as well as adults, and 51% for at least 36 months (63% protection for individuals older than 6 years of age). We expect protection to be present 7 days after completing vaccine administration.

Dukoral is not licensed in the UK for the protection against enterotoxigenic *E. coli* (ETEC), a common cause of travellers diarrhoea. It is licensed in some other countries for this indication. The vaccine induces short-term (approximately 3 months) protection of around 60% against travellers' diarrhoea caused by ETEC. In trying to put things into perspective, when considering all causes of travellers' diarrhoea, this vaccine is about 23% effective at reducing the incidence of diarrhoea, compared with placebo. This is a welcome additional effect of this vaccine for one-off trips for any traveller to developing countries and certainly for us medics when we travel abroad.

> The only vaccine that is currently licensed in the UK is Dukoral™

It is important that we emphasise to travellers that, even if vaccinated, they must continue to be prudent about food and drink. There are no current British recommendations as to who should receive the vaccine. However, the licence stipulates the use of the vaccine for active immunisation of adults and children over the age of 2 years who will be visiting areas with an ongoing or anticipated epidemic or who will be spending an extended period of time in areas in which cholera infection is a risk.

In my view, there are some groups of travellers who are at particular risk of cholera infection when travelling to endemic areas, see Table 7. For these travellers I would particularly recommend vaccination.

Chemoprophylaxis

This is not effective and we should avoid prescribing prophylactic antibiotics, since such practice could lead to rapid development of antibiotic resistance.

Certification

Back in the 1970s, the only available cholera vaccine was the parenteral vaccine, which was not shown to have appreciable effectiveness during cholera outbreaks, nor was it shown to be able to interrupt transmission of *V. cholerae* in communities. At the same time it was impeding other more useful sanitary and therapeutic interventions. For these and other reasons,

Table 7. Travellers to endemic areas at particular risk of cholera infection.

- Emergency relief and health workers in refugee situations
- Relief, healthcare workers, missionaries and others that will work in refugee camps or urban slum areas
- Humanitarian workers frequently travelling abroad
- Military personnel
- Pilgrims to endemic areas or where there are outbreaks of the disease
- People undertaking long-term work abroad
- People with pre-existing disease that may be aggravated by the symptoms of cholera
- Those travelling extensively to rural areas
- People visiting friends and relatives
- People intending to spend time with the locals
- Backpackers
- Women who, during travel, intend becoming or are currently pregnant or lactating
- Immunosuppressed (by disease or treatment) travellers
- People taking antacids
- People of blood group O

the World Health Assembly removed the requirement for cholera vaccination for international travel in 1973. Currently, no country requires cholera vaccination as a condition of entry. However, some countries may require documentation of cholera vaccination in individuals travelling during a cholera outbreak or entering their country from an actively endemic area.

Conclusion

Cholera is a disease that does not discriminate once it spreads to a particular area. During outbreaks of cholera, people of all ages are at risk. Two parallel strategies are required to prevent cholera infection.

Firstly, it is important to prevent local transmission by improving water quality and sanitary conditions as well as the education of the local populations, access to health facilities and adequate supplies of rehydration solutions. Many countries, especially in Africa, are not able to deal with outbreaks independently and collaborative international efforts are necessary.

Secondly, we must adequately prepare travellers to endemic areas, particularly those at high risk of infection.

We are unlikely to see eradication of cholera in the world because of its environmental reservoirs that will probably continue to cause infection for many centuries to come. Although the disease no longer posses a threat to countries with adequate standards of hygiene, it remains a challenge to those that lack adequate sanitation and provision of safe drinking water.

No country requires cholera vaccination as a condition of entry. However, some countries may require documentation of cholera vaccination in individuals travelling during a cholera outbreak or entering their country from an actively endemic area.

Key points

- Cholera remains an important global infection, and occurs in areas where water supplies, sanitation, food safety and hygiene practices are poor.

- Whilst cholera is rare in developed countries, the fear of cholera persists for those visiting countries where the disease is endemic.

- More than 8 million individuals travel to developing countries each year and therefore it is essential that they receive advice on how to remain healthy when they are abroad. It is also important that clinicians are confident in recognising signs of infectious disease when traveller returns home.

- Whilst it is unlikely to see a case of cholera presenting in a GP practice, it is important to be aware of the presentation of the disease. Laboratory investigations should be performed on stool specimens when a traveller returns with diarrhoea.

- A number of preventive measures can be adopted to minimise the risk of acquiring cholera. This includes ensuring that water sources are safe and free of potential infection.

- An oral cholera vaccine is available in the UK for immunisation of adults and children over 2 years who are visiting areas with an ongoing or anticipated epidemic or for those who are planning to spend an extended period of time in areas with a high risk of cholera infection.

- Whilst vaccination is important for travellers to endemic areas of cholera infection, it is still essential to emphasise the importance of preventive measures to vaccinated individuals.

9. Chronic pain

Dr Graham Archard
Chair, Clinical Networks Royal College General Practitioners
Chair of Pain Committee, Pain Society Council member

Summary

Chronic pain is a very common symptom, and is one of the main reasons for individuals to seek medical help. As such, it exerts a huge burden in terms of the consumption of healthcare resources. Probably of more importance to the patient though is the huge impact that chronic pain has on quality of life, with up to 20% reporting pain so intense that sometimes they would prefer to die. Despite the extent of the problem, pain control is poorly recognised in terms of training and currently there are no central Government- or Department of Health-led initiatives which focus on pain control in practice. Moreover, the available guidelines which are most closely adhered to are not detailed enough to be of value in general practice. Whilst it is relatively easy to identify patients with chronic pain, there are a number of steps which can be implemented that can help us audit our professional performance in patient management. Taking an appropriate pain history can help define a management approach, whether it is a pharmacological intervention alone or in combination with other non-pharmacological techniques such as physiotherapy and psychological intervention. It would then be possible to determine whether the same approaches to management are taken by individuals within a practice and to identify shortcomings which can be implemented in practice and personal development plans.

The burden on general practice

Chronic or persistent pain is one of the most common presenting complaints in general practice. One-in-seven, or 7.5 million people suffer chronic pain in the UK and 20% have suffered for more than 20 years.[1] Thus, one-third of UK households are affected by chronic pain. Not surprisingly, patients with chronic pain consult their GP up to five-times more frequently than the general population, accounting for nearly 5 million GP consultations a year.[2] Seven per cent of the UK population receive incapacity benefit, of which 22% cite diseases of the musculoskeletal system and connective tissues as the reason for their claim, representing a cost to the community of £6.6 billion.[3,4] Persistent pain is responsible for 208 million lost work days a year, at a cost of £18 billion.[5]

Men and women are equally affected by pain and it occurs across all age ranges. Forty per cent of patients suffer with chronic pain as a consequence of arthritis and osteoarthritis – the most common site being the lower back. In an ageing population, the prevalence of osteoarthritis and thus chronic pain is set to increase, placing a greater burden on general practice. It is therefore important to prioritise this condition now, in order to provide effective management.

The burden on patients

The Pain in Europe Study revealed that 50% of those patients with chronic pain feel tired, helpless, older than they really are, and do not remember what it feels like not to be in pain (Figure 1).[1] One-in-five patients said that the pain is sometimes so bad they want to die. Forty-seven per cent of patients with chronic pain surveyed stated they would invest all their money in pain treatments if they knew they would work. Chronic pain also affected daily activities, with one-in-four patients reporting losing a job and a similar number being diagnosed with depression as a result of their pain.

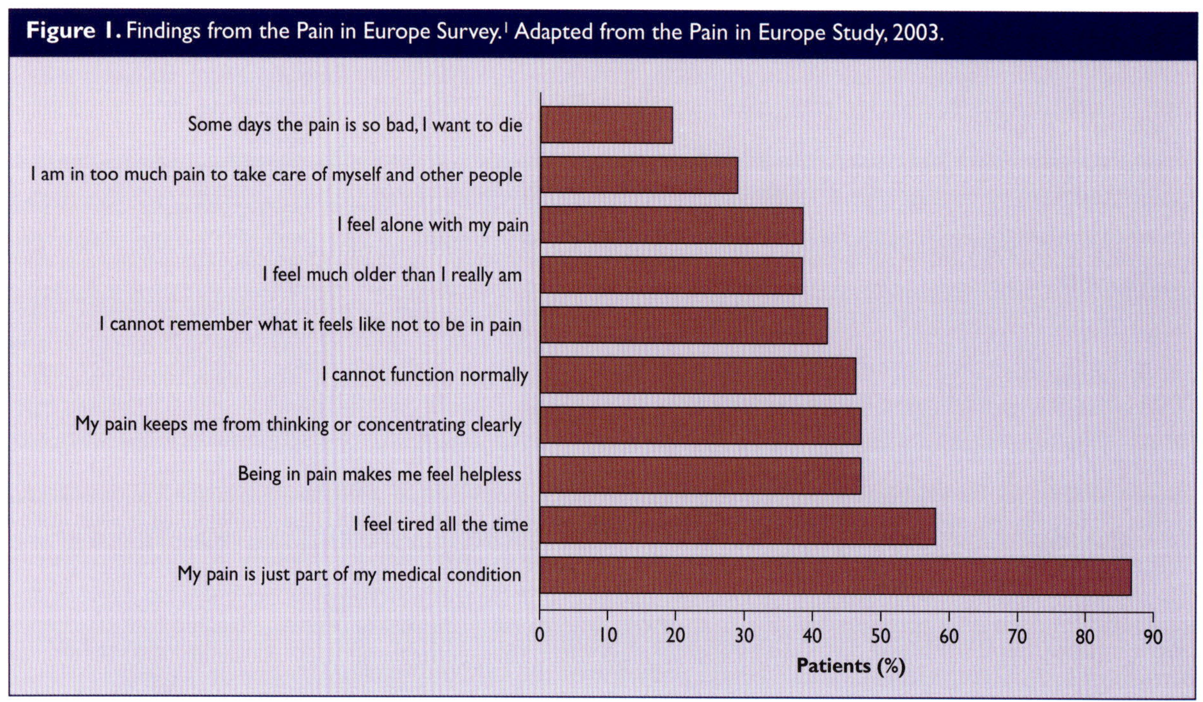

Figure 1. Findings from the Pain in Europe Survey.[1] Adapted from the Pain in Europe Study, 2003.

Despite all this, the majority of patients (70%) are very or extremely satisfied with the doctor who treats their pain, but 39% feel the doctor concentrates on the illness causing the pain rather than the pain itself. The most common prescription treatment is opioids but complementary therapies are popular with patients. Thus, 15% have massage, 12% acupuncture, 9% heat treatment and 8% exercise.

Challenges for general practice

Considering the impact of persistent pain on general practice and the population at large, it would be surprising if this condition was not a national priority. However, there appears to be little undergraduate training in pain control, no National Institute for Clinical Excellence (NICE) guidance and no inclusion of pain control in the new General Medical Services (GMS) contract. Thus, the burden of pain continues to be a Cinderella condition, with little emphasis from the centre on control despite the overwhelming evidence that this should be the case. The most commonly used guidelines are the World Health Organisation (WHO) pain guidelines, which are just not detailed enough for general practice.

Improving the management of chronic pain will reduce the burden on general practice, patients and the general population, both directly and indirectly, by reducing the social and financial consequences it produces.

How can we identify those patients with persistent pain?

At first sight this seems to be obvious. Those in pain will inform their GP, although this is not always the case, and many patients, as we have seen above, have inadequate pain control even if we have identified this as a problem.

The facts state that 30–50% of patients being treated for solid tumours and 70–90% of those with advanced cancer, are in pain.[3,6] More than 500,000 patients suffer from neuropathic pain, including 25% of diabetics.[7,8] If all members of the practice team are recording pathology in a consistent way, it will be a relatively easy task to identify those patients with painful conditions – those with arthritis, diabetic neuropathy, post-herpetic neuralgia and cancer. This in itself is a useful exercise to see if all members of the team are using the same Read codes for these conditions.

If we are serious about identifying those patients who are in pain, it may be worthwhile displaying a poster in the waiting room, inviting those patients experiencing pain to identify themselves to the team member who will be seeing them. There are several good pain scales that can be used in practice to see just how much pain a patient is suffering. These are available on the Pain Society website in a number of different languages.[9]

There are a number of misconceptions regarding pain. Some patients feel that unless they give exaggerated demonstrations of their pain by grimacing or other appropriate body language, they will not be believed. Conversely, other patients are concerned that they will not be believed if they act calmly. Patients who do not take painkillers may be considered uncooperative or are not in pain – this is just not the case either, as some patients find the side-effects of analgesia such as sedation worse than the condition – and some pains hardly respond at all to analgesia. It is also not true that pain does not exist where a cause cannot be found nor that the extent of pain a patient experiences is at all relative to the extent of pathology or injury found.

Pain management

A careful pain history is important to ensure that management is appropriate and effective and questions like those listed below are a good means of defining a management strategy for the individual patient.

- How long has the pain been present, and does the pattern change?
- Where is the pain and does it radiate anywhere?
- How severe is the pain? A pain score card can be used.
- Describe the pain – is it tight, stabbing, aching or burning?
- Does anything make it better or worse – position, activity, rest or analgesia?
- Does the patient feel depressed as a consequence of the pain?
- How is their quality of life affected – can the patient still work, do hobbies, exercise – is it affecting relationships and home life?

All types of non-neuropathic pain are managed in the same way through the use of the WHO analgesia ladder. Thus, breakthrough pain, bone pain and other chronic pain should be controlled quickly by quickly escalating the strength of analgesia used until the pain is controlled.

Although treating the underlying cause of pain is paramount, whilst this is improving, it is imperative that symptoms of pain are adequately controlled. Many causes of pain are untreatable, and so pain control becomes the main focus of attention.

Pharmacological pain control

Movement up and down the WHO pain ladder should be swift – starting at the appropriate step of the ladder. Paracetamol is frequently under utilised in pain control because of the perception that it is not particularly effective. In fact, taken at maximum dose, a large number of patients achieve very adequate analgesia using this. When used in combination with codeine, paracetamol has even greater efficacy.

Non-steroidal anti-inflammatory drugs (NSAIDs) and cyclo-oxygenase (COX)-2 inhibitors are effective analgesics particularly where inflammation is involved. Non-steroidals administered rectally still concentrate in the stomach so care must be taken in patients susceptible to gastrointestinal bleeds even using this route of administration. If in doubt a COX-2 selective inhibitor should be used or proton pump inhibitor (PPI) with a non-steroidal.[a]

Opioid analgesia should be used when non-opioid analgesia is ineffective. Opioid analgesics range in strength from codeine through to morphine analogues. It is obviously an easier management decision to use opioids in malignant pain rather than non-malignant pain, but they should not be withheld where they are needed. Patients needing strong opioids for the treatment for non-malignant pain should usually be referred to secondary care to ensure that a causative factor has not been missed and that there is no other suitable management. Patients should be warned about the common side-effects of opioids, including constipation, nausea and vomiting (which normally settles within a week or so) and dry mouth. Patients should also be warned about the possibility of sedation and be advised not to drive or use machinery until they are maintained on a stable dose. Opioids can also be used for the treatment of neuropathic pain, but antiepileptics, antidepressants, topical medications, steroids, bisphosphonates and hormone therapy have also been used with success.

Ultimately patients may need syringe drivers to deliver opioids for pain control. Syringe drivers are generally used when analgesics cannot be taken orally or that they have become ineffective. They are generally fairly freely available through the palliative care services. It is important to ensure that those caring for these patients understand how the drivers work, the dosage regimen, what to do if they go wrong and also to ensure that there is sufficient stock and prescribing authorisation for the analgesics used.

Non-pharmacological pain control

Physiotherapy is commonly considered for pain relief and can be particularly effective in some conditions – notably osteoarthritis. Ultrasound is less popular than it used to be as there is little evidence that it

---

[a]Editor's note: there is clearly some divergence in opinion between authors of the value of NSAIDs in chronic pain control.

is any more effective than placebo. Maintaining muscle strength improves joint mobility, and those who find it difficult to exercise regularly can find it helpful to join a club – such as yoga, Tai Chi, aerobics or aqua-aerobics – which helps to keep joints supple and muscles stronger.

Transcutaneous electrical nerve stimulation (TENS) is rarely used for the long-term control of pain though in the short term it can provide rapid and effective relief.

Complementary therapies such as massage, aromatherapy, reflexology and acupuncture can be extremely beneficial for some patients. Although there is little scientific evidence to support claims of their efficacy, more and more centres are using these techniques with much success in pain control. It is unlikely that patients will suffer as a result of these therapies, so they should not be discouraged from trying them.

Joint and soft tissue injection with steroids and local anaesthetics can be very beneficial in soft tissue pathology, whilst nerve blocks – either temporary or permanent – are effective when undertaken by those with the necessary skills.

Psychological approaches to pain control must not be forgotten as they are very effective for patients to accommodate their lives when they have intractable pain. This is usually undertaken in group sessions by a multidisciplinary team with the aim of getting people back to work and to be able to revert to their usual daily routines through cognitive behavioural therapy.

Patients also benefit by having an input into their own pain management. Self-help groups can provide patients with practical suggestions and advice on how to cope with their condition in particular, and their pain in general. These are listed on the British Pain Society website at (*www.britishpainsociety.org/gen_org_list.htm*).

When to refer

Patients with chronic pain who have been managed for a long time have the right to be reviewed to ensure that diagnoses have not been missed, that pharmacological and non-pharmacological therapies have been adequately explored and that there is nothing more that can be done to improve their lives. If the primary-care team cannot improve management then patients should be considered for referral to secondary care. It is important not to forget that social services can provide help not only to the patient but also to the carer in the form of respite care, patient sitting services and financial allowances for those caring for the chronically sick. In order to ensure that patients are properly managed it is essential to have the means to identify who they are – and this is where the computer coding is so important as a means of identifying the cohort to audit performance.

According to the Pain in Europe Study, patients felt that their chronic pain was not being adequately controlled. Primary care cannot possibly provide all the methods of pain control and so it is important to refer early rather than late if chronic pain is not controlled quickly. This is particularly important for patients who are likely to deteriorate – for example, those with cancer pain – and appropriate referral to the pain clinic or palliative care services should be made. Local factors will determine what facilities are available, but the secret of success in the management of chronic pain is through communicating with palliative care services, the local hospices, Macmillan nurses and other providers of specialised care. Most of these services are keen to work with Primary Care providers within an effective team. The Gold Standards Framework in Community Palliative Care provides examples of best practice on how to care for the patient in the last weeks and months of life and makes suggestions on how we can best organise palliative care services for our patients in the community.[10]

Hand over of care to the out-of-hours provider should be considered carefully. Local mechanisms of faxing through patient details can provide a lifeline for continuity of care. The message has to be: if in doubt fax through the details. There needs to be a mechanism to ensure that all practitioners actively consider the passing of this sort of information regularly, particularly before a weekend or bank holiday.

Clinical audit

Ensuring that we are practising as well as we feel we should is fundamental to our professionalism. There are a number of audit points that can be considered in the management of pain and the findings of the audit can then be used across the practice as part of the Practice Professional Development Plan as well as Personal Development Plans for all clinical staff.

- Are the same medications used across the practice for the management of chronic pain? If not, then this can be confusing if a patient does not see their usual doctor. It is worthwhile examining Prescribing Analysis and Cost (PACT) data (Sections 4.7.1 – non opioid analgesics and 4.7.2 – opioid analgesics) and discussing what should be used in your practice.
- Have patients been reviewed properly with regard to their pain? Should a pain scale be used and scores recorded to see how well pain is being managed?

- Does the practice have a pain pathway which can be used for each patient to ensure that all management techniques are used at the appropriate time? If not, would it be worthwhile producing one in collaboration with a local pain specialist?
- Do all members of the practice refer at the same rate and to the same specialist? If not is this because some are better at treating persistent pain, or do some dismiss pain control as a low priority? Examining individual patient records should identify the reasons behind this.
- Finally, all patients attending the surgery should be given a questionnaire asking if they are in pain, how long they have been suffering pain, if the pain is adequately controlled, if the patient feels the surgery takes their pain seriously and so on. The results can be enlightening, if not embarrassing, but can identify areas of practice that might need improvement.

GPs may find pain score sheets a useful adjunct in the assessment of pain. These are available in numerous languages on the British Pain Society website (*www.britishpainsociety.org/pain_scales.html*).

Patient expectations and perspectives

The Pain in Europe Survey has shown that many patients feel that their persistent pain is poorly controlled. This can be due to poor performance by health professionals, but can also be due to lack of understanding by the patient. Patients are often concerned about side-effects, dependency and addiction to medications and they should be carefully counselled about this. Many patients will stop taking analgesics because of their side-effects, thus treatment for constipation should be considered on an 'as necessary' basis whenever opioids are prescribed. Patients who understand possible side-effects and their management and who are reassured about the safety of their prescribed medication will be more likely to take them regularly and have better pain control.

Patients should be asked to make a subjective assessment and even keep a diary of their pain. This will assist the clinician to change medication appropriately and to identify such complications as breakthrough pain. It should be explained that a lower dose of analgesia may be needed to keep pain under control than was needed to control it in the first place.

The control of pain – particularly at the end of life – is much more effective with the active participation of patients and their carers. Strong opioids can control pain but they do not lengthen life. Indeed their respiratory depressant effects may even shorten life. The management of pain at the end of life must be considered and discussed before it is too late.

Patients should be assured that everything will be done to control their pain at the end of their life, and the degree of active intervention – such as hospitalisation – should be discussed with the patient and carers if at all possible when these decisions can be made soberly and in advance. The wishes of the patient and carer should be documented and instructions left in the patient's home as well as with the out-of-hours providers so that the wishes of the patient and carers can be addressed.

Euthanasia, rightly or wrongly, remains a criminal offence in the UK. Its practice can neither be condoned nor supported by the profession no matter what the personal views of the patient or professional.

Future directions?

So what of the future? Will there be NICE guidance on the management of pain? This is unlikely. There are a number of groups who recognise the importance of pain control and are striving to move this up the political agenda. There have been a number of questions asked in parliament recently and an early day motion was tabled asking for the prioritisation of pain management. There are no comprehensive pain management guidelines, but there are a number of good courses exist on pain management for those interested enough to attend.

In the light of little help from elsewhere it is vitally important that, as non-specialists in pain control, we try to ensure that we are doing all we can to manage pain to the best of our ability. All disciplines in primary care have an obligation to ensure that performance is monitored and that patients are being offered the best management possible. Auditing performance each year against medications, referrals and patient questionnaires is probably the best methodology for achieving this.

Practices should consider the possibility of identifying a practitioner within the team – be it a nurse or doctor – who may wish to extend their knowledge and skills to act as a resource for the practice or group of practices. Not only will patients benefit, but so will the primary heathcare team which will not be so overburdened with the huge number of appointments being taken up by patients with poorly controlled pain.

The Shipman Enquiry is about to make recommendations regarding the safe storage, prescribing, administration and destruction of controlled drugs. Most of what has been published so far is accepted as good practice by the profession. What we must not do, however, is react in a way which will deprive patients of the appropriate management of their pain. If strong opioids are needed, then they should be prescribed. Most patients will make a useful contribution to their management plan if kept educated and informed – and this includes the use of strong opioids.

> It is vitally important that, as non-specialists in pain control, we try to ensure that we are doing all we can to manage pain to the best of our ability.

Small definite steps are usually more effective than wholesale change of provision. The introduction of a simple assessment device – such as a pain score sheet – may be all that is required to demonstrate quality of practice and to be the catalyst for change.

Key points

- More than 7.5 million people suffer from chronic pain in the UK, with one-in-five suffering with persistent chronic pain that can last for more than 20 years.

- Chronic pain exerts a huge and negative impact upon the economy and upon the individual.

- Despite its impact on primary care resources, chronic pain is not regarded as a national priority, training is inadequate, and moreover, pain control is not included within the new GMS GP contract.

- Whilst identifying patients with chronic pain would appear to be relatively straightforward, there are a number of practical approaches that can be implemented to identify patients who 'slip through the net' and who would benefit from pain control.

- A pain history is vital in determining an appropriate management strategy for a individual.

- Pharmacological management of chronic pain may involve paracetamol, NSAIDs or opioids, whilst non-pharmacological pain control includes the use of physiotherapy, complementary therapy and psychotherapy.

- Auditing professional performance in the control of chronic pain can play a major role in improving patient management and can also as part of individual professional and practice development.

- Patient pain diaries and simple assessment devices may help to monitor pain control and overall performance.

References

1 Pain in Europe. A 2003 Report. Research project, by NFO Worldgroup. Funded by an educational grant from Mundipharma International Limited. Cambridge, England, October 2003.

2 Services for Patients with Pain. London: Clinical Standards Advisory Group, 2000.

3 *http://www.dwp.gov.uk/asd/asd1/ib_sda/ib_sda_may02_pub.pdf*

4 *http://www.dwp.gov.uk/asd/asd4/Table3.xls*

5 Arthritis: The Big Picture. Chesterfield: Arthritis Research Campaign, 2002.

6 Addington-Hall J, McCarthy M. Dying from cancer: results of a national population-based investigation. *Ann Oncol* 1995; **9**: 295–305.

7 Karlsten R, Gordh T. How do drugs relieve neurogenic pain? *Drugs Aging* 1997, **11**: 398–412 .

8 Chan AW, MacFarlane IA, Bowsher D, *et al*. Chronic pain in patients with diabetes mellitus: comparison with a non-diabetic population. *Pain Clinic* **3**: 147–59.

9 *www.painsociety.org*

10 Thomas K. *Caring for the dying at home: companions on the journey.* Abingdon: Radcliffe Medical Press Ltd, 2003.

10. COPD

Dr Rupert Jones MB, BS, BSc (Hons) Pharmacology, DCH, DRCOG, MRCGP, DipOccMed, Clinical Research Fellow, Respiratory Research Unit, Peninsula Medical School, Plymouth, Devon
General Practitioner, Plymouth, Devon

Summary

Chronic obstructive pulmonary disease (COPD) exerts a major burden on healthcare resources in addition to the significant morbidity it imposes on the affected patient. Much of this burden falls upon primary care, and therefore it essential that GPs respond with appropriate strategies to improve patient management. Accurate identification of affected patients will invariably require spirometry, and the new General Medical Services (GMS) contract recognises the importance of this diagnostic tool, and provides financial rewards to those practices which employ such services. Despite this, there are numerous problems in providing quality spirometry services in the community. The availability of practical guidelines may go someway to improve the management of the condition, and recently the National Institute for Clinical Excellence (NICE) have published COPD management guidelines from a UK perspective. However, there is some deviation between the NICE guidance and the quality indicators used within the GMS contract, particularly with regard to reversibility testing. Here, we outline the approaches to managing patients with varying severities of COPD including appropriate lifestyle advice, pharmacotherapy, pulmonary rehabilitation and palliative care.

The burden of COPD in general practice

COPD is becoming increasingly recognised as a massive and growing burden on the NHS and its patients. It has been estimated that a GP with an average list of 2000 patients will have 150 patients with COPD, with three-quarters of these undiagnosed. COPD affects about 2% of men aged 45–65 years and 7% of men over 75 years of age, though these figures are probably underestimates. As much as 15% of the population over 45 years of age report chronic cough and sputum production. COPD often presents at a late stage when most of the damage is already done, and is relentlessly progressive unless the patient stops smoking. Therefore, COPD can be prevented by smoking cessation when recognised at an early, often asymptomatic stage.

Primary-care professionals face a number of major challenges when dealing with the problem of COPD.

- The disease is often hidden, with patients not recognising and dealing with it, particularly in its earlier stages.
- Effective diagnosis of COPD requires spirometry. However, there are many problems in providing a quality spirometry service in primary care. Reversibility testing is confusing, and establishing a diagnosis can be complicated.
- Good care is time consuming and places a significant burden on already overstretched primary-care resources.
- COPD is not one of the major new priorities identified in the NHS (e.g. implementing the National Service Frameworks (NSF) on cancer and cardiovascular disease). Thus, even in enthustiastic practices it can be difficult to justify the time and resources spent on managing COPD.
- Comprehensive guidelines on appropriate management exist but are poorly understood and implemented. Indeed, in many practices there is overt apathy towards the condition – COPD is not recognised as a 'sexy' disease. Perceptions and ambivalence towards COPD are ingrained: patients are not young, the disease is 'self-inflicted' and, worst of all, patients usually fail to get better with treatment, a cardinal sin in the eyes of many GPs!
- Support services are lacking in many areas (e.g. expert outreach nurses, pulmonary rehabilitation services and early-supported-discharge schemes).
- Despite the fact that as many patients die of COPD as lung cancer, little or no palliative care is available for these patients. This is despite the fact that their quality of life tends to be significantly worse than that of lung cancer patients.

It is currently impossible to provide an excellent service for all our patients in primary care, with all the other demands on our time. We must provide education and training for GPs and nurses, respond to a growing list of new priorities such as the NSFs, perform appraisals, organise clinical governance procedures, update computer systems, develop electronic links with hospitals and others, employ and manage staff and complete the growing mountain of paperwork. It is not surprising that COPD is not dealt with brilliantly by all practices. Primary-care trusts (PCTs) have a major role to play in providing leadership, support and a structured approach in their area.

What reasonable strategies should a practice employ?

Spirometry

The first decision a practice needs to make is whether to get a spirometer. However, this should not be done unless there is a clear plan for its use. Far too many spirometers have been purchased with enthusiasm and at great expense but end up being unused. Frequently, spirometry can do more harm than good, inaccurate results possibly being misleading or even dangerous. The following matters should be considered before acquiring a spirometer.

Type of spirometer

Some authorities recommend using only those spirometers that produce a graphical output. The spirogram provides an assessment of the quality of the readings. For example, delayed start, cough and poor effort will usually be detected this way. However, these devices tend to be more expensive than small, hand-held spirometers, and usually need calibrating before use, which is time consuming. Such spirometers are therefore unsuitable for opportunistic screening. However, it is not unreasonable to use a micro-spirometer as a screening tool, and then to refer patients with abnormal results for accurate spirometry elsewhere.

Training in spirometry techniques

All spirometer users should have formal training, with appropriate assessment of their skills. Without training there are many pitfalls, and inaccurate results are very common, which is clearly not acceptable. Half-day courses have shown to be enough, but skills quickly decline if they are not used. Even after 6 months there is a significant and measurable fall in users' skills; this applies to both doctors and nurses. In reality, a top-up course every 5 years is the minimum requirement. Spending 30 minutes with the spirometry sales representative when the equipment first arrives is clearly not sufficient. The NICE guidelines recommend that spirometry can be performed by any healthcare worker who has undergone appropriate training and who keeps their skills up to date. This allows for the possibility of healthcare assistants or phlebotomists undertaking spirometry, and in some pilot studies, pharmacists are now also performing spirometry.

> The NICE guidelines recommend that spirometry can be performed by any healthcare worker who has undergone appropriate training and who keeps their skills up to date.

Interpretation

A suitably trained individual is needed to interpret spirometry readings accurately and to respond to them effectively. Many practices train their nurses in spirometry, whilst the GPs have no expertise. As practice nurses extend their role and see more patients with asthma and COPD, they are becoming the spirometry experts and GPs are becoming de-skilled. Thus, when a complex result is obtained, for example a restrictive picture, the nurse goes to the GP asking for help and if the GP is unable to respond, the patient is no further on, the nurse is demotivated and the GP unhappy. If in-house expertise is not available then there must be an external source of advice.

When a patient produces an obstructive spirogram, reversibility testing is often needed to differentiate a reversible cause (e.g. asthma) from irreversible causes such as a tumour or COPD (Table 1). According to the NICE guidelines, reversibility testing is not always needed if the diagnosis of COPD is clear on clinical grounds. However, as reversibility testing is included as a quality marker in the GMS contract, it appears to be sensible to perform it on new patients. To add to the confusion, asthma and COPD can coexist and give a partly reversible obstructive picture. Unless GPs are used to interpreting spirometry results, confusion and errors are the likely result.

Practices without a spirometer

COPD cannot be ignored and all practices should make arrangements so that it can be diagnosed and staged appropriately. The new GMS contract emphasises the need for spirometry, and also makes it financially worthwhile. However, in the absence of spirometry, various options are possible.

- Patients can be referred to an outpatient department for assessment. However, this is slow, often unnecessary and adds to waiting lists. Moreover, most hospitals are becoming increasingly reluctant to do this.

Table 1. Reversibility testing in chronic obstructive pulmonary disease (COPD). Such testing is not always necessary, but can help to distinguish asthma from COPD.

Bronchodilator
Salbutamol, 2.5 mg via nebuliser
Record FEV_1 before and 15 minutes after

Inhaled steroid
800–1000 mg beclomethasone or budesonide
400–500 mg fluticasone for 6 weeks
A positive spirometric response is a 200 mL or 15% increase in FEV_1 from baseline
A substantial response (e.g. 500 mL) may be an indication of asthma

FEV_1, forced expiratory volume in 1 second.

- Expert nurses can be employed solely for the purpose of auditing COPD patients, performing spirometry and acquiring the data necessary to meet the requirements of the GMS contract. In some cases, pharmaceutical companies may agree to fund such services.
- Direct-access spirometry clinics are available in some areas, often led by the PCT. Such clinics can be excellent, but they must be supported by appropriate expertise in interpreting the results. (Table 2).
- New systems are currently being assessed. For example, a trial of a mobile spirometry service in Plymouth was very successful. A specialist practice nurse visited practices and provided a one-stop service with interpretation of results, which were then verified by a GP with special interest in respiratory disease.

How should a practice respond?

Set up a register of COPD patients

Step 1

- Record patients who have had a proper assessment and an established diagnosis, even though often these procedures may have been through secondary care. This can be done electronically using Read codes.
- Record smoking status.
- Record smoking-cessation advice.

Table 2. Data output from a one-stop spirometry clinic.

Patient	
Results	FEV_1: 0.6; 35% of expected
	FVC: 2.8; FVC, 80% of expected
	FEV_1/FVC ratio: 25%
	No response to bronchodilators
Interpretation	Severe obstruction, mild restriction
Diagnosis	Probably severe COPD
Suggestions	Trial of inhaled corticosteroids and repeat spirometry
	Chest radiograph
	Consider referral for pulmonary rehabilitation

COPD, chronic obstructive pulmonary disease; FEV_1, forced expiratory volume in 1 second; FVC, forced vital capacity.

Step 2

- Confirm the diagnosis in patients with suspected COPD. Examine the notes and, where the diagnosis is in doubt, refer for a formal assessment using spirometry and reversibility testing.
- Record the date spirometry was performed and the results of reversibility testing if done.
- Record when the patient's inhaler technique was checked.

Step 3

- Screen patients at risk of COPD by spirometry. Such at-risk groups include:
  - asymptomatic smokers over 40 years of age
  - patients with acute bronchitis
  - patients with persistent cough, sputum production, dyspnoea, wheeze and chest tightness
  - asthmatics
  - those with occupational risk factors
  - those with smoking-related diseases.
- Record clearly in the patient's notes the basis for the diagnosis of COPD (consider Read codes) and the date of assessment.

Ensure that appropriate management steps have been taken

The main strategies for COPD management at the different stages of the disease are outlined in Table 3.

Step 1

- Recommend smoking cessation for all patients with COPD and for at-risk patients.

Step 2

For patients with mild COPD

Vaccination
- Influenza vaccination: there is excellent evidence of benefit in patients with chronic lung disease.
- Pneumococcal vaccination also protects against hospitalisation for serious pneumococcal infections such as septicaemia, and it is now recommended for COPD patients. However, it should be emphasised that pneumococcal vaccination will not prevent milder respiratory tract infections.

Table 3. Primary-care management at different stages of chronic obstructive pulmonary disease (COPD) (adapted from Global initiative for Chronic Obstructive Lung Disease (GOLD) and other guidelines).

Stage of COPD	Primary-care role
Stage 0: At risk	• Identification • Smoking cessation • Influenza vaccination
Stage I: Mild	• Antibiotics for exacerbations • Short-acting bronchodilators • Exercise encouraged
Stage II: Moderate	• Other drugs to achieve maximal bronchodilation • Inhaled oral steroids as appropriate • Chest radiograph • Pulmonary rehabilitation • Nutritional support
Stage III: Severe	• Support for exacerbations • Assessment for long-term oxygen treatment • Treatment of coexisting disease (e.g. anxiety, depression, osteoporosis)
Stage IV: Very severe	• Psychosocial support for patient and carer • Exacerbations may be life threatening and will normally require hospitalisation • Multidisciplinary palliative care as appropriate

Lifestyle advice

- Healthy eating: patients with a diet low in antioxidants are more at risk of developing COPD; fish oils and fresh fruit and vegetables are therefore recommended. The obese should lose weight, whilst the underweight should eat plenty of protein as they are likely to have reduced muscle bulk.
- Exercise: keeping fit maintains muscle bulk and improves the efficiency of oxygen consumption. Exercise is a critical factor in maintaining lung function. Many patients become breathless with exertion and therefore stop exercising. As they become more unfit, they require more energy to do the same tasks. This leads to a vicious cycle of breathlessness, lack of exercise, deconditioning and demotivation.

Exercise is a critical factor in maintaining lung function.

Drug treatment

- Bronchodilators: short-acting β_2-agonists should be used in combination with anticholinergics as their effects are additive. In an audit in our practice, 70% of COPD patients found anticholinergic inhalers helpful and continued them in the long term.

- Inhaled steroids: the place of inhaled corticosteroids is debated. In my view they should be reserved for patients with a proven element of reversibility, who have shown benefit in a 6-week trial or whose condition has deteriorated on their withdrawal. A benefit from oral steroids does not necessarily predict a positive response to inhaled steroids in COPD.
- Antibiotics: these are useful for exacerbations with purulent sputum. Recent research has shown that sputum colour reflects bacterial load and predicts who will respond most from antibiotics. Cream or yellow sputum is okay, whilst green is not, with a darker green indicating a more heavy infection. The widespread practice of starting antibiotics at the onset of an upper respiratory tract infection is probably sensible. Indeed, patients who have frequent exacerbations should have a home supply of antibiotics and/or prednisolone. Exacerbations are very serious and lead to a faster decline in lung function. Thus, the earlier treatment is started, the better the outcome. Exacerbations also have a prolonged impact on quality of life.
- β-blockers: check that all patients with COPD are taken off non-selective β-blockers. This is also the case with asthma.

For patients with moderate COPD

Drug treatment

> Maximal bronchodilation is critical to both symptoms and outcomes.

- Long-acting bronchodilators: whichever agent is selected, it should be tested for 4 weeks. The rationale for using these agents is that maximal bronchodilation is critical for both symptoms and outcomes. Every effort should be made to optimise lung function. This requires assessment of the drug regimen, the delivery system, inhaler technique, concordance and the patient's understanding of the treatment.

Pulmonary rehabilitation

- As most of the lung damage in COPD is fixed, the benefits of drug treatment are limited. Breathless patients have high levels of anxiety and depression, are unfit, underactive and demotivated. They are often angry, guilty and in denial. Their quality of life is poor, their relationships damaged and their self-esteem shattered. They get little or no sympathy, as they have previously smoked and therefore 'brought it on themselves'. They often do not understand what is wrong with them, except that they are very ill, getting worse and 'there is nothing that can be done for them'.

- Pulmonary rehabilitation is a programme of exercise and education for patients with chronic lung disease. It improves quality of life, reduces dependence and improves exercise tolerance, and the benefits can be remarkable. All this can be achieved without changing lung function. The NICE COPD guidelines require that pulmonary rehabilitation should be offered to all patients who consider themselves to be functionally disabled by COPD (usually Medical Research Council dyspnoea scale grade 3 and above). Pulmonary rehabilitation programmes must meet clinical needs in terms of access, location and availability. If it is not available to your patients, you should take this up with your PCT.

> Pulmonary rehabilitation is a programme of exercise and education for patients with chronic lung disease and the benefits can be remarkable.

For patients with severe COPD

The main aims of managing patients with severe COPD are providing social and nursing support at home and keeping patients out of hospital.

- Short-burst oxygen is of limited value and is often viewed as an expensive placebo. It should only be given in stable disease, as in acute exacerbations carbon dioxide retention can be a real danger. Pulse oximetry will not predict those who will develop hypercapnia.
- Long-term oxygen treatment (for 16 hours a day) improves the prognosis in selected patients. Referral for appropriate assessment is recommended in all patients with a forced expiratory volume in 1 second (FEV_1) of below 30% of the predicted value and in those with cyanosis, polycythaemia, peripheral oedema, raised jugular venous pressure or oxygen saturations of 92% or lower in air.
- Diuretics are needed for patients with cor pulmonale.
- Provision of palliative care is grossly inadequate for non-cancer diseases across the UK, with differences in local arrangements. Consideration should be given to referring patients with advanced COPD to specialist COPD nurses or general palliative care if it is available.

What should the practice record and audit?

Minimum data set

Minimum recorded data should be documented for each patient on the COPD disease register. Read coding for these is possible. A minimum dataset might include:

- date of diagnosis of COPD according to protocols
- spirometry results at diagnosis (e.g. FEV_1, forced vital capacity [FVC], FEV_1 % of expected, FEV_1/FVC ratio)
- staging (mild/moderate/severe)

- irreversible or partially reversible
- follow-up spirometry results and date recorded
- current smoker/ex-smoker/never smoked
- smoking history in pack-years (20 cigarettes per day for 1 year is 1 pack-year)
- date of advice to stop smoking
- exacerbations in past 6 months (number requiring extra treatment)
- unscheduled care (e.g. accident and emergency, GP visit, other)
- admissions (number of bed-days)
- date inhaler technique checked and whether satisfactory
- compliance discussed
- treatment reviewed
- significant comorbidity (e.g. depression/anxiety/osteoporosis/ischaemic heart disease)
- immunisation against influenza/pneumococcus
- referrals for smoking cessation/pulmonary rehabilitation/oxygen assessment/consultant chest physician.

Meeting the requirements for the new GMS contract

Read codes for COPD

Currently, there are numerous Read codes, but they often are duplicated or overlap. Despite this, they are insufficient to cover the complexity of primary care. How they are used and how they integrate into everyday use in a primary-care setting varies widely, and is significantly dependent on which computer system the practice employs.

For a full list of recommended Read codes, the reader is directed to the website of the General Practice Airways Group (GPIAG) (*www.gpiag.org*) or alternatively go directly to *www.gpiag.org/forum/final_codes_mark_levys_respiratory_codes_04022004.xls* for the full list. A sample of Read codes related to COPD is shown in Table 4, and their application in a diagnostic work-up and in the management of the condition is shown in Figure 1.

Assessing the COPD service in a practice

The following issues may be recorded:

- training of spirometer users (informal training; formal, assessed training course)
- COPD course (formal qualification; informal course[s])
- spirometer: quality controls built into the spirometer software.

Table 4. Chronic obstructive pulmonary disease (COPD)-related Read codes.

COPD read code:

H36	Mild COPD
H37	Moderate COPD
H38	Severe COPD
H3z	COPD nos

Consider recoding as COPD:

H31	Chronic bronchitis
H32	Emphysema

Need to exclude from COPD register:

H33	Asthma
H34	Bronchiectasis
H35	Alveolitis

N.B. If a diagnosis of COPD is suspected, but not confirmed, consider using 1J7 'Respiratory disease suspected'.

Audited outcomes

Audit standards need to be agreed in a practice. An annual review against set standards is very helpful for keeping the practice on target for good management. This can be part of the practice's clinical governance procedures.

The new GMS contract standards for quality in COPD came into force in April 2004 (Table 5). Practices can measure their own performance against these standards and establish realistic goals for future years in a number of areas. For example, an annual review of the recording of factors in the minimum dataset could be set up. This is relatively easy if Read codes have been used. One effective standard may be the percentage of patients with a chest radiograph in the past 5 years. Other areas for consideration include health economics, prescribing (e.g. percentage of patients on inhaled corticosteroids or anticholinergics) and hospital admissions. At present there is little authoritative guidance, but that will change in the near future. The GPIAG is working on producing a minimum dataset with Read coding. Encounter screens which can be used to record this information and allow very rapid auditing are also on the way. Of course, it is always preferable to collect data that can be compared with other practices both locally and nationally.

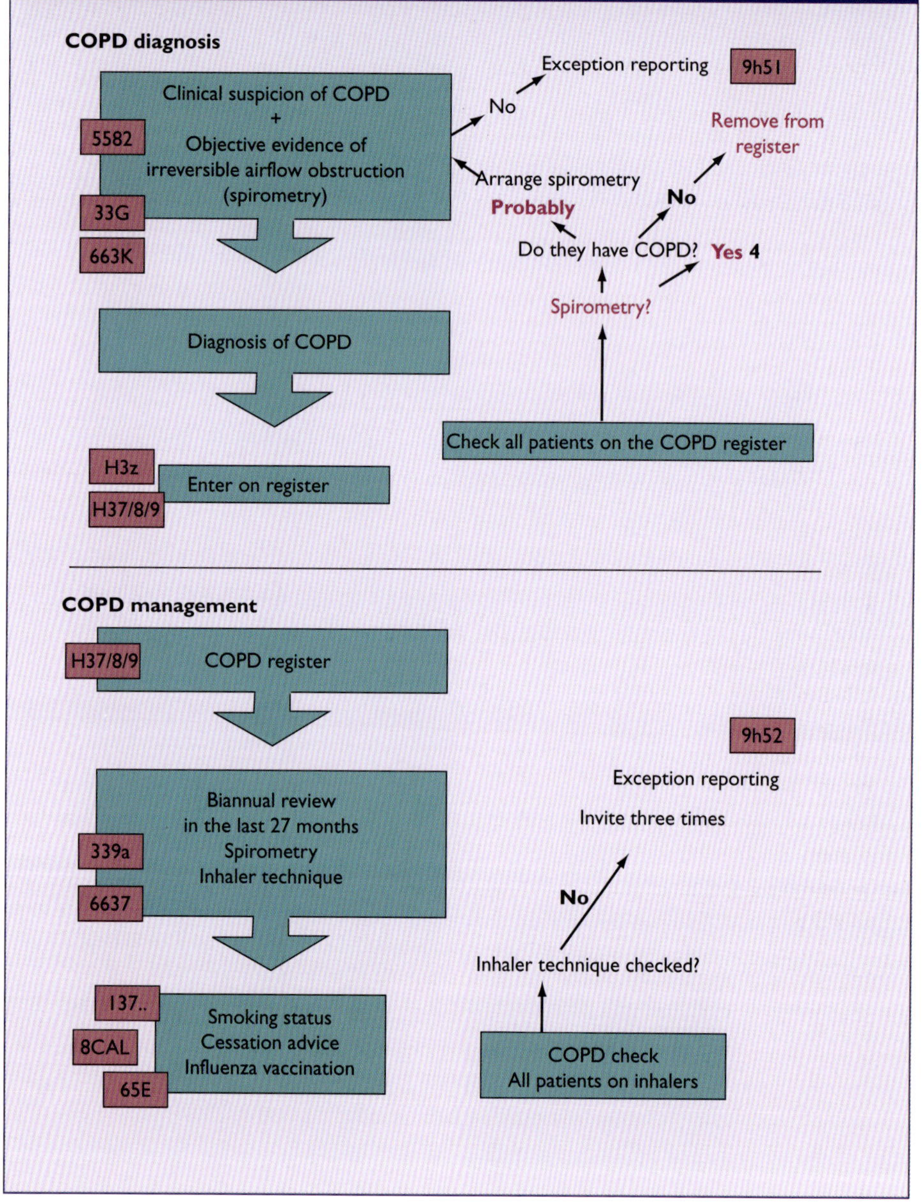

Figure 1. Assigning Read codes in COPD diagnosis (top) and management (bottom). Adapted with permission from Dr Hilary Pinnock, GPIAG Research Fellow, University of Aberdeen; GP, Whitstable, Kent. COPD, chronic obstructive pulmonary disease; GPIAG, General Practice Airways Group.

Table 5. New General medical Services (GMS) contract standards for quality care in chronic obstructive pulmonary disease (COPD) (*www.nhsconfed.org/gmscontract*)

Indicator	Points	Minimum threshold	Maximum threshold
Records			
COPD 1.			
The practice can produce a register of patients with COPD	5	N/A	N/A
Initial diagnosis			
COPD 2.			
The percentage of patients where diagnosis has been confirmed by spirometry including reversibility testing for newly diagnosed patients	5	25%	90%
COPD 3.			
The percentage of all patients with COPD where diagnosis has been confirmed by spirometry including reversibility testing	5	25%	90%
Ongoing management			
COPD 4.			
The percentage of patients with COPD in whom there is a record of smoking status in the previous 15 months.	6	25%	90%
COPD 5.			
The percentage of patients with COPD who smoke, and whose notes contain a record that smoking cessation advice has been offered in the past 15 months	6	25%	90%
COPD 6.			
The percentage of patients with COPD with a record of FEV_1 in the previous 27 months	6	25%	70%
COPD 7.			
The percentage of patients with COPD receiving inhaled treatment in whom there is a record that inhaler technique has been checked in the preceding 2 years.	6	25%	90%
COPD 8.			
The percentage of patients with COPD who have had an influenza immunisation in the preceding 1 September to 31 March period	6	25%	85%
Total points available	**45**		

N/A, not applicable.

Future directions

Practices should set out their own goals to improve COPD care. These may vary across practices, but one example would be to formalise the use of short courses of antibiotics and prednisolone at home. For example, a self-management card could be used, although few exist at present. Another example might be to purchase a pulse oximeter in order to detect those who desaturate, and then establish a protocol for referral for oxygen assessment. However, given the realities of daily clinical practice, over-ambitious plans are unlikely to be achieved. Changes will probably best occur if they are organised at a PCT level and facilitated by staff with appropriate expertise and support.

Key points

- COPD is a growing problem and should be taken seriously in primary care.
- The most important factors in improving the burden of COPD are:
  - accurate diagnosis using a spirometer by a trained operator according to established protocols
  - making early diagnoses, combined with smoking cessation to prevent disease progression
  - appropriate drug treatment to achieve maximal bronchodilation
  - non-drug treatment to prevent functional decline (e.g. exercise, nutrition, education, motivation and support)
  - early intervention in exacerbations with antibiotics and steroids
  - referral for long-term oxygen assessment for selected patients.
- In reality, many practices will not be able to tackle these issues in isolation and will need to raise them with the PCT in order to develop a unified strategy.
- The new GMS contract includes a number of quality indicators to evaluate the performance of individual practices with regard to COPD management.
- Additional guidance on what to record and which audits to perform is expected shortly from national bodies like the GPIAG. In the meantime, if core local services are not available (e.g. outreach nurses, mobile one-stop spirometry clinics and pulmonary rehabilitation), primary care should actively lobby for them.

11. Coronary heart disease

Dr Jonathan Morrell MB BChir. FRCGP DCH DRCOG
General Practitioner, Hastings, East Sussex

Summary

Coronary heart disease (CHD) and its principal clinical manifestation, myocardial infarction (MI), represent a significant burden on patients, the healthcare system and the economy. Patients who experience an MI are at a significantly enhanced risk of reinfarction or death. Their management upon discharge from the coronary care unit now falls to the GP and the primary healthcare team. Whilst there is convincing evidence supporting a variety of lifestyle, pharmacological and surgical interventions to optimise patient care after an index MI, many post-MI patients do not receive optimal preventative treatment. A number of initiatives are under way to resolve this treatment gap, including the National Service Framework (NSF) for CHD and the new General Medical Services (GMS) contract for GPs. By implementing the evidence base effectively for the various interventions discussed in this article, particularly by involving the whole multidisciplinary team, we can expect to see significant advances in care, which will translate to longer and better quality lives for our patients who have experienced an MI.

Introduction

MI is a dangerous condition and is the cause of death for about 330 people each day in the UK. Survivors are at greatly increased risk of reinfarction or death and represent a priority group for a range of evidence-based secondary prevention interventions that have become part of everyday activity in primary care. With a prevalence of around 4%, a GP with a list of 2000 patients might expect to look after 60–80 individuals diagnosed with CHD. With the increased potential to detect myocardial damage afforded by troponin estimations, the same GP can now expect up to 15 patients to present with an acute coronary syndrome each year.

Despite the scale of this problem and the validity of the appropriate interventions, there is evidence that many post-MI patients are not receiving optimal preventative treatment. Narrowing the 'implementation gap' that exists represents a major challenge to all healthcare professionals in

> Survivors of an MI are at greatly increased risk of reinfarction or death and represent a priority group for a range of evidence-based secondary prevention interventions that have become part of everyday activity in primary care.

both primary and secondary care. This problem is not specific to the UK, however. Indeed, this Europe-wide treatment gap is illustrated by data collected in a CHD secondary prevention survey across nine European countries up to February 2000 (Table 1).

As a response, blueprints for tackling heart disease have emerged, such as the NSF for CHD and these itemise explicit standards to guide health professionals at all organisational levels. For example, standard three of the NSF for CHD outlines the care expected for patients with established CHD and lists a number of criteria, whose implementation would go a long way towards eliminating variations and inconsistencies in service provision. (Table 2).

What interventions work?

Cardiac rehabilitation

Cardiac rehabilitation after MI facilitates patients' recovery and is associated with a reduction in mortality of 20–25%. This intervention is usually hospital-based, started just after discharge and is delivered by a specialist multidisciplinary team. Components should be tailored to the individual and include:

- information and education about CHD and its treatment
- an incremental exercise regimen
- advice about giving up smoking, modifying diet and controlling weight psychosocial support for the patient and their family.

In their contacts with post-MI patients, primary care professionals should endorse the value of structured cardiac rehabilitation, reinforce the

Table 1. Data from the EUROASPIRE II survey in 2001.

Audit criterion (European Task Force recommendations)	EUROASPIRE II (% of patients)
Smoking persistence	20.8
BMI >30 kg/m²	32.8
BP >140/90 mmHg	53.9
Aspirin therapy	83.9
β-blocker therapy	66.4
ACE inhibitor therapy	42.7
Lipid-lowering therapy	62.9
Total cholesterol (>5.0 mmol/L)	58.8

ACE, angiotensin-converting enzyme.

Table 2. 'Standard three' criteria from the National Service Framework for Coronary Heart Disease.

Criterion
Advice about smoking cessation, including nicotine replacement therapy
Advice about other modifiable risk factors including exercise, diet, alcohol consumption, weight and diabetes
Advice and treatment to maintain blood pressure (<140/85 mmHg)
Statins and dietary advice to lower serum cholesterol below 5.0 mmol/L (LDL-C <3.0 mmol/L) or by 20–25% (LDL-C by 30%) (whichever is the greater)
Meticulous control of blood pressure and glucose in diabetic patients
Low-dose aspirin therapy
ACE inhibitors for patients with left ventricular dysfunction
β-blockers for patients with a history of myocardial infarction
Warfarin or aspirin for people 60 years or older with atrial fibrillation

ACE, angiotensin-converting enzyme; LDL-C, low density lipoprotein cholesterol.

messages, identify and refer patients who may have slipped the net and cajole the reluctant into participation.

After the catastrophe of an MI, there are usually a number of practical issues for the patient and other members of the family and primary care professionals will often need to supply supplementary information concerning:

- driving
- employment
- smoking
- exercise
- sexual activity
- alcohol consumption
- holidays.

Primary care professionals should endorse the value of structured cardiac rehabilitation, reinforce the messages, identify and refer patients who may have slipped the net and cajole the reluctant into participation.

Lifestyle interventions

Lifestyle modification is clearly a critical element in a secondary prevention strategy after an MI. The range of lifestyle interventions thought to be effective are outlined in detail below.

Smoking cessation

Cessation of smoking is one of the most important interventions. Observational studies have shown that for smokers who quit, the risk of CHD reduces by 30–50% within 1–2 years, albeit that it may take as long as 10–15 years to return to the baseline risk of those who have never smoked.

Diet

The Diet and Reinfarction Trial (DART) found that post-MI patients who ate oily fish, rich in marine omega-3 polyunsaturated fats, twice a week, had a 29% reduction in all-cause mortality and a 33% reduction in CHD mortality at 2 years. The Lyon Diet Heart Study also showed reduced mortality using a rapeseed margarine, rich in the omega-3 polyunsaturated fatty acid a–linolenic acid, as a substitute for butter as part of a Mediterranean-style diet with less meat, more bread, fruit, vegetables and fish.

Exercise

The evidence strongly suggests that post-MI rehabilitation programmes with exercise can produce worthwhile reductions in cardiac mortality. One systematic review has found that exercise alone reduces mortality compared with usual care. Patients should be encouraged to increase their exercise over 4–6 weeks to their previous level, eventually incorporating moderate intensity exercise (i.e. feeling warm and slightly out of breath) for 30 minutes, most days of the week.

Psychosocial treatment

Most trials of psychosocial support or stress management are of poor quality and there is limited evidence of benefit, but two trials of psychological treatments have shown improved quality of life for patients.

Pharmacological treatments

Cholesterol lowering

Systematic review of the large statin trials has shown that lowering cholesterol reduces all-cause mortality by 21% and major cardiac events by 31%. Moreover, not only do the absolute benefits increase as baseline risk increases (e.g. in patients with diabetes) but also these benefits are independent of baseline cholesterol levels. Statins are the only non-surgical cholesterol-lowering treatment that have been shown to reduce mortality and, if tolerated, should be given to all post-MI patients. Cholesterol targets of <5.0 mmol/L (total cholesterol) and <3.0 mmol/L (low density lipoprotein cholesterol [LDL-C]) are likely to be reduced to <4.0 mmol/L and <2.0 mmol/L, respectively, as greater recognition accrues of the value of cholesterol reduction.

Antiplatelet therapy

A meta-analysis of 195 trials of aspirin has shown an odds reduction of 23% in the secondary prevention of MI and confirms the effectiveness of the 75 mg daily dose. The thienopyridine, clopidogrel, may have a small advantage over aspirin and provides a well tolerated and effective alternative for those patients who experience a further ischaemic event whilst already receiving aspirin and for the 10–15% of patients who are aspirin intolerant. Two new trials have shown that the combination of aspirin and clopidogrel together is more effective than aspirin alone in patients with unstable angina/non-STelevation MI or following percutaneous transluminal coronary angioplasty (PTCA). In both settings the combination should be continued for at least a year. The unanswered question is what to do then? Currently, this has to be a matter for clinical judgement.

Formal anticoagulation, with or without an antiplatelet agent, is no more effective than antiplatelet agents alone in reducing subsequent vascular events and carries a substantial extra risk of haemorrhage.

Observational studies have sparked recent concerns that ibuprofen may inhibit the antiplatelet effect of aspirin. If true, this would have far-reaching implications as the combination is common. On balance, more evidence is needed before definite recommendations can be made.

β-blockers

Long-term treatment with β-blockers has been associated with a reduction in all-cause mortality by about 20%, non-fatal reinfarction by about 25% and sudden cardiac death by about 30%.

β-blockers should be started early after an initial event. However, up to 25% of patients complain of adverse events and this may be a factor behind the relatively poor uptake of β-blockers in this patient population. The best evidence available is for timolol, metoprolol and propranolol. However, atenolol is the most commonly used β-blocker.

One trial has shown that sotalol is associated with increased mortality and, therefore, this should not be used.

Angiotensin converting enzyme (ACE) inhibitors

Large trials have now confirmed the benefit of ACE inhibitors in post-MI patients with and without left ventricular dysfunction. Following the results of the HOPE (Heart Outcomes Prevention Evaluation) study, the EUROPA (European Trial on Reduction of Cardiac Events with Perindopril in Patients with Stable Coronary Artery Disease) study has shown a 24% reduction in MI after 4 years' treatment with the lipophilic ACE inhibitor perindopril, in a large CHD secondary prevention population already receiving optimal background therapy. This means that, in addition to a statin, an antiplatelet agent and a β-blocker, clinicians should also consider an ACE inhibitor for all new post-MI patients. Most new MI survivors are discharged on this quartet of agents. Emphasising to the patient the relative merits of each drug at this stage is a powerful influence in maintaining long-term compliance with therapy.

Fish-oil capsules

The large GISSI-Prevenzione trial has demonstrated a reduction in all-cause mortality of 20% at 3.5 years in the treatment group allocated to daily treatment with 850 mg of highly purified marine omega-3 polyunsaturates (Omacor™). Sudden death was reduced by 45%. These findings are consistent with the huge epidemiological literature on the association between fish oil and cardiovascular protection and support the findings of the DART study.

Blood-pressure lowering

The absence of a specific blood pressure-lowering trial in post-MI patients means that recommendations for the control of blood pressure in this situation are based on observational studies and extrapolation from the primary prevention trial database. The optimum target is also consensus-based and is normally <140/85 mmHg, and <130/80 mmHg for patients with diabetes.

Insulin

People with diabetes are not only more likely to have an MI but also experience worse outcomes when they do. Metabolic derangements at the time of an MI increase infarct size and impair the compensatory mechanisms of surrounding viable tissue. The DIGAMI (Diabetes Mellitus Insulin-Glucose Infusion in Acute Myocardial Infarction) study showed that reversing this adverse metabolic status by converting patients who had not previously received insulin to glucose and insulin infusions resulted in a

52% reduction in the death rate. Patients may still be on subcutaneous regimens at discharge and intensive glycaemic control remains essential.

Surgical interventions

Revascularisation

Revascularisation is offered to patients for symptomatic or prognostic reasons. Nowadays routine investigations such as exercise testing, nuclear scanning, echocardiography and coronary angiography are able to evaluate prognostic risk on an individualised basis and the potential benefit of performing either percutaneous coronary interventions (PCI) or coronary artery bypass surgery (CABG).

CABG is most valuable for patients with significant stenosis in the left main stem or where there is three-vessel disease (left anterior descending [LAD], circumflex and right coronary artery) or two-vessel disease including proximal LAD stenosis. CABG is particularly effective where there is left ventricular dysfunction (ejection fraction <50%).

PCI is used both in two- or three-vessel disease with proximal LAD stenosis or one-to-two-vessel disease without proximal LAD stenosis.

What interventions don't work?

A number of secondary prevention interventions have fallen by the wayside over the years. These include:

- hormone replacement therapy
- vitamin supplements (particularly vitamins E, C and β-carotene)
- calcium antagonists
- oral glycoprotein IIb/IIIa receptor inhibitors
- class 1 anti-arrythmics.

Implementing effective interventions in primary care

The prevention of CVD has become one of the most important activities in primary care. Driven by the severity of the epidemic of CHD in the UK and the consequent evidence-based counter initiatives, all GPs are to be charged with identifying patients with CHD and optimising their management. The new GMS contract includes 101 quality points (nearly 10% of the total) for CHD secondary prevention (Table 3), with an additional 20 points for the care of those with left ventricular dysfunction.

Hopefully, the new contract will promote the structured review of CHD patients on a regular basis and improve the implementation and persistence of evidence-based therapies. Continuing compliance remains a challenge for all therapies, particularly when the individual feels well, but regular review

Table 3. Secondary prevention of coronary heart disease (CHD) quality indicators – summary of points from the new General Medical Services (GMS) contract 2003.

Indicator (must be recorded in last 15 months)	Points	Standard (% of patients)
CHD register	6	
Newly diagnosed angina (after 1/4/03) referred for exercise testing or specialist assessment	7	90
Smoking status (those who have never smoked need only one record)	7	90
Smokers offered smoking cessation advice	4	90
Blood pressure reading	7	90
Last blood pressure reading of 150/90 mmHg or less	19	70
Cholesterol reading	7	90
Last cholesterol reading of 5.0 mmol/L or less	16	60
Antiplatelet agent (or anticoagulation or contraindication)	7	90
β-blocker (or contraindication or side-effect)	7	50
ACE inhibitor (for MI after 1/4/03)	7	70
Influenza immunisation in the preceding September–March	7	85

ACE, angiotensin-converting enzyme; MI, myocardial infarction.

in the surgery fosters the sort of therapeutic alliance between patient and primary care professional that, in the light of the quality marker scheme, can only be mutually beneficial.

Much of the structured review of patients with CHD will be conducted by nurses. A demonstration project from the Grampian region of Scotland showed improvements after 1 year in terms of aspirin uptake, blood pressure and lipid control, physical activity and diet in CHD patients who attended a nurse-led clinic. At 4.7 years, most of the improvements were sustained and the differences against a control group translated into significant reductions in both all-cause mortality and CHD events.

Whoever is responsible in the practice for the continuing review of patients with CHD, the essential elements that should be covered include:
- review of lifestyle and coronary risk factors
- review of drug treatment
- review of compliance with all therapies
- confirmation of patient understanding
- review of targets (i.e. blood pressure, lipids, diabetes)
- psychological assessment
- functional assessment

- identification of those needing further treatment or investigation
- data recording.

Conclusion

The challenge posed by ischaemic cardiac events is not new. Progressive refinement of the evidence base now means primary care can offer its patients a range of interventions, that with continuing compliance and structured follow-up will translate into longer, better quality lives after the trauma and setback of the denominating event.

Key points

- The clinical management of MI survivors has become a routine everyday activity in primary care.

- Despite the availability of a wide range of interventions, the management of these patients remains suboptimal. A number of initiatives are currently being implemented to tackle this treatment gap.

- A number of non-pharmcological interventions have been shown to improve the outcomes of patients after an MI.

- These include cardiac rehabilitation (structured care involving patient education, an incremental exercise regimen, lifestyle advice and support), which is initiated in secondary care and reinforced in the community.

- Specific lifestyle interventions which can improve patients' outcome include smoking cessation, consumption of a healthy diet containing omega-3 fatty acids and exercise.

- A wide range of pharmacological interventions are available to primary care to reduce the risk of reinfarction and improve outcome. The evidence base for the management of patients post-MI is strongest for the following drug classes: statins, antiplatelet therapy (with aspirin or clopidogrel), β-blockers, ACE inhibitors and fish-oil supplements. Intensive glycaemic control is also important in diabetic patients.

- Revascularisation interventions may be useful in certain patients for symptomatic or prognostic reasons.

- Implementing the evidence underpinning this variety of interventions is a significant challenge and GPs are at the forefront of identifying patients with CHD who require such control. The support of other integral members of the healthcare team, particularly nurses, can serve to improve the care of all our patients.

12. Depression

Dr George Kassianos MD (Hons), FRCGP DRCOG LRCPEdin. LRCSEdin.
LRCP&SGlasg. DFP DMedAcup. DMedHypn MILT
General Practitioner, Bracknell, Berkshire

Summary

Depression is a highly prevalent condition, with the majority of patients diagnosed and managed in primary care. Despite the fact that depression is so common, many patients are still not appropriately identified when they first present to their GP. Moreover, some patients do not even present to their doctor because of the stigma that is still associated with the condition. This under-recognition is principally a function of the complexity of the condition, as depression usually presents as a constellation of signs and symptoms, compounded further by the fact that patients often feel helpless in their ability to communicate how they feel. Such factors make diagnosing depression particularly challenging in the primary-care setting. Good interviewing skills lie at the heart of establishing a correct diagnosis, whilst as GPs we can also motivate our patients to persist with the treatments we prescribe by establishing 'contracts' with them. By providing quality education and reaffirming the fact that neurochemical imbalances are central to the development of mood disorders such as depression, we also stand more of a chance of improving compliance and positive outcomes from the wide array of effective treatments that are currently available to treat depressive disorders.

The challenge in primary care

The widespread occurrence of depressive disorders in our society and the consequences for depressed patients, their families and society as a whole of under-recognition or poor management of this disorder means that it is our responsibility as GPs to be continually on the lookout for ways to improve practice.

Recognising depression in patients who present in a busy primary-care setting, often with totally unrelated complaints or with poorly defined or hidden signs or symptoms, can be quite a challenge. Despite depression being so common, there is evidence to suggest that we do not recognise

We do not recognise about half of our patients with depression at first consultation.

about half of these patients at first consultation. Although we may pick up some of these patients in subsequent consultations – and some get better spontaneously – about a fifth of patients are depressed for up to 6 months before being diagnosed in primary care. And that is just the patients that we get to see.

Identifying patients

One of the main difficulties in recognising depression arises from the fact that clinical depression, a mood disorder, is a syndrome (i.e. a constellation of signs and symptoms). All too often these are attributed by the patient, the relatives, or even the physician, to a normal reaction to life's difficulties or events. As we know, the contrary is true, and depression is primarily the result of a biochemical deficiency, though life events may trigger the symptoms and signs that accompany depression. If we can make our patients understand that there is a neurobiological basis for their 'mood disorder', we have a better chance that they will accept and comply with the treatment we prescribe, and of achieving a successful outcome for both the patient and their doctor.

In the following sections I will discuss the many factors that can add or lead to a delay in the diagnosis and treatment of depression.

Social and other patient factors

A stigma still surrounds depression in our communities – such that patients are reluctant to admit to themselves or others that there is anything wrong medically (or worse, 'mentally'). Sometimes, a patient may simply lack insight and be unable to recognise or communicate their symptoms. The co-existence of a physical illness with symptoms can mask depression, and mean that it is not recognised by patient or clinician; and because patients may feel helpless in their ability to communicate how they feel, for reasons of education, culture or language, they may fail to present to us at all and therefore forego the opportunity of having their condition diagnosed and treated.

A stigma still surrounds depression in our communities

Practice factors

From the GP's point of view, diagnosing depression in a patient presenting with physical illness as a primary symptom can be terribly difficult. You may remember the elderly patient with hypothyroidism, the woman with cancer of the breast or the middle-aged man after he has suffered a myocardial infarction. Once the opportunity to make the diagnosis of depression is missed (or at least the index of suspicion is raised in our minds, resulting in "I would like to see you again in a week's time"), it may be some time, if ever, before we get another opportunity. A lot depends on our interviewing skills, motivation and knowledge, as well as our general attitude as people – as well as clinicians – towards depression.

We would all like to have more time for face-to-face consultation with our patients, so that the patient feels comfortable and not under pressure to 'get on with it', and good communication between the patient and the clinician is effected. We must also believe that the cause is not hopeless, that there is something that we can do to help, that effective treatment is possible and available to us, and that the diagnosis of depression is the beginning of the process of restoring normality for our patients.

> The diagnosis of depression is the beginning of the process of restoring normality for our patients.

Patient groups

If any of us were asked to paint a picture of the typical depressed patient, she might be the widow who has cancelled the newspapers, doesn't visit her friends, no longer borrows books from the mobile library and rarely visits the food store. She stays in her flat all day, not always answering the phone, goes to bed late and wakes up very early, having been unable to get back to sleep. Although typical perhaps, there are other groups of patients for which we should be on the lookout, and in whom it can be more difficult to establish the diagnosis of depression. For example, in children and adolescents, depression is not always characterised by sadness. They may present with an inability to find fun in the things their peers do or to experience pleasure in the clearly pleasurable. They (or more likely their parent or guardian) will complain of an unnatural propensity to or level of boredom or irritability.

In an elderly patient the presentation of depression can be covert. They are likely to have had depression for some time before coming to the surgery, they are less likely to complain of depressive symptoms or to even look depressed and they often have co-existing physical illness. Managing depression is also part of palliative care. Depression affects as many as three out of every four terminally ill patients. Although this statistic may not be surprising, we need to do better at tackling depression as part of the palliative care of some of our most needful patients.

> In children and adolescents, depression is not always characterised by sadness …in an elderly patient the presentation of depression can be covert.

The size of the challenge

The majority of patients with depression are diagnosed and treated in primary care. With an average number of 20 patients per surgery, we should expect to see at least one case of depressive illness in every surgery session. A good working knowledge of the condition, a high index of suspicion, well-honed consultation techniques and skills, and having the latest information on the treatment options available are vital to the accurate recognition, assessment and management of depression.

Numerous tools and techniques are available to help us in our aim of achieving a successful outcome. Perhaps it is because of the complex and multi-faceted nature of general practice in today's NHS that we tend to rely mainly on our personal skills and experience. Very rarely do we use tools such as questionnaires and rating scales in our everyday work.

Goals of management

1 *Recognise the signs and symptoms and take the opportunity to make the diagnosis.*

Once missed, depression is doubly difficult to recognise at subsequent consultations. It is therefore important to:

- allow patients time to express themselves in an unhurried environment
- help patients to communicate their feelings by asking open rather than closed 'yes/no' questions
- listen carefully and try not to interrupt
- maintain an open body posture and sensitive eye contact
- watch carefully for non-verbal behaviour, signs and symptoms.

2 *Make a careful and complete assessment of the presenting symptoms.*

The main and obvious symptoms are depressed mood and/or a general loss of interest and pleasure in everyday life activities, including hobbies. The following symptoms are more difficult to identify, and it may take some time for patients to volunteer if they have one or more of these:

- difficulty concentrating
- feelings of guilt or worthlessness
- insomnia (or even the opposite, hypersomnia)
- loss of energy and general and unnatural fatigue
- change in appetite and weight
- retardation or agitation
- thoughts of suicide.

The existence of suicidal ideation clearly puts the patient at a higher risk and in particular need of careful follow-up. Furthermore, it is important to assess concomitant conditions such as hypothyroidism, Cushing's syndrome, therapeutic use of corticosteroids, pregnancy or recent delivery, premenstrual syndrome or menopause and establish a differential diagnosis.

3 *Alleviate the patient's fears about the treatment of depression.*
The patient may already have pre-existing ideas about depression as an 'untreatable disease' or fears of addiction to antidepressants. Good practice includes ensuring that patients understand that:

- depression is common
- it has a biochemical basis and is not a failure on their part to 'cope'
- antidepressants are not addictive, and taking them is not a sign of weakness or madness
- by co-operating with treatment, a successful return to oneself is perfectly possible.

4 *Establish a contract with the patient.*
A very important part of the contract with our patients is the expected length of treatment and what constitutes a result. Traditionally, clinical trials have measured response as a 50% reduction from baseline in a chosen scoring system. This is more of a quantitative analysis of improvement. In the real world of a primary-care setting, we may often look to a more qualitative outcome (i.e. have the patients achieved a degree of improvement in their symptoms [remission] that has allowed them to return to their 'premorbid', or as they see it, 'normal' state?) The aim is, of course, to render the patient completely asymptomatic from their depressive symptoms. Just 'feeling better' (response to treatment) is not good enough, because residual symptoms are predictors of relapse, suicide and functional impairment.

Just 'feeling better' (response to treatment) is not good enough, because residual symptoms are predictors of relapse, suicide and functional impairment.

Once the patient has returned to a normal 'premorbid' function (i.e. is in remission) we should aim to ensure that they continue their medication for a minimum of 6 months before a decision is taken jointly to reduce, and then stop, therapy. Some patients need to continue for longer than this in order to achieve the treatment goal and occasionally some have to continue with their medication long term.

We should try to make it clear that:

- antidepressants can take about 2 weeks to start working and 4–8 weeks to show their full effect at the dose prescribed
- initial side-effects such as nausea and headaches are common, to be expected, but transient, and should disappear after 1–2 weeks
- taking once-daily medication at night to start with can go some way to making these side-effects more acceptable. (You may like to explain that, once stabilised on the treatment, patients can switch to taking their medication in the morning if they wish, as this may help them get into a routine that aids compliance.)

Antidepressants can take about 2 weeks to start working and 4–8 weeks to show their full effect at the dose prescribed.

5 *Select the right treatment for the individual patient.*
The choice of drug is often the most difficult decision we have to make, not least because of the often conflicting advice we are subjected to, and which is available from a variety of sources. This publication is not prescriptive in the sense that it does not set out to provide you with a 'Which Drug?' analysis but rather to provide a definitive and evidence-based analysis of the significant data available on one particular drug. This you will, no doubt, want to consider against other information at your disposal. We stand firmly by the principle that very many factors will affect your treatment decision – a decision that is yours to make. However, I would like to make some suggestions.

- Ensure that you prescribe an adequate dose of the antidepressant you select. The aim is to restore normal function in the patients and enable them to return to their daily routines at home and at work.
- I believe that it is important to select drugs that are safer in overdose, especially in the elderly and in those patients who exhibit suicidal ideation who, in addition, will need to have supportive psychotherapy.

Switching antidepressants

A patient may need to change to an alternative antidepressant if the initial drug is either ineffective or poorly tolerated. This can be performed by:
- a direct switch to another antidepressant
- leaving a washout period before starting another antidepressant
- cross tapering (i.e. the dose of the drug to be discontinued is slowly reduced while the new drug is slowly introduced).

However, the switching of antidepressants is a contentious issue: there is a lack of accurate, reliable and unbiased advice on this subject, and what little exists is often contradictory. If the appropriate course of action is to discontinue one drug before starting another, should a washout period be used, and if so, how long should this last? If it is decided to cross-taper antidepressants, exactly how should this be performed? It is difficult to give specific advice as patients' needs vary. For example, patients switching between the same antidepressants but for a different reason (poor tolerability or poor efficacy) may switch in a different manner. Thus, it is clearly inappropriate to recommend specific regimens that are appropriate for every patient switching from 'drug A' to 'drug B'. It is recommended that local prescribing guidelines are consulted and/or specialist psychiatric advice is obtained when switching antidepressants, in addition to reviewing the specific summary of product characteristics for each of the medications. However, it is possible to make some generic recommendations.

- When switching from a tricyclic antidepressant (TCA) to a selective serotonin reuptake inhibitor (SSRI), or vice versa, cross-tapering is recommended. The exceptions are clomipramine, which should not be given with an SSRI, and fluoxetine, which should be stopped for several days in order to allow the peak level to fall before adding a TCA with caution and at a low dose. The dose of the TCA can then be titrated upwards slowly, though potential drug interactions should be monitored for at least 4 weeks before starting a TCA.
- The speed of cross-tapering is best judged by monitoring the person's tolerability.
- When switching between SSRIs/serotonin and noradrenaline reuptake inhibitors (SNRIs), the first SSRI/SNRI should be withdrawn before the second SSRI/SNRI is started. After stopping fluoxetine, a different SSRI/SNRI should not be started until 4–7 days later, as it has a long half-life and active metabolites.
- Monoamine oxidase inhibitors (MAOIs) should be discontinued for at least 2 weeks before starting therapy with another antidepressant.
- SNRIs should be discontinued for at least 1 week and SSRIs for 2 weeks before starting MAOI therapy.
- Potential dangers of simultaneously administering two antidepressants include additive effects (e.g. serotonin syndrome) and pharmacokinetic interactions (e.g. some SSRIs raise TCA plasma levels). Thus care should be taken when switching antidepressants.
- In view of the fact that mirtazapine has multiple routes of metabolism, problems when switching to other antidepressants would appear to be unlikely. However, some caution is advised when switching to the SNRI, venlafaxine. The same warnings given above regarding switching to and from MAOIs also apply to mirtazapine.

Improving practice

We all set out to manage our patients as well as we can, given the limitations of what it is possible to achieve within our healthcare system. And, like me, I am sure that you hope that you are doing a good job. But how do we know? One way to find out is to regularly audit our management of depression so that we can identify any possible shortcomings and formulate a plan of action to improve our practice. Hopefully, clinical audit is no longer seen as it once was – as a stick to beat us with – but rather as a tool that we can employ in primary care to assess objectively how well we are doing. It enables us to identify areas that are in

Clinical audit enables us to identify areas that we feel are in need of attention, set realistic goals for ourselves, make changes to achieve these goals and then reassess our practice.

need of attention, set realistic goals for ourselves, make changes to achieve these goals and then reassess our practice at a later date to check on the progress that we have made. We are not only likely to make measurable gains for our patients, but also for ourselves as clinicians and the whole of the primary-care team. The following are a few aspects of depression that can be audited.

Antidepressant therapy

- Patients are receiving the optimum dose of the drug we have selected for the treatment of their depression, as recommended in the summary of product characteristics and the *British National Formulary.*
- The length of pharmacological therapy is appropriate.
- Patients are compliant with the prescribed medication.

Postnatal depression

- Postnatal patients have completed the Edinburgh Postnatal Depression Scale (EPDS). (This is usually completed in conjunction with the health visitor at 6 weeks and 3 months after delivery. About 85% of patients are expected to score less than 10 points.)
- Mothers scoring over 11 points on the EPDS have been followed-up appropriately.

Lithium prescribing and monitoring

- The lithium level has been checked during the last 4 months.
- The last serum lithium level is within the therapeutic range (as per local laboratory advice).
- The thyroid function test, electrolytes, urea and creatinine have been checked during the last 12 months.

Suicides

- The number of suicides is no higher than the number expected in the community (4000 people commit suicide every year in England and 5000 in England and Wales). It is a *Health of the Nation* objective to reduce suicides by 20% by the year 2010.
- The practice has carried out critical event analysis on all completed suicides.

Key points

- Depression is a highly prevalent condition in the UK and is diagnosed and managed principally in primary care.

- Accurate and effective diagnosis, however, is a major challenge for primary care. Good interviewing skills are vital for identifying depressed patients and also in motivating patients to persist with their prescribed treatment.

- Despite being widely available, disease-specific questionnaires and validated rating scales are rarely used when diagnosing depression in primary care, mainly because the majority of practitioners prefer to draw on their own personal skills and experiences.

- To improve the management of depression, it is vital that GPs have a good working knowledge of the condition, maintain a high index of suspicion, employ good consultation techniques and keep abreast of the latest information on the available treatment options.

- It is vital to alleviate patients' fears about the condition and its treatment and to emphasise that depression has a biochemical basis and is not caused by a failure to 'cope'.

- Establishing a 'contract' with the patient will give the individual patient an idea of the length of treatment necessary, its likely outcomes and possible side-effects.

- The ultimate aim of treatment is complete remission, as residual symptoms can predict relapse. It is particularly important to identify patients with suicidal thoughts because they are at higher risk and in need of regular follow-up.

- Selecting an appropriate treatment for an individual patient is an individual decision by the doctor, but by ensuring an adequate dose is used and by selecting agents that are safer in overdose, we can optimise treatment.

- It is critical to follow some general recommendations when switching between different antidepressants if the original agent is ineffective or poorly tolerated.

- Clinical audit is a useful and objective tool to assess how well we manage depression in primary care and allows us to identify areas in need of attention and to set realistic goals in order to re-evaluate our progress.

13. Diabetes

Dr Eugene Hughes MB BS MRCGP,
General Practitioner, Isle of Wight
Editor, Diabetes and Primary Care
Executive Member, Primary Care Diabetes Europe

Summary

As GPs we are bombarded with guidelines, targets and service frameworks concerning diabetes, and now the new General Medical Services (GMS) contract awards up to 99 points for the management of diabetes, reflecting the seriousness which the government now accords this condition. In this section a ten-point plan is outlined that unifies all the existing guidelines and strategies and meets the requirements of the GMS contract. This will help GPs to pick their way through the morass of information on this subject and to improve the management of diabetes in their practice.

Signposts towards optimal care

The world is faced with an epidemic of diabetes. The World Health Organization (WHO) predicts that by 2010 there will be 3 million sufferers in the UK. The increasing prevalence of the condition, particularly type 2 diabetes, is reflected in a greater primary care workload. For practitioners seeking to provide optimal care, there are a number of influences which have made themselves apparent over the past few years:

- evidence-based medicine
- therapeutic targets
- the Nation Service Framework (NSF) for diabetes
- the new GMS contract.

Evidence-based medicine

We are awash with evidence to support our management of diabetes. The Diabetes Control and Complications Trial (DCCT) and UKPDS studies clarified our understanding of the progress of type 1 diabetes and type 2 diabetes respectively. The 4S study, West of Scotland Coronary Prevention Study (WOSCOPS) and Heart Protection Study (HPS) pointed the way in lipid management, and Hypertension Optimal Treatment (HOT) study, Heart Outcomes Prevention (HOPE) trial and Antihypertensive and Lipid Lowering Treatment to Prevent Heart Attack Trial (ALLHAT) have enabled us to logically assess antihypertensive therapy.

Therapeutic targets

As a result of the previously mentioned studies, various august bodies such as Diabetes UK, NICE, and the British Hypertension Society have recommended treatment targets for type 2 diabetes (Table 1).

The NSF for diabetes

2001 saw the publication of the long-awaited *National Service Framework for Diabetes: Standards* document. It was followed a year later by *National Service Framework for Diabetes: Delivery Strategy*. Together, these documents set out a 10-year strategy for primary care trusts (PCTs) with some important milestones. The 12 standards are shown in Table 2.

The new GMS contract

Whilst we were still digesting the above document, 76% of GPs voted to accept the new contract. A core component of this is the Quality and Outcomes Framework – 1050 points for GPs to 'collect'. Ninety nine of the points are for diabetes management, reflecting the seriousness which the government now accords the condition. The 99 points are split into 15 'indicators' (Table 3).

Practical strategies

Faced with all these possible directions, how are we supposed to proceed? Is it possible to adopt a practice strategy that can unify all the above

---

Table 1. Recommended treatment targets for type 2 diabetes.

Parameter	Target
HbA_{1C}	<7%
Blood pressure	140/80 mmHg
Total cholesterol	<5.0 mmol/L
LDL cholesterol	<3.0 mmol/L
HDL cholesterol	>1.2 mmol/L

HDL, high density lipoprotein; LDL, low density lipoprotein.

Table 2. Diabetes National Service Framework (NSF) standards to be reached by 2013.

Prevention of Type 2 diabetes	*Standard 1* The NHS will develop, implement and monitor strategies to reduce the risk of developing type 2 diabetes in the population as a whole and to reduce the inequalities in the risk of developing type 2 diabetes.
Identification of people with diabetes	*Standard 2* The NHS will develop, implement and monitor strategies to identify people who do know they have diabetes.
Empowering people with diabetes	*Standard 3* All children, young people and adults with diabetes will receive a service which encourages partnership in decision-making, supports them in managing their diabetes and helps them to adopt and maintain a healthy lifestyle. This will be reflected in an agreed and shared care plan in an appropriate format and language. Where appropriate, parents and carers should be fully engaged in this process.
Clinical care of adults with diabetes	*Standard 4* All adults with diabetes will receive high-quality care throughout their lifetime, including support to optimise the control of their blood pressure and other risk factors for developing the complications of diabetes.
Clinical care of children and young people with diabetes	*Standard 5* All children and young people with diabetes will receive consistently high-quality care and they, with their families and others involved in their day-to-day care, will be supported to optimise the control of their blood glucose and their physical, psychological, intellectual, educational and social development. *Standard 6* All young people with diabetes will experience a smooth transition of care from paediatric diabetes services to adult diabetes services, whether hospital or community-based, either directly or via a young people's clinic. The transition will be organised in partnership with each individual and at an age appropriate to and agreed with them.
Management of diabetic emergencies	*Standard 7* The NHS will develop, implement and monitor agreed protocols for rapid and effective treatment of diabetic emergencies by appropriately trained health care professionals. Protocols will include the management of acute complications and procedures to minimise the risk of recurrence.
Care of people with diabetes during admission to hospital	*Standard 8* All children, young people and adults with diabetes admitted to hospital, for whatever reason, will receive effective care of their diabetes. Wherever possible, they will continue to be involved in decisions concerning the management of their diabetes.
Diabetes and pregnancy	*Standard 9* The NHS will develop, implement and monitor policies that seek to empower and support women with pre-existing diabetes and those who develop diabetes during pregnancy to optimise the outcomes of their pregnancy.
Detection and management of long-term diabetes	*Standard 10* All young people and adults with diabetes will receive regular surveillance for the long-term complications of diabetes. *Standard 11* The NHS will develop, implement and monitor agreed protocols and systems of care to ensure that all people who develop long-term complications of diabetes receive timely, appropriate and effective investigation and treatment to reduce their risk of disability and premature death. *Standard 12* All people with diabetes requiring multi-agency support will receive integrated health and social care.

Table 3. Indicators for patients with either type 1 or type 2 diabetes.

Diabetes mellitus (diabetes)

This set of indicators refers to patients with both type 1 and type 2 diabetes

Indicator	Points	Payment stages
Records		
DM 1. The practice can produce a register of all patients with diabetes mellitus	6	
Outgoing Management		
DM 2. The percentage of patients with diabetes whose notes record BMI in the previous 15 months	3	25–90%
DM 3. The percentage of patients with diabetes in whom there is a record of smoking status in the previous 15 months, except those who have never smoked where non-smoking should be recorded once	3	25–90%
DM 4. The percentage of patients with diabetes who smoke and whose notes contain a record that smoking cessation advice or referral to a specialist service, where available, has been offered in the last 15 months	5	25–90%
DM 5. The percentage of patients with diabetes who have a record of HbA_{1C} or equivalent in the previous 15 months	3	25–90%
DM 6. The percentage of patients with diabetes in whom the last HbA_{1C} is 7.4 or less (or equivalent test/reference range depending on local laboratory) in last 15 months	16	25–50%
DM 7. The percentage of patients with diabetes in whom the last HbA_{1C} is 10 or less (or equivalent test/reference range depending on local laboratory) in last 15 months	11	25–85%
DM 8. The percentage of patients with diabetes who have a record of retinal screening in the previous 15 months	5	25–90%
DM 9. The percentage of patients with diabetes with a record of the presence or absence of peripheral pulses in the previous 15 months	3	25–90%
DM 10. The percentage of patients with diabetes with a record of neuropathy testing in the previous 15 months	3	25–90%
DM 11. The percentage of patients with diabetes who have a record of their blood pressure in the past 15 months	3	25–90%
DM 12. The percentage of patients with diabetes in whom the last blood pressure is 145/85 or less	17	25–55%
DM 13. The percentage of patients with diabetes who have a record of micro-albuminuria testing in the previous 15 months (exception reporting for patients with proteinurial)	3	25–90%
DM 14. The percentage of patients with diabetes who have a record of serum creatinine testing in the previous 15 months	3	25–90%
DM 15. The percentage of patients with diabetes with proteinuria or micro-albuminuria who are treated with ACE inhibitors (or A2 antagonists)	3	25–70%
DM 16. The percentage of patients with diabetes who have a record of total cholesterol in the previous 15 months	3	25–90%
DM 17. The percentage of patients with diabetes whose last measured total cholesterol within previous 15 months is 5 or less	6	25–60%
DM 18. The percentage of patients with diabetes who have had influenza immunisation in the preceding 1 September to 31 March	3	25–85%

components? If we take as our starting point the 15 indicators, arranged in sensible groups, we can devise a work schedule which will:

- make best use of the available evidence
- allow us to strive to achieve therapeutic targets
- adhere to the principles of the NSF
- earn maximum points under the new contract.

1. Practice register

This is worth six points. You are required to set up a register of all patients (type 1 and type 2 are lumped together) for systematic care, recall and audit purposes. The rules do not specify how the diagnosis should be made, but it would seem sensible to follow the WHO criteria (Table 4). This is the ideal opportunity to clean-up the data on your existing system, whether it is manual or computer based. This register is going to be the focus for obtaining all the other points, so it is important to get it right. All patients with diabetes should be on the register, and all people on the register should have diabetes. This may sound self-evident, but I found several people with a computer diagnosis of diabetes where assumptions had been made, and even one where the diagnosis related to another family member as in 'diagnosis DIABETES' – then in free text –'mother has it!'

Set up a register of all patients (type 1 and type 2 are lumped together) for systematic care, recall and audit purposes.

2. BMI

Three points for a record of BMI in the preceding 15 months. Remember that patients frequently get weighed at hospital appointments – it is important to be able to utilise data from various sources. A trained clerk can process all communications from clinics and extract the necessary data.

Table 4. Diagnostic values for diabetes using the oral glucose tolerance test.

| | Glucose concentration (mmol/L) | | | |
| | Whole blood | | Plasma | |
	Venous	Capillary	Venous	Capillary
Diabetes mellitus				
Fasting value *or*	≥6.7	≥6.7	≥7.8	≥7.8
2 hours after glucose load	≥10.0	≥11.1	11.1	≥12.2
Impaired glucose tolerance				
Fasting value *and*	<6.7	<6.7	<7.8	<7.8
2 hours after glucose load	6.7–10.0	7.8–11.1	7.8–11.1	8.9–12.2

Note: for epidemiological or population screening purposes the 2-hour value after administering 75 g oral glucose may be used alone. The fasting value alone is considered to be less reliable since true fasting cannot be assured and the spurious diagnosis of diabetes may more readily occur.

Weight control in overweight patients with diabetes is associated with improved glycaemic control.

3. Smoking status and advice

Smoking is an established risk factor for cardiovascular and other diseases. Achieving smoking cessation in people with diabetes is the single most important risk reduction factor. There are three points for recording smoking status, and five points for *a record* that smoking cessation advice or referral to a specialist clinic has been offered – an *assumption* is not good enough.

4. Glycaemic control

The big one – a total of 30 points. There are three points for a record of HbA_{1C} in the previous 15 months. There are two tiers of glycaemic control for which points are awarded. The first, for 16 points, is the percentage of patients for whom the last HbA_{1C} is 7.4% or less. It is important to note the range of payment stages associated with this indicator (25–50%). This means that full points will be awarded if 50% of your patients are below this level. This is just as well, as studies in this country and others show that the average percentage of patients achieving the target HbA_{1C} of 7.0% is about 45%. The contract has some built-in leeway. In recognition of the fact that these levels are difficult to achieve, there is a second tier with an upper limit of HbA_{1C} of 10% and a range of 25–85%. Most practices should be able to achieve these levels.

There are a variety of agents available to us in our battle for improved glycaemic control, and the merits of these have been discussed elsewhere in this journal. There are, however, some guiding principles.

- For most patients requiring oral hypoglycaemic agents, metformin would be the first drug of choice, particularly if the BMI is over 25. It is important to recognise that some ethnic minorities, especially Asians, have a high prevalence of insulin resistance, with central obesity despite a low BMI. In these individuals, it may be appropriate to start metformin if the BMI is over 22.
- If HbA_{1C} levels remain above 7.0%, despite maximum tolerated doses of metformin (there is little benefit in exceeding 2000 mg/day), then *early* combination therapy will be required, using a sulphonylurea, a postprandial glucose regulator or a glitazone as appropriate, and depending on tolerability.
- Similarly, if oral therapies are failing, the *early* introduction of insulin, alone or in combination with metformin, should be considered. In the past, there has perhaps been a reluctance *on the part of the healthcare*

professional to suggest this direction, reserving it as 'the last resort'.
Thankfully, attitudes are changing, and patients are able to benefit from
improved glycaemic control and improved well being.

5. Retinal screening

There are five points available for a record that patients have had retinal
screening by an approved retinal screening service within the previous
15 months. This may be by digital photography, or an optometrist-led
service. It is, once again, important to be able to extract this data from
source – this may mean liaising with optometrists to obtain a report of
findings rather than depending on the patient to report that they 'have
had their eyes checked'.

6. Foot care

A total of six points, three for recording peripheral pulses, and three for
neuropathy testing. Interestingly, there is no Read code for pulse present,
and the preferred Read codes will be for 'pulses left' and 'pulses right' with
'present' or 'absent' added in free text. There is also no Read code for
'neuropathy testing', so 'neurological screening' will be used. Most patients
with diabetes will benefit from a referral to a specialist diabetic chiropody
service, but liaison will be important to enable recording of the all-
important data.

7. Blood pressure control

Second only to glycaemic control as a 'pointgrabber' with a total of
20 points, three for a record of blood pressure in the past 15 months and
17 points for attaining levels of 145/85 in 55% of patients. UKPDS
showed that tight control of blood pressure in type 2 diabetes is central to
cardiovascular risk reduction, furthermore any reduction in blood pressure
confers a lower risk of developing complications. If lifestyle changes do not
reduce blood pressure levels to target levels, antihypertensive agents need to
be considered. There is no optimal recommended first-line antihypertensive
agent, but in patients with microalbuminuria, an ACE-inhibitor or an
angiotensin II receptor blocker should be used. Again, *early* combination
therapy to achieve target levels should be considered, as agents often have a
synergistic effect. A useful rule of thumb is the AB/CD plan where:

A = ACE-inhibitor or angiotensin II receptor blocker
B = β-blocker
C = calcium-channel blocker
D = diuretic.

If a patient is receiving 'A' or 'B', and a second-line agent is required, use 'C' or 'D', and *vice versa*. Many patients will end up on three or more agents, but as blood pressure control was shown to be more effective than glycaemic control in reducing complications in the UKPDS, and as hypertension is present in as many as 70% of type 2 diabetics, this is cost-effective treatment, if adding to the burden of polypharmacy in our patients.

8. Renal function

There are nine points available in this category, and it is the area where I feel most practitioners may have the most difficulties. The breakdown is simple enough:

- three points for a record of serum creatinine
- three points for a record of microalbuminuria testing
- three points for using an ACE inhibitor or an angiotensin II receptor blocker in appropriate cases.

Serum creatinine should provide no problems. NICE recommends that patients with type 2 diabetes should have annual microalbuminuria testing. If this is positive, it should be repeated twice; if it remains positive, an ACE inhibitor should be started with regular monitoring of creatinine and electrolyte levels. However, there are logistical problems:

- the test-retest reliability of stick tests is poor
- there are many reasons for a positive reading, necessitating further investigation
- the definitive test is timed urine collection
- some people would argue that the test is irrelevant in the presence of existing cardiovascular disease, as risk factors are already being addressed
- some people suggest that it is of limited value in the over-70 population.

Perhaps it is for these reasons that repeated surveys and audits show that microalbuminuria testing is the lowest ranking indicator in diabetes care. This is despite the fact that ACE inhibitors and angiotensin II receptor blockers have been shown to reduce progression to renal failure, following early detection of microalbuminuria, and that it represents an independent risk factor for cardiovascular disease. Thus, more work needs to be done to clarify this situation.

9. Lipid management

Three points are given for a record of total cholesterol, and a further three points for achieving a value of 5 mmol/L or less. The evidence base for lipid management in diabetes is complex and somewhat overwhelming, with claim and counter-claim appearing almost weekly. Some would advocate a 'statins for all' policy, others prefer individual risk assessment. However, claims are made that the Framingham tables do not apply to diabetes (and indeed there were only about 300 diabetics in the Framingham study), and the more recent HPS has raised further questions about intervention levels. I have a simple strategy:

- Secondary prevention: no problem – put all patients on a statin.
- Primary prevention: if the total cholesterol is above 5 mmol/L, put them on a statin. Targets for individual lipid subfractions are also important, so I would also use a statin if these levels were out of target range. It is worth arguing that there is no such thing as primary prevention in type 2 diabetes, as this group has the *same risk of having a major cardiac event as someone without diabetes who has already had an MI.*

10. Influenza immunisation

Finally, three points are awarded for following the advice of the Joint Committee on Vaccination and Immunisation with respect to 'flu jabs.

Concluding comments

So there you have it. A ten-point plan to unify all existing guidelines and strategies. Careful analysis of the above will reveal that there is nothing new about this plan. All the above elements are those you would have checked in an annual review (with the exception of thyroid function – curiously missing from the indicators).

The differences are that performance is now going to be related to pay, and that data collection *and recording from whatever source*, be it primary or secondary care, will be necessary to demonstrate that you have done what you said you would do (and should do!).

A final thought – routine blood testing in other clinics frequently throws up results which place patients in the 'IFG' range (6.0– 6.9 mmol/L). There is increasing evidence that targeting individuals with states of impaired glucose metabolism may be beneficial. These groups have a higher risk of progressing to type 2 diabetes, and have, independently, an increased cardiovascular risk profile. Lifestyle intervention in the form of weight reduction, increased exercise levels and dietary change has been shown to reduce the risk of progression to type 2 diabetes by as much as 58%. We have started to keep a 'sub-register' of these individuals to assess the effect of our interventions on their progress (as if we didn't have enough to do looking after our existing patients with diabetes)!

Key points

- The increasing prevalence of type 2 diabetes has resulted in a greater workload in primary care.

- GPs are bombarded with guidelines and targets for the treatment of patients with diabetes, particularly arising from the GMS contract and the NSF.

- Ten practical strategies, as outlined in this section, can be used to meet these targets.

- The identification of patients with impaired states of glucose metabolism and advocating diet and exercise in these cases may help prevent the progression to diabetes.

14. Erectile dysfunction

Dr David Edwards MBBS DRCOG
General Practitioner, Chipping Norton, Oxfordshire
Member of Primary Care Subcommittee, European Society for Sexual
Medicine Member of Steering Committee for Sexual Health Teaching at Oxford
Medical School

Summary

With the expanding global prevalence of erectile dysfunction (ED) and a growing awareness of the condition amongst both physicians and patients, the management of the condition has fallen firmly into the domain of primary care. Indeed, the condition can be effectively managed in a GP's surgery without the need for specialist referral in the majority of cases. However, despite this, confusion prevails relating to the rules of prescribing oral therapy for the condition, making the task of balancing patient expectations and appropriate care even more challenging for the individual practitioner.

ED should be considered as an important independent marker for other potentially life-threatening conditions, including cardiovascular disease and diabetes. However, it is infrequently applied as a screening tool for these conditions, principally due to communication issues in this sensitive area. Indeed, effective doctor–patient communication is essential to effect an accurate diagnosis of ED and to initiate an appropriate management strategy.

The burden of ED in primary care

ED is a common disorder in the UK, whilst across Europe it is estimated that as many as 1 in 10 men over 16 years of age will, at some stage in their life, experience ED of some severity. Various epidemiological studies and surveys have estimated the prevalence of ED to range from 12 to 69%.

Each of these studies are consistent in that they have demonstrated a strong age-dependence of the condition, with both the severity and prevalence of ED increasing with age. This reflects the chronic nature of the condition, and its association with many other chronic and potentially fatal conditions, such as coronary heart disease (CHD) and diabetes.

Protective factors for ED appear to be exercise and moderate levels of alcohol intake, whilst the probability of experiencing ED is inversely related

With this expanding global prevalence of ED, coupled with a growing awareness of the condition among physicians and patients alike, the management of the condition has become firmly rooted in primary care.

to the level of high density lipoprotein cholesterol (HDL-C), suggesting that this too may also be a protective factor.

The prevalence of ED is on the increase, partly due to ageing populations in developed countries and general population growth in developing countries. By 2025, the total global estimate predicts that the current number of cases (152 million) will more than double to 322 million.

With this expanding global prevalence of ED, coupled with a growing awareness of the condition amongst physicians and patients alike (not least because of the availability of the PDE5 inhibitors), the management of the condition has become firmly rooted in primary care. Indeed, given that about 50% of ED cases that present in day-to-day clinical practice are of mild severity, the condition can be managed effectively in a GP's surgery, without the need to refer to specialist secondary care.

The importance of sexual functioning and patient expectations

Discussing sexual problems can represent a significant challenge, both for the patient and their doctor. However, sex is clearly an important part of any patient's life. This has been elegantly demonstrated in a survey of 26,000 men across 28 countries aged between 40 and 80 years. Eighty-three per cent of men who responded, stated that sex was either moderately or very important to them. Consequently, the impact of ED and other syndromes of sexual dysfunction on patients and their partners is profound, and can severely impact on their relationships.

ED is unique in that patient choice is a major driver in determining the treatment programme, whilst patients have definite expectations that they look for in terms of the management of their condition.

ED is unique in that patient choice is a major driver in determining a treatment programme, whilst patients have definite expectations that they look for in terms of the management of their condition. Such factors include:

- a cure of the ED, ideally a 'quick, one-stop fix'
- increased pleasure
- partner satisfaction
- reproduction needs
- 'naturalness' and spontaneity
- confidentiality
- a sympathetic and knowledgeable clinician
- easy access to a non-threatening but professional clinic.

Patients often expect an NHS prescription for an oral treatment. However, currently only certain categories of patient are eligible for treatment, and these only account for about 15% of patients with ED.

Thus, treatments for ED are currently available at NHS expense only for men treated for prostate cancer; men receiving dialysis for kidney failure; those with spinal cord injury, diabetes, multiple sclerosis, single gene neurological disease, spina bifida, Parkinson's disease, polio, severe pelvic injury or radical pelvic surgery or in men who have had a prostatectomy or kidney transplantation; for those men who were already receiving drug treatment for ED on 14 September 1998; through specialist services for men suffering severe distress because of ED.

This makes the task of balancing patient expectations and delivering appropriate care even more challenging for the practitioner. The rules of prescribing are clearly complex, and even more difficult to implement when at the front line in a busy and pressurised surgery environment.

Case finding

A typical patient presenting with ED has the following profile:

- 54 years of age
- married
- has hypertension or diabetes
- is receiving medication for a pre-existing condition
- has not had sex for several months
- presents to his doctor at 18–60 months after the onset of ED.

Data from my own ED clinic concur with the above and also reflect the findings of epidemiological studies. For example, the age range of patients with ED presenting in my clinic ranges from 18 to 87 years.

When enquiring about erectile function, it should be kept in mind what are the characteristics of a normal erection. Ideally, an erection should have the following qualities:

- firm enough to allow penetration
- not too firm that it is painful
- should be maintained long enough to allow successful completion of intercourse to the satisfaction of both parties
- consistency (i.e. that any drugs used to treat ED should produce the same success in nine out of ten subsequent occasions).

ED as a marker for comorbid disease

ED is an independent marker for a number of other serious and potentially life-threatening conditions. These include diabetes, peripheral vascular disease, hypertension, cardiovascular disease and depression. Consequently, ED can be viewed as a useful 'red flag' warning which can alert a GP to the presence of these other conditions. However, given the issues revolving around patient–doctor communication in this sensitive area, ED is infrequently applied as a screening tool for these other comorbidities. This is clearly an area that can be improved upon within the primary-care setting, and the involvement of the whole multi-disciplinary primary-care team may ensure that warning signs are effectively and promptly identified.

Diabetes

It has been estimated that between 12 and 20% of patients with ED have previously undiagnosed diabetes. One specific study examined patients that were apparently not diabetic. One-third had no sexual problems, one-third had premature ejaculation and one-third had ED. On testing all of them, over 12% of patients who experienced ED were found to have previously undiagnosed diabetes. However, this association was not observed in patients with premature ejaculation or in those without sexual dysfunction.

In another large multicentre study, patients with recently diagnosed type 2 diabetes were screened for other complications. Twenty per cent were found to already have ED at the initial diagnosis.

Cardiovascular disease

The association of ED with cardiovascular disease has been well documented. For example in one study:

- 23% of patients from a group of patients with established coronary artery disease, were shown to have had ED prior to developing their coronary symptoms
- 18% of patients with ED also had undiagnosed hypertension
- 5% of patients with ED had undiagnosed ischaemic heart disease.

To identify the link between other cardiovascular risk factors and ED, we have examined patients' cholesterol and glucose levels in our GP-run ED clinic. These studies have shown that:

- 59% had serum cholesterol levels above 4.8 mmol/L
- 31% had a fasting glucose level above 5.5 mmol/L
- 23% had a body mass index (BMI) greater than 28
- 21% of patients had both elevated cholesterol and elevated fasting glucose.

These 'real life' observations are supported by laboratory studies which have shown that decreased smooth muscle function in the corpora cavernosa is associated with elevated cholesterol levels.

Depression

ED is a significant prognostic marker for depression. Conversely, depression and, paradoxically, its treatment, can also result in ED. It has been clearly established that it is important to treat ED effectively, as this can have a beneficial impact upon the depressive condition. However, it would be considered negligent to stop treatment for depression in order to correct ED. Thus, this is a difficult balance to achieve in practice. In practical terms, it is best to negotiate with patients and, where appropriate the psychiatrist, to trial different antidepressant medications in order to treat both the depression and to correct the ED simultaneously. For example, drugs that cause ED in one patient may not cause ED in another. When taking a history in such cases, it is particularly important to determine whether the dominant sexual dysfunction problem is anorgasmia or retarded ejaculation as opposed to ED, as this can be a very common finding with some selective serotonin reuptake inhibitors (SSRIs).

ED is a significant prognostic marker for depression. Conversely, depression and, paradoxically, its treatment, can also result in ED.

Dealing with the consultation

A typical patient with ED presenting to his GP will usually only mention difficulties with erectile function towards the end of a routine consultation, for example during a hypertension check. In many cases, the patient will be virtually out of the surgery, before he will finally pluck up the courage to say something about his erectile difficulties. The next minutes of the consultation are critical in establishing a rapport with the patient, in order to effect an accurate diagnosis. You may wish to consider employing the following strategy during the remainder of the consultation.

- Invite the patient to sit down and then sit down yourself, which will reassure the patient that you take the matter seriously.
- Ensure that you are both talking about ED. It is absolutely essential that the clinician is comfortable about discussing sexual matters.
- Reflect the patient's language back to him in order to make him feel comfortable about discussing what is, in fact, a very intimate and personal matter.
- Thank him for having the courage to discuss the problem, and share with him how common ED is, emphasising that it affects 2–3 million men in the UK alone.
- Explain that the problem needs a full and thorough investigation, rather than just issuing a simple and quick prescription.
- If you have a colleague with a special interest in ED, invite the patient to set up an appointment to see them.

In many cases, the patient will be virtually out of the surgery before he will finally pluck up the courage to say something about his erectile difficulties.

I like to suggest to my partners that they arrange for the patient to have the following initial blood tests performed:

- thyroid function tests
- fasting glucose
- cholesterol and lipid profiles
- full blood count
- testosterone.

Additional blood tests may be required subsequently, depending on the outcome of the initial tests and on the history of the patient and the outcome of their physical examination. Further blood tests may include:

- creatinine and electrolyte levels if a renal problem is suspected
- a prostate-specific antigen (PSA) test if a prostate problem is suspected
- follicle-stimulating hormone (FSH)/luteinising hormone (LH)/prolactin (PRL)/sex hormone binding globulin (SHBG)/insulin-like serum growth hormone (GH) if testosterone levels are low
- HbA_{1C} (sometimes as an initial blood test if it is difficult to get a fasting blood glucose).

A diagnostic, self-administered, questionnaire can then be given to the patient which may assist in reaching a diagnosis (Figure 1). In addition, the questionnaire serves two other purposes. Firstly, it helps to speed up the second consultation and secondly, it makes it easier for the nervous patient to broach the subject. Both doctor and patient can focus on the questionnaire until a rapport is built up, and thus doctor–patient communication is improved.

After the initial consultation, a second appointment with the patient can be carried out either by the interested GP or by referral to a colleague that has an interest in ED. At this stage further history taking is mandatory.

Medical history

First of all you need to look at the patient's medical history, comorbid conditions (e.g. diabetes, drug history, cardiovascular risk factors), previous surgery, any penile problems such as trauma, neurological illness such as spinal cord injury, endocrine disease (e.g. thyroid disorders) and any psychiatric illness (e.g. anxiety and depression).

Sexual history

When taking a sexual history, one needs to ask further questions about the nature of a patient's erectile difficulty to establish an accurate diagnosis. For example, it is necessary to determine the onset, duration, rate of progression and when sexual activity tends to take place. Additionally, it is important to determine what penile sensation is like (for example does the penis feel cold

---

Figure 1. Diagnostic screening of suspected erectile dysfunction in primary care.

Thank you for completing this questionnaire, which will help us to understand more about you and your problem with erections. This is a common problem and can affect men of all ages.

What is your age?   What is the age of your partner?

How long have you been together?

How much do you smoke?   How much alcohol do you drink?

Have you had any illnesses such as diabetes, depression, high blood pressure, operations and admission to hospital?

Are you on any medication? If so what, and for how long have you been taking it?

Do you regard your sex drive (libido) as normal compared to say 5 years ago?

Each question below has several possible responses. Please circle ONE response for each question that best describes your own situation over the past 6 months.

1. How do you rate your confidence that you could get and keep an erection?		Very low 1	Low 2	Moderate 3	High 4	Very High 5
2. When you had erections with sexual stimulation, how often were your erections hard enough for penetration (entering your partner?)	No sexual activity 0	Almost never or never 1	A few times (much less than half the time) 2	Sometimes (about half the time) 3	Most times (much more than half the time) 4	Almost always or always 5
3. During sexual intercourse, how often were you able to maintain your erection after you had penetrated (entered) your partner?	No sexual activity 0	Almost never or never 1	A few times (much less than half the time) 2	Sometimes (about half the time) 3	Most times (much more than half the time) 4	Almost always or always 5
4. During sexual intercourse, how difficult was it to maintain your erection to completion of intercourse?	Did not attempt intercourse 0	Extremely difficult 1	Very difficult 2	Difficult 3	Slightly difficult 4	Not difficult 5
5. When you attempted sexual intercourse, how often was it satisfactory for you?	No sexual activity 0	Almost never or never 1	A few times (much less than half the time) 2	Sometimes (about half the time) 3	Most times (much more than half the time) 4	Almost always or always 5
Score						

What does your partner think of your problem?

Have either of you thought what might be causing the problem and have you tried anything to correct it?

What do you and your partner hope to gain from any treatments that might be available?

or is it painful?), is there any alteration in penis shape, reduced libido, or problems with ejaculation or orgasm. Finally, it may also be helpful to record any relevant additional factors, for example illness or death of a spouse or partner.

Physical examination

A physical examination should include recording blood pressure, height and weight, checking peripheral pulses and recording any signs of aneurysmal disease, together with an examination of genitalia and secondary sexual characteristics (e.g. for signs of Peyronie's disease or hypogonadism).

Other examinations

Depending on the outcomes of the medical history and physical examination, other examinations may be indicated. Such tests include a digital rectal examination (DRE), clinical signs of under/over activity of the thyroid, liver failure, anaemia, hypotension, serious cardiovascular pathology or end stage renal failure.

Treatment options

The questionnaire serves two other purposes. Firstly, it helps to speed up the second consultation and secondly, it makes it easier for the nervous patient to broach the subject.

It is important to take a holistic approach when treating ED, and this is something that primary care can offer. Lifestyle modification is easy to discuss with the patient, but more difficult to put into practice! It is important to offer support from the dietician and smoking cessation sister. It is not the remit of this article to list the various treatment options available in great detail, however, below I have outlined some of the more recent developments in treatment options.

- Oral medications including the PDE5 inhibitors sildenafil, tadalafil and vardenafil, and the centrally acting agent, apomorphine, are now available.
- Vacuum therapy devices are now available on prescription under the same guidelines as other treatments for ED.
- Testosterone is now available in a gel form if the patient has proven hypogonadism.
- In my experience intraurethral and intracavernosal medications are second-line treatment options. Likewise penile prosthesis insertions and other forms of corrective surgery are now considered third-line treatment options.
- Sexual psychotherapy is useful in certain situations. However, its availability varies significantly across the country. Also, as it is often only available privately, some patients prefer to try medication initially. Time will tell whether this is the best long-term treatment solution for them.

Irrespective of the treatment option chosen to manage ED, it is important to arrange a follow-up appointment to reassess the treatment needs. Some patients may need tertiary referrals to other specialities. For example, looking at my own clinic statistics from April to June 2003 we have referred patients with ED to the smoking cessation sister, dietician, cardiology, cardiothoracic surgery, urology, neurology and back to GP colleagues for treatment of newly diagnosed hypertension and diabetes.

Conclusion

ED is a common disorder, and as such falls very much into the day-to-day routine of the primary care team. Indeed, the GP can effectively deal with the majority of cases. However, it is paramount that the clinician is comfortable in discussing sexual matters. Importantly, ED has now been shown to be a useful prognostic marker for the presence of other comorbid diseases, and thus in terms of global disease management, we owe it to our patients to arrange for them to be fully investigated. Given this link, one can view the penis as the barometer of the body for both organic and psychological problems. Together with a growing understanding of the condition, and its pathophysiology, there is now an increasing array of treatment options, which can restore the couple's sexual needs, improve their relationships and thus increase the quality of their lives.

Irrespective of the treatment option chosen to manage ED, it is important to arrange a follow-up appointment to reassess the treatment needs.

ED is a common disorder, and as such falls very much into the day-to-day routine of the primary care team.

Key points

- ED is a very common disorder in the UK, with 1 in 10 men experiencing the condition at some point in their lifetime.

- There has been an increasing awareness of ED amongst both physicians and the general population, particularly since the introduction of agents that are effective in its treatment.

- Patients are now managed routinely in primary care. As such, the GP and other primary healthcare professionals must be comfortable and confident in discussing matters of male sexual functioning.

- In addition to the impact ED has on patients' quality of life, it is important to remember that it is also an independent marker for a number of serious and potentially life-threatening comorbid conditions. The penis can therefore be viewed as a 'barometer' for both physical and psychological health.

- A number of techniques can be employed in a consultation to ensure that the patient feels comfortable about discussing their erectile difficulties.

- It is critical to take a thorough medical and sexual history, as well as conduct a physical examination once ED is suspected. The use of diagnostic sexual function questionnaires can assist in the diagnosis of ED and may also be useful in evaluating patients' response to treatment.

- A wide range of effective treatments are now available for patients with ED, although the physician must balance patients' expectation for therapy with current restrictions on who should receive treatment. Sexual psychotherapy may also help in certain situations.

15. Fungal infections

Dr Tim Mitchell, MBChB MRCGP DRCOG DPD
General Practitioner, Bristol
Secretary, Primary Care Dermatology Society

Summary

Fungal infections are extremely common in the UK and can be managed effectively in primary care in the majority of cases without the need for referral to a dermatologist. However, there is a chronic lack of dermatology training for healthcare professionals within primary care that needs to be addressed in order for us to deliver better patient care. Fungal infections vary in their severity and their impact on patients' lives – severe nail infections in the elderly can often be disabling for those with already limited mobility, whilst other infections are completely asymptomatic. Thus, there is significant debate as to whether all fungal infections need treatment. Establishing an accurate diagnosis is a vital step in the management of these conditions, particularly as there are a number of differential diagnoses which can complicate the clinical presentation. The entire primary-care team has an essential role to play in case finding, diagnosis and clinical management, although appropriate training must be given to ensure that this is successful.

Introduction

Fungal infections are very common. Fungi are primitive organisms closest to plants in structure and live as saprophytes or parasites. Looking across the range of all infections that afflict humans, fungal infections are the most prevalent and their incidence seems to be increasing. Various studies have produced different estimates of prevalence, but I am most impressed with figures of over a million cases of fungal nail infection in adults and a 15% incidence of tinea pedis overall in the UK population.

The prevalence of tinea capitis is more difficult to determine as it varies geographically. It is almost endemic in inner city areas, especially amongst children of African–Caribbean origin.

This imposes a large burden on the health service in terms of the need to spend time diagnosing the infections and the cost of treating them. At one end of the spectrum, there are many cases of tinea pedis that can be

There are over a million cases of fungal nail infection in adults and a 15% incidence of tinea pedis overall in the UK population.

effectively self-managed with advice from a pharmacist, whilst at the other end are some very resistant cases of onychomycosis.

The incidence of all fungal infections is increasing, even in the developed world. Various reasons have been proposed to explain this including:

- increasing age of population
- increased use of swimming pools and leisure clubs.

It is known that fungal nail infections increase with age. This is due to changing growth rates in the nail itself (the infection is rare in children), difficulty with foot care (if your hips are arthritic, you cannot reach your feet) and an increasing incidence of concomitant disease (in particular, diabetes and HIV infection). Communal bathing and washing facilities add to the chance of spreading infections and, although national service and the mining industry were responsible for many infections in the past, most communal washing now takes place in connection with the pursuit of fitness and the rise of the sporting and leisure club sector. Men are more likely to suffer fungal infections than women, and this may reflect a difference in behaviour in communal bathing areas along with a suggestion that progesterone affects the ability of fungi to establish an infection.

Opinion is divided over the question of whether all fungal infections need treating. This debate is focused on onychomycosis as treatment can often be prolonged, expensive and systemic with the attendant risks of side-effects and drug interactions. Some studies have shown that the majority of patients with nail infections did not seek advice about treatment, but that 80% of them would seek advice if they were aware of an effective and safe treatment. One such study in 1990 was linked to the availability of a new treatment. However, we must be aware of the influence of marketing on the decision to treat and seek out cases. Many nail infections may be quite superficial and asymptomatic with little progression over the years and treating all of these would leave little money for the rest of the NHS! The most frequent reason for treatment in these cases is on cosmetic grounds, so those who control the budgets will have to make some tough decisions.

On the other hand, there are certainly many cases that need treatment on medical grounds. Severe fungal nail infection can be very disabling and can be the 'last straw' for older patients with compromised mobility, leading to isolation and a rapid decline in health. Chronic fungal infection in the nails and feet also compromises the barrier function of the skin leading to a higher risk of bacterial infection. In older patients, those with diabetes and those with impaired circulation in the legs, this can result in cellulitis or erysipelas.

Severe fungal nail infection can be very disabling and can be the 'last straw' for older patients with compromised mobility, leading to isolation and a rapid decline in health.

Tinea capitis is another presentation when treatment is important due to the high incidence of this disease in the inner city and the risk of scarring alopecia when the infection progresses into a kerion. This occurs almost exclusively in children when a superficial infection leads to a fierce immune response causing a rapidly growing boggy mass on the scalp. Prompt recognition and treatment is important to avoid permanent cosmetic problems. Fungal infections on the scalp are the only ones to buck the trend of increasing incidence with age. It appears that increased sebum production over the head and scalp with the onset of puberty protects against infection.

The challenges for primary care

The challenges for the NHS in identifying and managing fungal infections appropriately are great. As with the rest of skin disease, which accounts for around 15% of a GP's workload, they do not feature anywhere in the new General Medical Services (GMS) GP contract so will not be subject to targets and monitoring. However, the cost of treating these conditions will show up in prescribing budgets so, without the backing of national guidelines, GPs will come under intense pressure to restrict the use of some very effective drugs.

Practical strategies

Case-finding

Each primary healthcare team, under the umbrella of the local Primary Care Organisation (PCO) needs to look at priorities for treating patients with fungal infections and this should include a programme of education to raise awareness and encourage appropriate self-management.

Case-finding should take into account the reasons for picking up the infection and any specific health problems that would make it more of a problem. PCOs have a public health brief and so should be targeting schools, sporting and leisure clubs and swimming pools with poster information or material that could be incorporated into the school curriculum where appropriate. This should especially apply to boarding schools where much higher incidences of tinea pedis have been found than in day schools (22% as opposed to 8.5% in one study). Inner city schools should also attract a special emphasis on the problem of tinea capitis.

Primary healthcare teams could also mount awareness campaigns but might want to concentrate on specific at-risk groups. All diabetics are offered annual checks which include actively looking for foot problems and, therefore, nursing and podiatry staff must be trained to spot the signs of fungal infection and be encouraged to take scrapings or clippings for further investigation. Nurses working in the practice and in the community will also be involved with the care of patients with leg ulcers and should not miss the opportunity to check for infections on the feet when patients attend for dressing changes. Healthcare assistants will also be involved in washing and bathing isolated and immobile patients in the community and must be given specific training to allow them to approach a colleague to follow up a suspected infection.

This whole issue of training is of paramount importance. The All-Party Parliamentary Group on Skin, in several reports, has highlighted the lack of training in dermatology for almost all healthcare staff. Therefore, PCOs need to look at what is needed and allocate resources from training budgets to ensure that patients receive the care they deserve. It may also be worth asking the Strategic Health Authorities what they are doing with the ring-fenced money they will have received after the report of the first *Action on Dermatology* programme.

Diagnosis

As far as diagnosis is concerned, this can be divided into two groups. The first group will contain simple, superficial infections of the skin. These will be mainly tinea pedis between the toes (or Athlete's foot) and some small areas of tinea corporis presenting as 'ringworm'. Patients with previous occurrences may well self-diagnose and others could seek advice and be diagnosed by a community pharmacist. Both situations should entail the purchase of an appropriate over-the-counter cream with the proviso that lack of clearance in a couple of weeks will need further assessment by a GP.

Other presentations should be seen by a GP or appropriately trained nurse/nurse practitioner for fuller assessment and investigation. There are many differential diagnoses for fungal infections as illustrated in Table 1.

The golden rule is to investigate whenever an infection is suspected. This could be a typical site or an unusual presentation of what otherwise might look like eczema or psoriasis. It is always worth investigating an asymmetrical rash, as eczema and psoriasis tend to occur symmetrically (i.e. on both sides of the body). Almost any rash on one limb should have fungal infection as a differential diagnosis.

Sample collection and laboratory investigations

Investigation must be carried out properly to minimise the number of false negatives from even the best laboratories. The taking of an appropriate sample is the first step in this process. The skin or nail should first be cleaned with surgical spirit, especially if creams or powders have been applied.

Table 1. Differential diagnosis of fungal infections.

Fungal infection	Differential diagnosis
Tinea corporis	Lichen simplex
	Pityriasis rosea
	Candidiasis
	Pityriasis versicolor
	Discoid eczema
	Psoriasis
	Secondary or tertiary syphilis
Tinea capitis	Alopecia areata
	Seborrhoeic dermatitis
	Traumatic alopecia
	Psoriasis of the scalp
	Impetigo secondary to head lice infestation
	Lichen planus
	Discoid lupus erythematosus
Onychomycosis	Psoriasis
	Eczema
	Lichen planus
	Paronychia
	Onychogryphosis

- *Nails*: affected nails should be clipped as proximally as possible with good quality clippers to obtain a full thickness sample. Any debris under the nail can be scraped out and included with the specimen.
- *Hair*: plucked hairs which include the root and scalp brushings should be sent. Cut hair is of no value in diagnosis. The small disposable toothbrushes often given out by airlines are ideal for brushings, especially if case-finding during an outbreak of tinea capitis.
- *Skin*: scrapings should be taken from the active edge outwards. The central part of a fungal rash often shows clearing and will contain very little fungal material. Scraping should be done with a blunt scalpel blade held perpendicular to the skin to avoid cutting it. Blisters or vesicles can be de-roofed to send the skin, and it is easy to peel soggy skin from interdigital spaces.

Investigation must be carried out properly to minimise the number of false negatives from even the best laboratories.

Any of these specimens can simply be wrapped in black paper and sent to the mycology lab. It is important to use a specialist mycology lab where the staff have expertise in examining and culturing specimens. Their job is made much easier if the correct information is sent with the sample. For example, it is of little help to write 'rash ? fungal infection' on the accompanying form as there are so many different types of fungi, and labs will often limit their search to the common types for each presentation. Essential information to provide with the sample includes:

- age and sex
- part of body affected
- clinical history including treatments already used
- concomitant diagnoses including any immunosuppression
- contact with animals as pets or through work
- recent foreign travel (exotic fungi can be difficult to detect unless specifically looked for)
- previous trauma in the case of nails (some moulds and yeasts are able to attack damaged nails but not healthy ones).

Most laboratories will carry out microscopic examination on the day that the specimen is received so confirmation may be possible quite quickly. Culture to identify the particular fungus can take 14 days. GPs with their own microscope might like to do some initial microscopy but it is important to ensure that enough material is left to send to the lab as well!

Remember that false negative mycology can be a problem so scrapings, clippings and pluckings should all be repeated if the presentation is still clinically suspicious.

One further investigation that is of limited value these days is to examine the suspected rash under Wood's light. This was useful for cases of tinea capitis in the past when *Microsporum canis* was the most common infecting fungus. It fluoresces under ultraviolet light and so provided a very quick clue to the diagnosis. These days, however, the principal cause of fungal infections, especially in the inner cities, is *T. tonsurans* which does not fluoresce.

Disease management

Drug treatment

Firstly, always take a good history of what has already been tried by the patient as there is little point in prescribing something that has already been tried over-the-counter. The speed of clearance may be very important for some patients – terbinafine cream can work for skin infections in a matter of days as opposed to 2 weeks for the imidazoles. This can lead to better results and fewer recurrences, as compliance with treatment tends to fall away after the first few days.

Nail infections will cause some problems and, as mentioned above, it is a matter for the local health community to debate the value of treating

---

It is important to use a specialist mycology lab where the staff have expertise in examining and culturing specimens.

asymptomatic infections in patients who are not at risk of complications. Systemic treatment is best, except for very superficial cases affecting one or two nails, and will need to be given for 3 months if a fungicidal agent is used, and much, much longer if a fungistatic one is used. The affected nails may not look much better after treatment but it is very important not to give in to any pressure to prescribe another course. If the fungus was susceptible, it will have been adequately treated and only time will make a difference. Nails, especially toenails, will take a good year to grow back to normal so the only action needed might be to repeat the clippings to reassure patients and give advice about prevention of reinfection.

Tinea capitis is probably the most difficult area to treat as it mainly affects children. Only one agent is licensed for paediatric use – the fungistatic agent griseofulvin. It is relatively ineffective and must be given for at least 4–6 weeks. To make matters worse, the liquid formulation is currently unavailable and so only tablets can be prescribed. Itraconazole is available in a liquid form, but it too is fungistatic and is therefore less effective than the fungicidal agent terbinafine. Terbinafine tablets do seem to be the best option in cases of serious infection in the scalp, especially if there is any hint of kerion formation. Even then, it is worth combining oral treatment with ketoconazole shampoo. In the case of simple, superficial infections, griseofulvin with or without the shampoo is a much cheaper first-line option, switching to terbinafine if there is little progress after 4 weeks.

Preventing recurrent infections

If the cause of the infection is known, prevention must start by addressing it. Animals may be a source of infection and so any pets should be seen and treated by a vet. In most cases, however, the source of infection can only be assumed to be due to exposure in communal washrooms or from direct contact at school. With the former, patients can be advised to eradicate any spores or residual infection in socks, towels and bathmats by washing them using a hot wash of at least 60ºC – I have come across patients who microwave their socks but this seems a little excessive! Some shoes, such as trainers, can also be washed but others cannot so an alternative is to use one of the proprietary powders sold to treat Athlete's foot. They are of little use as a treatment but can reduce the risk of reinfection if sprinkled inside shoes. Affected areas of skin or nails should be kept dry and cool and shoes should fit well to avoid trauma and should not be worn for too long if they cause the feet to sweat. Nails should not be permanently covered in varnish as this can prevent the evaporation of excess moisture. Patients should also avoid going barefoot in public places and be reminded not to share towels or shoes.

In the case of tinea capitis, an outbreak of *T. tonsurans* infection should be referred to the local public health advisers so that preventive treatment can be used for school pupils. Many pupils will carry spores, so widespread use of particular shampoos may be of benefit even in the absence of clinical infection. This should also be recommended for family members and other close contacts of cases. Shampoos containing selenium sulphide, zinc pyrithione or ketoconazole are suitable. *T. tonsurans* spores can also survive on furniture, combs and brushes, so cleaning these will help prevent reinfection in the home.

Conclusion

In summary, fungal infections are very common and can be managed effectively in primary care in the majority of cases. Accurate diagnosis is vitally important as there are a number of differential diagnoses for each common presentation. This should, ideally, be made on the basis of clinical suspicion backed up with positive mycology especially if costly systemic agents are required to achieve a cure. Many healthcare professionals working in primary care will play a part in case-finding, diagnosis and management as follows:

- community pharmacists can identify and treat uncomplicated superficial infections (e.g. tinea pedis)
- GPs can diagnose and manage all presentations of fungal infections
- practice and district nurses can screen opportunistically for signs of infections and take appropriate samples for mycological assessment
- health visitors can advise on nappy rash, which often has a fungal component, and liaise with school nurses in cases of tinea capitis
- podiatrists/chiropodists can be involved in the prevention and treatment of fungal nail disease as well as in opportunistic case-finding.

Referral to a dermatologist should rarely be necessary for straightforward cases but may be required in cases of diagnostic doubt and infection with rare moulds or with a mixed aetiology. It should go without saying that all team members must be adequately trained to play their parts in management and this will be the key to improving care of patients in the future.

> Fungal infections are very common and can be managed effectively in primary care in the majority of cases.

Key points

- Fungal infections are extremely common and are managed principally in primary care without the need for referral to a dermatologist.

- The incidence of fungal infections is increasing as the population ages and as a result of the increased use of communal washing facilities in swimming pools and other leisure facilities.

- The severity of fungal infections varies considerably – from debilitating nail infections in the elderly and in those with diabetes, to infections that are completely asymptomatic.

- Skin conditions account for a significant proportion of a GP's workload but are neglected in the new GMS contract. On account of this, GPs will be under pressure to justify the use of effective drugs to manage these conditions.

- An accurate diagnosis is an essential first step in the effective management of these infections. This involves appropriate sample collection for laboratory assessment and providing essential information to assist in establishing the diagnosis.

- All of the primary-care team (GPs, community pharmacists, practice and district nurses, health visitors, podiatrists/chiropodists) have a role to play in case finding, diagnosis and disease management.

- Appropriate training of the primary-care team is essential to improve patient care.

16. GORD

Dr Richard Stevens MA BMBCH DRCOG FRCGP
General Practitioner, Oxford

Summary

Heartburn represents a significant diagnostic challenge to GPs. It is a very common disorder with prevalence estimates of up to 40%, with about 10% of these experiencing the most severe symptoms reflective of 'true' gastro-oesophageal reflux disease (GORD). Sufferers of GORD can be badly affected by its symptoms, with some estimates likening its impact upon quality of life to being equivalent to that imposed by more 'serious' conditions such as angina. Both GORD, and more worryingly, oesophageal cancer, are on the increase, with factors such as obesity, changing diets and declining *H. pylori* infection proposed to account for this increase. A major challenge for the GP is discriminating between GORD and oesophageal malignancy, and making a judgement as to whether to treat empirically with an acid-suppressing therapy or to refer the patient for secondary assessment with endoscopy. However, the majority of patients will be managed effectively within primary care and as such the responsibility to ensure best practice falls upon the GP. Patient education and reassurance is important in the overall management plan, with lifestyle interventions playing a major role in controlling symptoms. Such changes can also benefit the general health of the patient. However, most patients will also require acid-suppressing therapy to control symptoms fully, and such treatment should be regularly reviewed by the GP and adjusted accordingly.

Introduction

Whilst my academic interest in gastroenterology is satisfied by my involvement with the Primary Care Society for Gastroenterology, like most of us in primary care, I am confronted daily with the practical difficulties of my improving practice as much in this area of medicine, as in any other aspect of my work. Whilst writing this piece I have been able to reflect on some of the challenges that we all face in day-to-day practice and to focus on how we might set out to improve the management of GORD to the benefit of our patients.

The challenge in primary care

The wide spectrum of severity and type of symptoms seen with heartburn represents a significant diagnostic challenge to the GP. As we are all aware, heartburn is very common among our practice populations, with some studies reporting prevalence rates of up to 40%. As a consequence, heartburn can almost be described as a 'normal' consequence of dietary indiscretion. At the more severe end of this spectrum are those patients who experience disabling symptoms three or more times a week leading to marked sleep disturbance. Of heartburn sufferers who present with these severe symptoms, 8–10% tend to be diagnosed with 'true' GORD.

The disabling and painful symptoms associated with GORD can impact on patients' quality of life so profoundly that is equivalent to the negative impact on well-being seen in patients with angina. Of course, angina is not considered a trivial condition – unlike many GPs' current perception of GORD.

Concern that these severe symptoms may stem from an oesophageal malignancy is real for the GP, who has to balance the resource implications of referring the patient for upper-gastrointestinal endoscopy against treating empirically with acid-suppressing therapy. Selecting those patients who should receive appropriate investigation is a challenge which is often dictated by the availability of local resources, and national or local guidelines.

The cost of treating heartburn often seems disproportionate to the perceived size and consequences of the problem, and has therefore become a target for cuts by prescribing advisors and others who regard the problem as trivial. Indeed, heartburn is often perceived as a 'lifestyle' condition that is often selfinflicted and therefore not worthy of serious and often costly intervention. Such 'labels' are rarely used for conditions such as angina despite, as mentioned earlier, the similar impact of the two conditions on a patient's well-being.

Population factors

To those of us in day-to-day practice, it is clearly not an illusion that heartburn has become more common in recent years. There seems to be a real increase in prevalence which is not simply the result of a change in diagnostic labelling. Perhaps more worryingly, the rate of oesophageal cancer is also increasing and affected patients are being diagnosed at a younger age. Although the reasons for this are not fully understood, changes in diet and the falling prevalence of *H. pylori* infections are postulated to be likely causes. Heartburn is more common in overweight people and, given the growing incidence of obesity in the UK, the problem is likely to increase

---

GORD can impact on patients' quality of life so profoundly that is equivalent to the negative impact on well-being seen with angina.

Heartburn is more common in overweight people and, given the growing incidence of obesity in the UK, the problem is likely to increase further.

further. In many patients, symptoms probably arise from increased intra-abdominal pressure, which forces gastric contents to reflux into the oesophagus. In addition, we are now aware that foods with a high fat content remain in the stomach longer and therefore increase the length of time that gastric contents are available to reflux.

The reduction in the prevalence of *H. pylori* infection seems to be inversely correlated with an increase in oesophageal disease. Although there is currently no clear evidence for a causal relationship, one possible mechanism may help to explain this correlation. *H. pylori* often causes atrophic gastritis and, as a consequence, a reduction in acid secretion from the stomach. Absence of *H. pylori* and its associated gastritis can therefore lead to higher output of gastric acid and possible increases in the occurrence of heartburn. The decrease in the number of individuals carrying *H. pylori* stems from improvements in standard of living and hygiene, such as clean water supplies and food refrigeration.

The rise in the incidence of oesophageal cancer mirrors the rise in heartburn symptoms. Indeed, there is some evidence that prolonged acid reflux is a major risk factor for developing oesophageal cancer. Prolonged acid exposure is also thought to be a factor in the genesis of Barrett's oesophagus, which is characterised by a change in the epithelial cells lining the oesophagus. This change is essentially a protective mechanism that renders the oesophagus better able to tolerate the lower pH of the gastric juices. However, Barrett's oesophagus is itself a risk factor for oesophageal cancer.

> There is some evidence that prolonged acid reflux is a major risk factor for developing oesophageal cancer.

Patient factors

A number of informative studies on consultation behaviour in dyspepsia management are probably also relevant for the more specific symptoms of heartburn. Dyspeptic symptoms are common in the community, with only a minority of sufferers consulting their GP. The severity and frequency of symptoms are no different between those who consult their GP and those who do not, and generally, a patient's decision to consult their GP reflects their concern about what the symptoms may represent. High health anxiety or specific concern about gastrointestinal or heart disease particularly influences the decision. People with positive family histories for gastrointestinal cancers are also more likely to consult. Therefore, by the time patients present to us in primary care, their concern about their condition is serious enough to warrant our professional attention, even if the condition itself is not.

These issues are not the only factors that influence a patient's consulting behaviour. As we all know, many patients take the time and effort to visit their GP because of mildly bothersome symptoms or occasional sleep disturbance.

Increasingly, heartburn is seen as a side-effect of other pharmacological treatment, principally the non-steroidal anti-inflammatory drugs (NSAIDs). With an ageing population and an increase in the number of patients with arthritis of one form or another who require NSAIDs, heartburn as a side-effect of treatment will become increasingly common.

Finally, there is a group of patients whose heartburn arises from an incompetent LOS. These patients may have no other risk factors for the disease and may be young, slim and active yet still have severe symptoms that can in no way be attributed to their lifestyle. Interestingly, long-distance runners are believed to be particularly prone to heartburn, though this and its probable cause remain to be confirmed.

The size of the challenge

About 10% of the UK population consult their GP with dyspeptic symptoms each year. The majority are treated entirely in primary care, with only about a tenth being referred for specialist consultation. On the face of it, the cost of acid-suppressing drugs appears to be high, and some may even say disproportionate, but cost–benefit analyses reveal significant advantages of treatment that may justify the continued and even increased use of these drugs. In the UK alone, almost £500 million is spent annually on acid-suppressing drugs, with the majority of these prescribed to treat reflux symptoms. There is therefore no doubt about the huge responsibility placed on us to ensure best practice in management of GORD.

The value of endoscopy in the management of heartburn is debated. GORD can be endoscopy positive (showing signs of ulceration or inflammation in the lower oesophagus) or endoscopy negative (where the oesophagus looks normal), whilst symptoms do not correlate well with the endoscopy findings. This complicates the role and interpretation of endoscopy. However, there are cases, often where the presentation is atypical, where timely endoscopy is undoubtedly helpful. In many areas, waiting times for endoscopy are long and endoscopy units are under intense pressure. The rising incidence of heartburn is a major contributor to this pressure.

Improving practice

GORD is a disease defined by its symptoms and thus the primary goal of management is to control these symptoms. Until we have clarified the risk of complications such as stricture or cancer arising from prolonged acid exposure and silent refluxing, it is probably sufficient for good symptom control to be the primary goal of management.

Our growing understanding of what triggers a patient to consult their GP provides the opportunity for some quality general practice. Careful exploration of the severity, frequency and impact of symptoms, together with how the patient interprets the symptoms, can lead to a successful consultation. Reassured that their heartburn does not stem from any serious disease, an explanation alone or minimal therapy is often all that is needed by most patients. In addition to good consultation skills, the GP needs to be confident in distinguishing mild and intermittent symptoms (which can be regarded as 'normal') from the more persistent and chronic symptoms of true GORD.

Treatment of heartburn

Below I outline the hierarchy of interventions that should be considered when treating heartburn.

Reassurance and explanation

When the patient's concern centres on the possible significance of the symptoms rather than the symptoms themselves, then reassurance and explanation that there is no significant underlying disease, together with advice to continue with over-the-counter (OTC) medication as required, may be all that is necessary.

Lifestyle

There is good reason to believe that a number of lifestyle changes would be effective in alleviating the symptoms of heartburn in many patients. Although their success in controlling reflux is limited, lifestyle changes should always be suggested. Moreover, many of these lifestyle changes (e.g. weight loss and diet changes) also provide other health advantages. However, as any experienced GP knows, such lifestyle changes are notoriously difficult for patients to implement. The following lifestyle changes are recommended.

- Moderation in the amount and frequency of alcohol consumption should always be recommended.
- Any particular precipitating foods should be avoided.
- Weight loss should be encouraged.
- Consumption of fatty foods should be discouraged.
- Eating close to bedtime should be avoided to lessen the chance of gastrooesophageal reflux.

- Raising the head of the bed can also be helpful, but in my experience such advice is often greeted with a compliant nod of the head and little else.

Antacids

Many patients will have tried OTC antacid preparations before consulting their GP. Although antacids are of limited potency, they do have the advantages of being cheap and rapidly acting. They can sometimes be beneficial for milder cases of heartburn, particularly if adequate doses are used.

Histamine H2 receptor antagonists

H2RAs were once heralded as wonder drugs and in their day represented a major step forwards in the treatment of acid-related gastrointestinal disorders. However, they have now largely been superseded by the more potent PPIs. Like antacids, they can be a step in the treatment of milder symptoms and have the advantages of being available OTC and are relatively rapidly acting.

Proton-pump inhibitors

PPIs provide more potent acid suppression and symptom control. As a class they are generally well tolerated and usually extremely effective in achieving symptom control. The National Institute of Clinical Excellence (NICE) has published guidelines on the use of PPIs and acknowledges that they are the most clinically effective and cost-effective agents to heal severe GORD and to prevent its recurrence.

When treating heartburn, there is debate as to whether it is best to step up the dose in response to symptoms or to step down having quickly brought the symptoms under control. In either case, the key seems to be to review the patient regularly and titrate the amount of acid suppression according to symptoms.

There is evidence that once initial healing or symptom control is achieved with a higher or healing dose, then patients can be maintained on lower doses. In any event, regular review of patients taking long-term PPI therapy is encouraged and dose adjustments should be made according to the patient's symptoms. Although at present this review is not normally the responsibility of practice nurses, there is no reason why it could not be, with adequate training. Reviewing all patients on long-term medications represents good practice and long-term acid-suppressing drugs should be no exception.

Repeat prescribing of PPIs represents a suitable topic for an audit of a practice's prescribing, and factors such as diagnosis, investigations and reviews can be incorporated into this. Patients who develop complications of GORD, Barrett's oesophagus or oesophageal cancer can form the basis of a critical-incident analysis.

Some PPIs have 'intermittent courses as required' as part of their licensing. This is an attractive option that offers symptom control with minimum intervention. There is good evidence that patients have always taken their acidsuppressing therapy in this way, but it is reassuring to have a licensed indication for this.

Conclusion

Whatever therapy is used, it must be understood that GORD is often a condition with chronic and relapsing symptoms. Consideration should be given to matching symptom severity with the level of intervention needed to relieve the symptoms, together with the fact that this level may change both between and within relapse episodes. The key message, endorsed by NICE, is that regular review and, if necessary, adjustment of therapy is good practice.

Key points

- Heartburn is a very common symptom that presents in primary care with an estimated prevalence of about 40%. Up to 10% of these patients will have 'true' GORD.

- GORD has a major impact upon quality of life and its symptoms can be extremely disabling for the sufferer. Its impact has been likened to the burden of more 'serious' conditions such as angina.

- The increase in prevalence of oesophageal cancer mirrors the increase in the prevalence of GORD. Possible reasons for the increase in both conditions include changes to the diet, increases in obesity and a decrease in *H. pylori* infections in the community.

- The majority of patients who seek help for their symptoms are treated in primary care, with only a small fraction being referred for further specialist investigation. Thus, the responsibility to ensure best practice in GORD management falls upon GPs.

- The primary goal of clinical management in GORD is the control of patients' symptoms. Reassurance that there is no underlying disease, an explanation of why symptoms occur and prescription of appropriate pharmacotherapy is often all that is needed by the majority of patients.

- Pharmacotherapy with acid-suppressing agents is regarded as the most effective tool for managing GORD in primary care. However, lifestyle changes can also help control patient's symptoms and may also provide other health advantages.

- Patients receiving acid-suppressing therapy should have their treatment reviewed regularly and adjusted accordingly.

17. Heart failure

Dr Richard Lehman MA, BM, BCh. MRCGP, DRCOG
General Practitioner, Banbury, Oxfordshire
Senior Research Fellow, Department of Public Health and Primary Care
University of Oxford

Summary

The principal challenges of heart failure for primary care are to identify affected patients and optimise their treatment. The National Institute for Clinical Excellence (NICE) has recently published guidelines on how best to do this. Basic diagnostic investigations should include electrocardiography (ECG), chest X-ray, baseline blood tests and evaluation of pulmonary function. In addition, measurement of plasma levels of natriuretic peptides may also have diagnostic value. Treatment of heart failure should start with angiotensin-converting enzyme (ACE) inhibitor therapy (or an angiotensin-receptor blocker [ARB] if poorly tolerated), followed by the addition of a β-blocker. Diuretics should be administered to control congestive symptoms and fluid retention. If the patient remains symptomatic, aldosterone antagonist therapy should be considered. A structured approach to the management of heart failure, involving the whole primary-care team, is central to its success, as is the education of patients with heart failure about their illness and its treatment.

Heart failure in primary care

Heart failure is a term which confuses doctors and terrifies patients. It can be used to describe anything from asymptomatic left ventricular dysfunction to imminent death from pulmonary oedema. Somewhere between the two lie the vast majority of patients who are diagnosed with heart failure in primary care – those with symptomatic cardiac impairment known as 'chronic stable heart failure'. The stability of heart failure is frequently threatened by factors which lead to 'decompensation', usually involving a rapid worsening of breathlessness and very often leading to acute hospital admission.

The principal challenges for primary care are to:

- identify patients who have heart failure, usually alongside other problems of old age

- optimise their treatment so as to relieve symptoms, improve daily function, and prolong life
- identify decompensation and intervene rapidly, hopefully before hospital admission becomes necessary
- support the patient and their carers throughout the course of the illness by involving the whole multidisciplinary healthcare professional team
- provide appropriate end-of-life care.

Heart failure with left systolic dysfunction, severe enough to cause breathlessness during normal activity, is a malignant condition with a prognosis that can be worse than many disseminated cancers. However, appropriate treatment undoubtedly improves both the length and quality of a patient's life. Properly structured team-led care and better use of biochemical markers may transform the care of what is currently seen by many GPs as an intractable and unpredictable condition.

The size of the problem

Despite much community-based research effort over recent years, it is very difficult to quantify the burden of 'real life' heart failure in UK primary care. The British Heart Foundation website *www.heartstats.org* contains very useful summaries of what is known, and estimates that there are currently 880,000 patients with chronic heart failure (CHF) in Britain. However, the case definition of CHF is so broad and debatable, and access to diagnostic testing so patchy, that we cannot place much reliance on current data derived from general practice. However, we can say with relative certainty, that the average age of a patient is around 75 years, that men outnumber women, and that most GPs will be looking after between 20 and 40 patients with CHF.

Identifying patients with heart failure

Risk groups

The practice team will be familiar already with the majority of patients with heart failure, whether or not the diagnosis has been established. This is principally because the vast majority of heart failure arises in patients with pre-existing conditions, such as ischaemic heart disease (particularly previous myocordial infarction [MI]), diabetes and hypertension. Consequently, any community screening programme for heart failure would logically begin with these groups, but active case finding is not currently encouraged. However, if new symptoms of breathlessness and peripheral oedema arise in these groups, there is a much higher likelihood of heart failure than in patients with no known risk factors. Smaller, but more specific risk groups include those with valvular heart disease or those with a family history of cardiomyopathy or haemochromatosis.

Acute precipitants

Patients presenting with heart failure usually have an acute precipitant as well as a predisposing cause. Common precipitants include:
- respiratory infection
- anaemia
- atrial fibrillation
- drugs causing fluid retention, especially non-steroidal anti-inflammatory drugs (NSAIDs) and thiazolidinediones (glitazones)
- new MI (sometimes silent)
- renal failure
- thyroid dysfunction.

Symptoms of heart failure may disappear following treatment of the precipitant, but anyone who has had 'a touch of failure' for any reason should have further cardiac investigation.

Practice registers

Even if the correct Read codes have been used consistently, practice heart failure registers are unlikely to provide the necessary information on left ventricular systolic function required by the new GMS contract (Table 1).

Table 1. General Medical Services (GMS) contract quality standards for left ventricular dysfunction.

	Points	Maximum threshold
LVD 1. The practice can produce a register of patients with CHD and left ventricular dysfunction	4 points	
LVD 2. The percentage of patients with a diagnosis of CHD and left ventricular dysfunction (diagnosed after 1/4/03) which has been confirmed by an echocardiogram	6 points	90%
LVD 3. The percentage of patients with a diagnosis of CHD and left ventricular dysfunction who are currently treated with ACE inhibitors (or angiotensin II receptor antagonists)	10 points	70%

Prescribing audit

Audits of particular drug class prescribing have been used over the last decade to help establish accurate heart failure registers. In the majority of practices, checking all patients prescribed loop diuretics and ACE inhibitors, either alone or in combination, will identify more than 90% of patients with heart failure. Obviously this requires individual case review and, as such, this can be time-consuming. There may be a small extra yield from checking prescriptions of digoxin, angiotensin receptor blockers and thiazide diuretics.

Confirming the diagnosis

The evidence base for treating heart failure is largely based on studies of patients below 70 years of age, mostly male and usually with a history of MI or cardiomyopathy. A key entry criterion has always been a reduced left ventricular ejection fraction (LVEF) as measured by radionuclide ventriculography or angiography. Unfortunately most of our patients with CHF in primary care are not like this and we cannot make patients conform to a 'gold standard' in order to merit treatment. Half of the patients we diagnose with heart failure have a normal LVEF. This does not mean that heart failure can be excluded. It simply means that we do not have a solid category in which to put their heart failure, or a good evidence base for their treatment.

Patients with symptoms of heart failure, but without a history of MI, valve disease or cardiomyopathy, are likely to have normal systolic function. This is an important point to which we will return.

NICE has published an algorithm on appropriate investigations for heart failure (Figure 1). Basic investigations that can be conducted within a primary care setting encompassed within these guidelines are outlined below.

- **ECG** – a normal ECG makes heart failure with systolic dysfunction unlikely. Systolic heart failure is almost always (90–95%) accompanied by major abnormalities such as Q-waves, left bundle branch block (LBBB), and/or extensive T-wave inversion.
- **Chest X-ray** – the chest X-ray is often normal in compensated heart failure, but it can provide useful information such as heart size, whether there is pulmonary oedema or co-existing lung disease. Remember that pulmonary fibrosis can mimic heart failure, with lung crackles and peripheral oedema due to right ventricular overload.
- **Baseline blood tests** should include a full blood count, creatinine and electrolytes, with glucose, lipids and thyroid stimulating hormone (TSH) as useful additions.

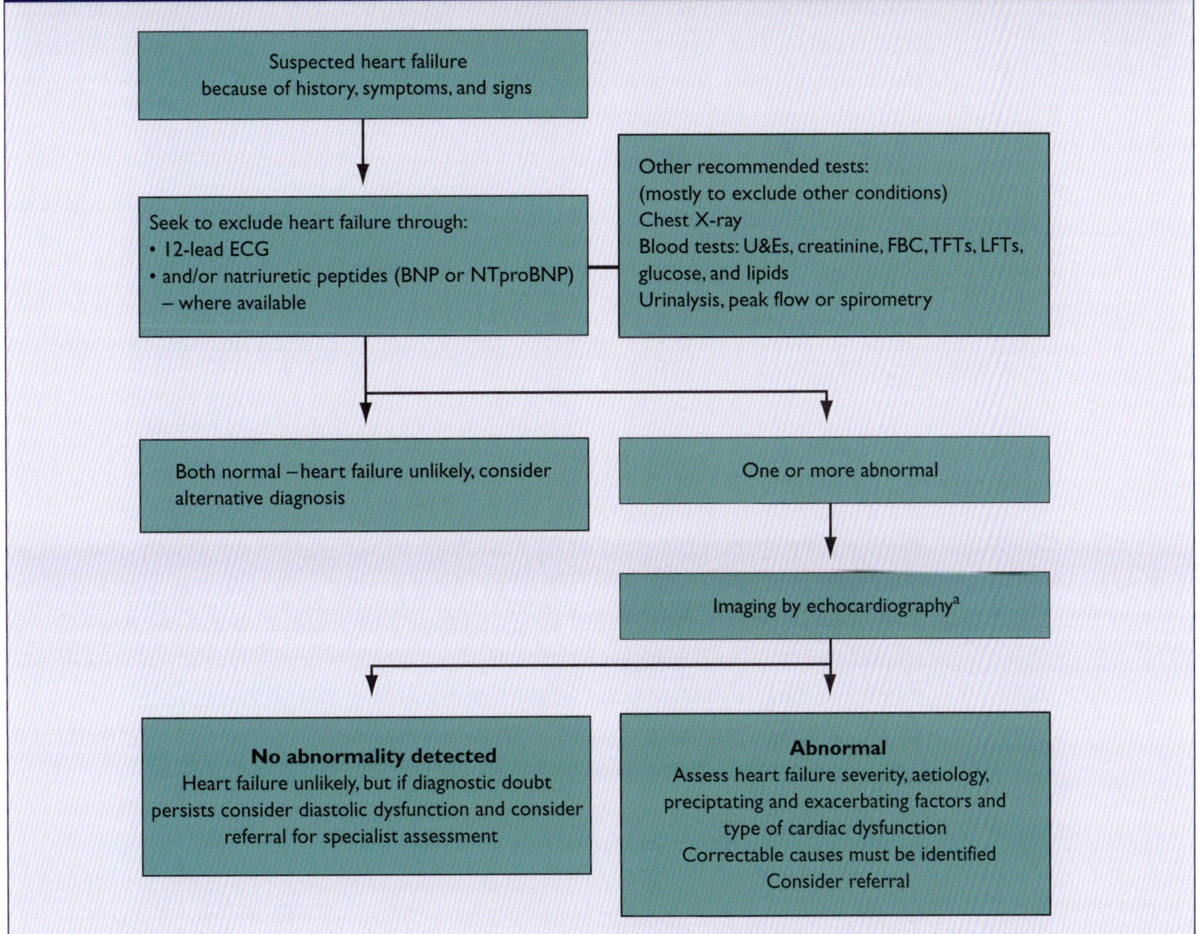

Figure 1. A diagnostic algorithm for the management of patients with suspected heart failure (adapted from the National Institute of Clinical Excellence [NICE] Clinical Guideline on Chronic Heart Failure; *www.nice.org.uk*). BNP, B-type natriuretic peptide; ECG, electrocardiogram; FBC, full blood count; LFTs, liver function tests; NTproBNP, N-terminal pro-B-type natriuretic peptide; TFTs, thyroid function tests; U&Es, urea and electrolytes.
[a]Alternative methods of imaging the heart should be considered when a poor image is produced by transthoracic Doppler 2D echocardiography – alternatives include transcesophageal Doppler 2D echocardiography, radionuclide imaging or cardiac magnetic resonance imaging.

● **Pulmonary function testing** may also be helpful. A positive diagnosis of chronic obstructive pulmonary disease does not necessarily rule out heart failure, because both conditions are common in elderly smokers. Heart failure itself may also cause a mildly obstructive picture on spirometry.

B-type natriuretic peptide

B-type natriuretic peptide (BNP) is released by both cardiac ventricles in response to strain (excessive stretch). Confusingly, it is sometimes called brain natriuretic peptide because it was first isolated from pig brain. However, it is a cardiac hormone, of such basic importance that it is present in fish and reptiles as well as mammals. It is impossible to have uncompensated heart failure without elevation of BNP, though successful treatment of heart failure may normalise BNP levels. The NICE guidelines therefore suggest that a normal level of BNP or N-terminal pro-BNP can be useful in excluding newly presenting heart failure. This is true, although whether it adds useful information to doing an ECG is debatable.

BNP has much greater potential value than this. In the future, it is likely that we will be using serial measurements to guide treatment and to establish a diagnosis of heart failure with normal systolic function. Also, BNP is the best prognostic marker we have in heart failure: very high levels indicate that death is imminent. This may have important consequences for the deployment of palliative care.

Systolic and diastolic function

We have seen that it is possible to have heart failure despite a normal ejection fraction. This type of dysfunction (often described as 'diastolic', although this is misleading) becomes more prevalent as the heart gets stiffer and older, by processes which are accelerated in those patients with hypertension and diabetes. Virtually all patients with 'diastolic' heart failure will have had left ventricular hypertrophy and may still have a high pulse pressure. This may be difficult to reduce because their heart and capacitance vessels are irreversibly stiffened.

Measuring the systolic ejection fraction, or something similar, like the wall motion index, is consequently not the 'gold standard' for diagnosing heart failure. It does, however, help us to identify those patients for whom we have a good therapeutic evidence base. Those with preserved systolic function ('diastolic' heart failure) will have to await the results of numerous diagnostic and interventional studies that are currently under way.

Echocardiography

So where does echocardiography fit in? Even if it was a good way to measure systolic function, it would not be the 'gold standard'. In fact, there are far more accurate ways to obtain the ejection fraction, for instance with angiography, MRI and radionuclide scanning. Nevertheless, echocardiography is so easily performed and yields so much information

that it remains the most useful investigation that primary care can
access – when it is permitted to. Provided the patient is not too obese or
emphysematous, the structure and function of the valves and ventricles can
be observed and measured. The systolic EF can be roughly estimated ('eye-
balling'), and if it is reduced, the patient can enter into the happy realm of
evidence-based medicine.

In summary, the diagnostic strategy outlined above depends on:

- a high index of suspicion in risk groups
- basic tests to rule out heart failure
- echocardiography to rule in systolic dysfunction.

Medical management of heart failure with left systolic dysfunction

Most of the NICE guideline is concerned with the management of heart
failure with left ventricular systolic dysfunction (most commonly as the
result of an MI) and it is to this we will now turn. A proposed treatment
algorithm for such a patient population is illustrated in Figure 2.

Treating the precipitating cause

Do not forget that heart failure usually has an immediate trigger as well as
an underlying cause. A list of precipitating factors has already been given,
and should be recalled each time there is an episode of decompensation:

- breathlessness and cough – these may be due to heart failure *per se*, but
  do not overlook a developing chest infection
- anaemia – is often present and treatable in early heart failure, but
  becomes more common and more difficult to treat in advanced disease
- atrial fibrillation – requires rate control, anticoagulation and referral to a
  specialist
- drugs – NSAIDs should never be given to patients with CHF
- treatment non-adherence – a common problem, as most patients do not
  understand their treatment, and are on many different drugs
- silent MI
- renal failure – is easily missed, but common in this group of patients
- thyroid dysfunction.

Treating fluid overload

Furosemide (frusemide) remains the first-line treatment choice to manage
fluid overload. However, resistant oedema may sometimes respond to a
change of loop diuretic (e.g. to indapamide or bumetanide), or the addition
of a powerful thiazide diuretic such as metolazone. Postural hypotension

Figure 2. A treatment algorithm for the management of patients with symptomatic heart failure as a consequence of left ventricular systolic dysfunction (adapted from the National Institute of Clinical Excellence [NICE] Clinical Guideline on Chronic Heart Failure; *www.nice.org.uk*)

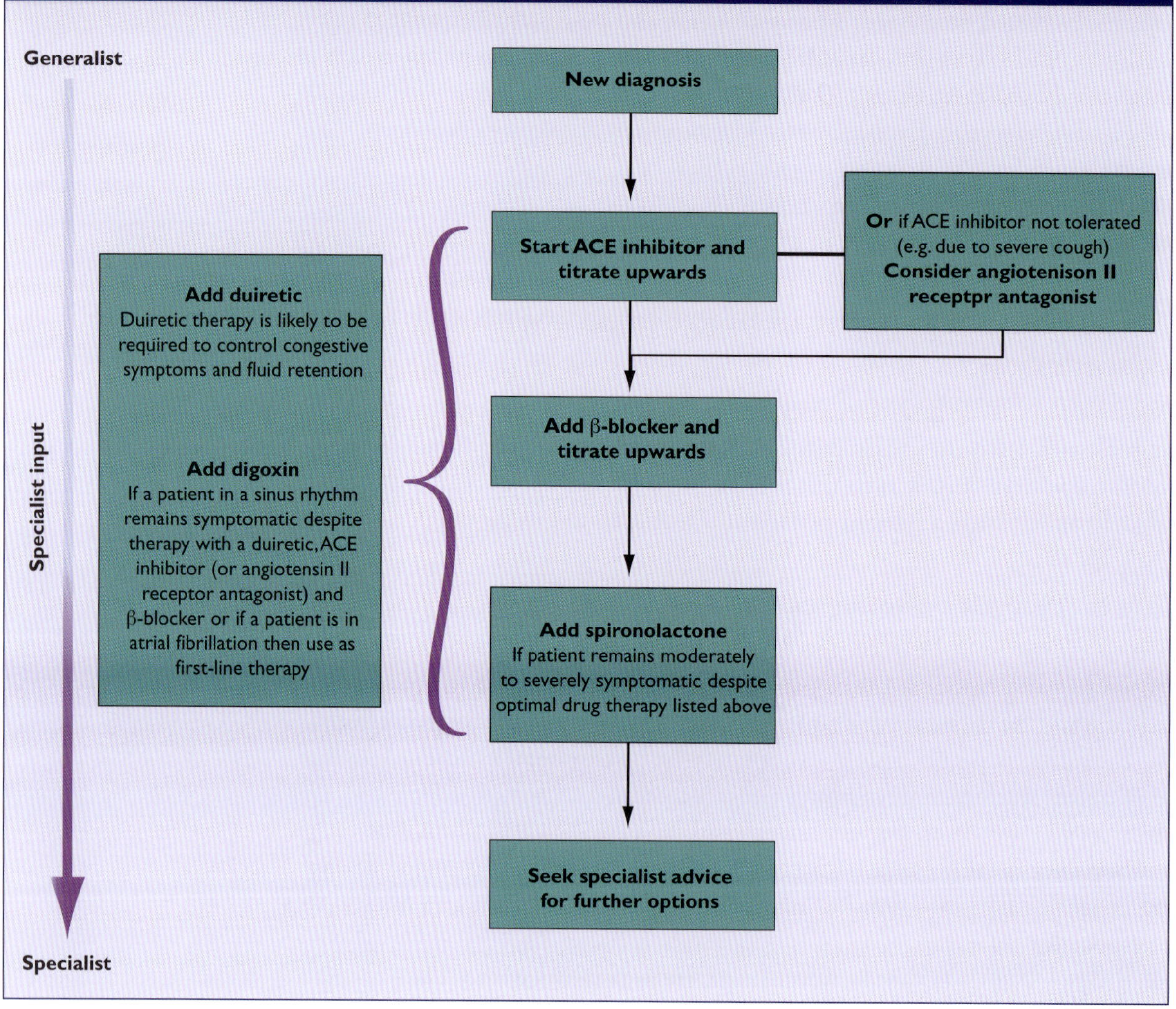

and electrolyte disturbances can, however, often follow, so it is important to:

- measure both sitting and standing blood pressure
- ask patients to weigh themselves daily
- check creatinine and electrolytes frequently
- use trained nurse help if available.

Drugs modifying the renin–angiotensin–aldosterone system (RAAS)

The management of heart failure was transformed 20 years ago by the discovery that the inhibition of ACE leads to an improvement in symptoms and prolongs life. Since that time, several other stages of the RAAS have been used as pharmacological targets:

- renin blockers (currently under development)
- ARBs
- direct aldosterone antagonists.

Most trials have used new agents in combination with existing treatments, and the benefits derived from such an approach appear to be additive.

The recently reported CHARM trial, however, looked at the effect of an ARB, candesartan, in combination with ACE inhibition, and alone. Combined treatment is best, but this trial also provides the first convincing evidence that ARBs are as effective as ACE inhibitors used alone. Thus we can feel reasonably comfortable about changing patients who cannot tolerate ACE-inhibitors to an ARB.

Each new drug requires introduction at a low dose together with close monitoring of blood pressure and renal function. The majority of evidence suggests that most GPs do not up-titrate the doses of an ACE inhibitor as recommended in most guidelines. However, there is only weak evidence that high-dose ACE inhibition is advantageous, so this caution may not be too disastrous: however, it is also worth remembering that the side-effects of ACE inhibitors are not dose dependent, and that groups randomised to high doses in clinical trials generally had the fewest adverse events!

It could be argued that the trial evidence supports triple RAAS blockade in every patient with left systolic heart failure. Potentially, therefore, there are at least nine steps of RAAS-modifying treatment at which monitoring of symptoms, BP and electrolytes is required – leaving aside the consequences of adding β-blockers and other drugs! This definitely requires nurse assistance if it is ever to be implemented in reality.

Beta-adrenergic blockade

β-blockers introduce another set of problems:

- in the past, doctors have been warned against using them in heart failure
- patients given β-blockers may get worse before they get better
- many patients have supposed contraindications to β-blockade
- there has been much debate about which agent to use and at which dose
- careful up-titration is absolutely essential.

The evidence that β-blockers prolong life and eventually relieve symptoms is incontrovertible. Studies have also shown that the majority of patients with mild asthma or COPD with a reversible component can be safely started on cardio-selective β-blockers given at low dosage.

Other drugs and therapies

The NICE guideline mentions digoxin as a potentially useful drug for heart failure in sinus rhythm. However, this is highly debatable. If by a miracle of organisation (see below) you have introduced at least one RAAS-modifying drug and a β-blocker at adequate dosage to your patient with CHF, and you are still having problems, referral to a specialist centre is best. There are many further potential interventions which include:

- anti-arrhythmic drugs
- biventricular pacing
- continuous positive pressure ventilation
- revascularisation of hibernating myocardium
- left ventricular assist devices.

Other measures: patient education, exercise and lifestyle

'Failure' is a word we tend to avoid in normal life, because it is so entirely negative. However, we are stuck, at least for now, with the term 'heart failure', even though it has little scientific meaning and less than no value as a communication tool. Just as we generally explain to patients what we mean if we use the word 'cancer', it is always worth going over with the patient what we do and do not mean when we refer to heart failure. Most people think it means a heart attack or sudden death.

The full agenda of patient education in heart failure needs to be addressed over several consultations with an expert professional, ideally a specialist heart failure nurse. The aims are to:

- understand the illness
- foster coping mechanisms
- understand the basis of drug treatment
- know when to seek help
- make necessary lifestyle changes.

Lifestyle changes which may be of benefit in heart failure include:

- salt avoidance
- exercise preferably encouraged by a cardiac rehabilitation unit – functional capacity in heart failure is more closely related to skeletal muscle fitness than to systolic ejection fraction

- maintenance of body weight as a high body mass index is positive in heart failure
- regular alcohol intake – there is currently no evidence that introducing alcohol newly into the diet improves heart failure, but there is significant evidence that regular drinkers have a decreased rate of heart failure and MI or reinfarction.

All patients with heart failure should be offered polyvalent pneumococcal vaccine and annual influenza vaccine.

The patient's agenda

While you are puzzling over which drug to use next and at what dosage, looking for the latest blood results and ringing the cardiology secretary's answering machine, your patient will be counting away the 10 minutes during which they may have hoped to raise an entirely different set of concerns. If we listen to our patients' stories, the themes which almost always emerge are of:

- little understanding of diagnosis or prognosis
- occasional improvements after treatment but overall seems to get worse
- social life becoming less and less
- relatives becoming anxious and exhausted
- a daily grind of hopelessness
- other medical problems (e.g. arthritis, visual impairment etc.)

However much we pride ourselves on being holistic and caring GPs, the fact is that the medical agenda for heart failure is awesomely complex and crowded, and leaves us little time to consider the wider context. If we communicate anything, it is often our own anxiety and uncertainty.

Thus, the management of heart failure needs a structured approach involving the whole primary-care team.

> The management of heart failure needs a structured approach involving the whole primary-care team.

Who will do the work?

The model of care which has so far been shown to work best in CHF is a hospital-based specialist nurse service with outreach to the community – but is this a logical model for a primary care-based NHS?

As we have seen, there may be about 880,000 patients with CHF in the community. Currently, there about 100 specialist heart failure nurses in post. There may be about 1000 cardiologists providing heart failure services in the UK, whilst there are about 30,000 GPs and perhaps 10,000 practice nurses. Clearly, the potential burden on already overstretched resources is huge.

Diabetes provides a possible model to meet this demand. Here, general practices who wish to provide a primary-care service deploy practice nurses trained in diabetes care. A GP runs a regular clinic alongside the nurse and other relevant health professionals (e.g. dietician, podiatrist, optometrist). In most localities there is a specialist nurse who is hospital based whose skills are used to look after difficult cases and to liaise with the hospital clinic.

To apply the same model to the structured disease management of heart failure, each practice would need:

- a practice nurse trained in the basic management of CHF
- a GP with sufficient time, interest and training to work alongside the nurse-led clinic.

We need much greater involvement of GPs with a special interest, and trained members of the primary care team, particularly nurses.

Consequently, this may not be practical for every GP partnership, and therefore practices and Primary Care Trusts should look at a range of models for structured care. What is apparent, however, is that cardiologists and specialist nurses on their own cannot cope with the whole burden of heart failure care in the community. We need much greater involvement of GPs with a special interest, and trained members of the primary-care team, particularly nurses. Training schemes for practice nurses as well as specialist nurses are now available (see Table 2).

Table 2. Useful heart failure-related website resources.

General

British Heart Foundation	*www.bhf.org.uk*
British Society for Heart Failure	*www.bcs.com/affiliates/bsh.html*
Primary Care Cardiovascular Society	*www.pccs.org.uk*

Patient experience

Database of Individual Patient Experiences	*www.dipex.org.uk*

Patient information

British Heart Foundation	*www.bhf.org.uk*
HertNet	*www.heartsforlife.co.uk*

NICE guideline

National Institute for Clinical Excellence	*www.nice.org.uk*

Training

For primary care nurses and other staff	*www.heartsave.org.uk*
For specialist nurses (contact Glasgow Caledonian University)	*m.wright@gcal.ac.uk*
Macmillan Gold Standard Framework	*www.macmillan.org.uk*

Dying from heart failure: palliative care

Even with the best treatment, heart failure remains a seriously life-shortening condition. An ideal pattern of care would be supportive throughout the disease process, rather than involving a sudden insertion of palliative care at some arbitrary point near the end stage.

Patients with heart failure have an approximately 'evens' chance of dying in one of two ways:

- suddenly, perhaps due to fatal arrhythmia or MI, and usually outside hospital
- slowly, due to pulmonary oedema, almost always in hospital.

A large amount of work needs to be done to improve the availability of palliative care, to develop means to relieve dyspnoea, and to give patients a genuine choice of place of death, based on intensive support at home. We can begin in a small way, by bringing the needs of our patients with advanced heart failure to the attention of the whole practice team and the palliative care nursing service. Pilot projects are already under way to incorporate heart failure into the Macmillan Gold Standard Framework for Palliative Care.

Key points

- Most GPs will be looking after 20–40 patients with heart failure.

- The majority of heart failure cases arise in patients with pre-existing conditions (e.g. ischaemic heart disease, MI and diabetes).

- NICE guidelines advocate that suspected cases of heart failure should be confirmed by clinical investigations such as ECG, chest X-ray, baseline blood tests and pulmonary function tests.

- Measurement of natriuretic peptide levels may be a useful prognostic tool.

- Treatment of heart failure should start with ACE inhibitor therapy (or ARB therapy if poorly tolerated), followed by the addition of a β-blocker.

- In those patients who remain moderately or severely symptomatic, treatment with an aldosterone antagonist (e.g. spironolactone) should be considered.

- Diuretic therapy should be administered to control congestive symptoms and fluid retention.

- A structured approach to heart failure, involving the whole primary-care team, is the key to its successful management.

18. Hepatitis A

Dr George Kassianos MD (Hons) FRCGP DRCOG LRCPEdin. LRCSEdin.
LRCP&SGlasg. DFP DMedAcup. DMedHypn MILT
General Practitioner, Bracknell, Berkshire

Summary

The risk of contracting hepatitis A is drastically increased when travelling to those regions of the world in which the disease is highly endemic, often as a result of poor living standards and inadequate sanitation. Thus, the prevention of hepatitis A in the individual traveller and the limitation and containment of isolated disease outbreaks, are both important and realistic goals. When abroad, travellers can reduce their exposure to potential sources of hepatitis A infection through the avoidance of high-risk food and drink substances and the adoption of simple hygienic procedures. Undergoing vaccination against hepatitis A prior to travelling to endemic areas is advisable both in adults and children and a number of effective and well-tolerated hepatitis A vaccines (monovalent or combined) are currently available in the UK. Young children, in whom the disease is frequently asymptomatic, represent a key source of disease transmission owing to their less-scrupulous hygiene standards, which further highlights the importance of vaccination in this age group in particular. The identification and careful monitoring of high-risk individuals (e.g. older people, patients with pre-existing liver disease or immunocompromised status) is strongly advised, in view of the more serious implications of hepatitis A infection herein. Vaccination against hepatitis A of individuals at high risk of contracting the disease, such as travellers to regions of high or intermediate endemicity, or homosexuals with multiple partners, is an important task for UK healthcare professionals.

Introduction

Hepatitis A is a common disease worldwide. It is highly infectious and thus able to spread easily, particularly within families and amongst children. Hepatitis A is closely associated with economic under-development, poor living standards and inadequate sanitation and hygiene in individual countries or areas. Its elimination is an important task for every government, whilst its prevention is the responsibility of all of us working in primary care.

> The elimination of hepatitis A is an important task for every government, whilst its prevention is the responsibility of all of us working in primary care.

The history of the hepatitis A

Hepatitis is one of the oldest diseases known to mankind. Hippocrates was the first to describe an epidemic of jaundice as early as the fifth century BC. It was not until 1973 that the virus responsible for hepatitis A was identified, and this was not grown effectively under laboratory conditions until 1979. The hepatitis A virus (HAV) is a single-stranded ribonucleic acid (RNA) virus belonging to the Picornaviridae family, which replicates exclusively in the cytoplasm of the host cell. The virus is heat stable and will survive for up to 1 month at the ambient temperature in the environment. However, it can be inactivated by ultraviolet radiation, autoclaving and by chemical inactivation (e.g. with sodium hypochlorite and iodine). The first HAV vaccine was introduced in the UK in 1992.

The global challenge of hepatitis A

The HAV does not recognise national or international borders. The growth in travel and the movement of produce between areas of high and low endemicity encourages transmission of this infection.

Hepatitis A is common in places where water supplies and sanitation are of a poor standard, and where personal and food hygiene standards are also substandard. Africa, South America, the Middle East, China, the Indian subcontinent and south-east Asia are high-risk areas, whilst southern and eastern Europe and the Russian Federation are considered to be intermediate-risk areas.

In about 95% of cases of hepatitis A, the disease is transmitted from *person to person,* particularly in children, and by *exposure* to contaminated food or drinking contaminated water. The remaining cases appear to be derived from contaminated blood or by anal intercourse. The illness can spread easily within families and where people live closely together, as the virus is shed in the stools of an infected individual. As such, hand-washing and good personal hygiene standards are very important control measures to reduce the spread of the infection.

Common-source outbreaks may occur as a result of faecal contamination of food and/or drinking or coastal water. In general, HAV infection is related to poor housing with poor hygiene and sanitary conditions, and where sewage comes into contact with drinking water. The epidemiology of hepatitis A is closely related to the level of economic development within a country or region. As such, an improvement in living standards appears to reduce the incidence of the disease leading to a decline in its prevalence.

Sewage has been implicated in hepatitis A outbreaks whilst a wide range of foods have been implicated in food-borne outbreaks. These include

> Hand-washing and good personal hygiene standards are very important control measures to reduce the spread of the infection.

shellfish (from sewage-polluted waters eaten raw or poorly cooked), milk, orange juice, ice cubes in drinks, mineral water, salads, strawberries, bread, caviar, hamburgers, spaghetti, sandwiches, pasties and cream. Watermelons are known to have been injected on occasions with (sometimes contaminated) water in order to increase their weight. An outbreak of food-borne infection can be imported from another country. As an illustration, in the autumn of 1999 there was an outbreak of hepatitis A centred on the Valencia area in Spain, which was caused by the consumption of previously frozen clams imported from Peru. Another example was the outbreak of HAV infection amongst customers of a restaurant in Monaca, Pennsylvania in 2003, which was associated with consumption of uncooked or minimally cooked green onions imported from Mexico.

Blood-borne transmissions are reported rarely and are due to the brief viraemia which occurs during the incubation period and the early acute phase of illness.

Viral inactivation during the preparation of blood products for patients depends on disrupting the lipid envelope of a virus. Since HAV is a non-enveloped virus, it resists such treatment and, therefore, can be transmitted by *blood products*. Patients with clotting factor disorders who are likely to require Factor VIII or IX are, therefore, at risk of HAV infection, particularly if the blood-donor was in the early stages of infection, prior to clinical presentation. In the UK, blood and blood products are routinely screened in order to eliminate this risk. Transmission from mother to newborn infant (*vertical transmission*) is uncommon.

Sexual practices most likely to spread HAV include penetrative anal intercourse and oral–anal contact. Another risk factor is sharing contaminated needles. Casual contact, such as kissing or sharing of utensils, is not an efficient source of transmission.

The challenge in primary care

After travellers' diarrhoea and malaria, hepatitis A is the most common infectious disease reported amongst UK visitors overseas. It is also the most common vaccine-preventable disease. A common source of acquiring hepatitis A is travel to endemic areas (Table 1). The Indian subcontinent has remained the most reported region for hepatitis A infection amongst foreign travellers. However, the widespread availability of HAV vaccines on the NHS in conjunction with improvements in the quality of travel clinics and increased access to them by travellers, may have contributed to the sustained reduction in the number of 'imported' cases of hepatitis A over recent years. Moreover, there have been parallel improvements in the

After travellers' diarrhoea and malaria, hepatitis A is the most common infectious disease reported amongst UK visitors overseas. It is also the most common vaccine-preventable disease.

Table 1. Hepatitis A laboratory reports in England and Wales (1990–2003) according to travel history by country. Adapted from the Health Protection Agency (*http://www.hpa.org.uk/infections/topics_az/hepatitis_a/data_lab_travel.htm*)

	Year												
	1992	1993	1994	1995	1996	1997	1998	1999	2000	2001	2002	2003[a]
Total reports	6762	3957	2412	1750	1086	1310	1104	1391	1047	801	1352	974
Reports associated with travel history	1771	939	736	453	305	318	193	159	116	68	56	28
Reports associated with travel history (%)	26.19	23.73	30.51	25.89	28.08	24.27	17.48	11.43	11.08	8.49	4.14	2.87
Reports according to country visited												
India	79	64	48	28	17	14	6	7	1	3	1	0
Pakistan	70	51	63	34	28	16	7	13	19	7	3	3
Bangladesh	22	12	3	21	10	4	2	1	1	4	0	0
ISC not specified	5	2	3	4	2	2	1	0	0	0	0	0
Spain	22	12	8	14	5	4	2	0	5	1	1	1
France	14	5	3	6	2	0	0	1	0	1	0	0
Portugal	4	8	17	3	1	0	0	0	0	0	0	0
Italy	4	2	2	2	0	2	0	0	0	0	0	0
Turkey	8	7	11	12	4	2	3	1	1	0	0	0
Greece	10	3	10	5	2	1	2	1	0	0	2	0
Other	203	145	128	100	94	141	108	72	54	39	17	7
Total	441	311	296	229	165	186	131	96	81	55	24	11
Proportion of cases by travel (%)	24.9	33.1	39.2	50.6	54.1	58.5	67.9	60.38	69.83	80.88	42.86	39.29

[a]Provisional data for 2003. ISC, Indian subcontinent.

provision of clean drinking water, food hygiene and accommodation for visitors to the majority of the tourist destinations, measures which have also benefited the local populations.

The introduction in the UK of the first hepatitis A vaccine in 1992 appears to have been a major factor in the marked fall in disease notifications in England and Wales – from 7856 cases in 1992, to 4457 in 1993 and 2715 the year after (Table 2). Before 1992, the only form of hepatitis A immunisation practised in the UK was passive immunisation with human normal immunoglobulin. Vaccination was made available on the NHS for those at increased risk of the disease, particularly travellers to highly endemic areas, in conjunction with health advice to remain prudent about food and drink.

One-in-ten children under 14 years, and one-in-five young adults aged 15 to 39 years are hospitalised for the symptoms of hepatitis A. The expected period of absence from work is about 1 month but can often

Table 2. Statutory notifications of hepatitis A by region in England and Wales (1990–2002). Adapted from the Health Protection Agency (*http://www.hpa.org.uk/infections/topics_az/hepatitis_a/data_not.htm*)

Region	1990	1991	1992	1993	1994	1995	1996	1997	1998	1999	2000	2001	2002
Northern and Yorkshire	2391	3099	2777	984	501	291	189	138	125	141	118	224	120
Trent	432	393	1296	662	407	217	172	100	77	120	113	97	475
Eastern	327	266	338	374	209	130	68	104	78	128	64	52	38
London	531	560	582	345	330	548	338	712	630	363	213	237	135
South East	1411	1038	563	391	404	384	187	276	195	362	272	169	114
South West	414	167	274	119	61	68	74	103	85	213	191	120	146
West Midlands	402	454	722	573	279	157	100	167	148	183	125	92	206
North West	1257	1209	858	505	334	248	139	187	127	125	148	119	126
Wales	151	244	446	504	189	77	72	50	50	41	27	31	21
Port Health Authorities	–	–	–	–	1	–	–	–	–	–	–	–	–
Total	7316	7430	7856	4457	2715	2120	1339	1837	1515	1676	1271	1141	1381

extend beyond 2 months. Thus, hepatitis A can exert a profound influence on productivity for the individual and the economy as a whole. After infection with the HAV, lifelong immunity is conferred.

Practical guidance for hepatitis A vaccination

There are four HAV vaccines available in the UK: Avaxim®, Epaxal®, Havrix® and Vaqta®. The schedule of immunisation is similar for all available vaccines (Table 3). However, there are some variations in their respective licenses relating to patient age and the timing of the reinforcing second dose, which is necessary to promote long-term protection as the first dose provides antibodies for protection for 6 months to 1 year. This applies to Epaxal, Havrix and Vaqta vaccines. There are serological data to show that there should be continuing protection against hepatitis A for up to 36 months after a first dose of Avaxim in subjects who responded to the initial vaccination.

Although the licensed time for the second dose differs from 6 to 36 months depending on the vaccine used, this dose can be given as a reinforcing dose regardless of the period of time that has elapsed since an initial dose. Thus, for example, a vaccinee who received the first dose of HAV vaccine 4 years ago and who subsequently returns for their second dose, does not need to have the first dose repeated and the second dose can be given.

Vaccines are also available in the UK that combine hepatitis A and typhoid (Hepatyrix®, Viatim®) for travellers exposed to waterborne diseases.

Table 3. Primary immunisation schedules for the various hepatitis A vaccines available in the UK.

Vaccine	Age group	Primary and booster dose	Route of vaccine administration (deltoid muscle)	Reinforcing (booster) dose period
Avaxim®	Adults 16 years and over	0.5 mL	i.m. injection	6–36 months
Epaxal®	Adults and children 2 years and over	0.5 mL	i.m. injection	6–12 months
Havrix® Junior Monodose	1–15 years	0.5 mL	i.m. injection	6–36 months
Havrix® Monodose	Adults 16 years and over	1.0 mL	i.m. injection	6–36 months
Vaqta® Paediatric	2–17 years	0.5 mL	i.m. injection	6–18 months

i.m., intramuscular.

For those exposed to waterborne diseases as well as sexual and blood transmission, two combination hepatitis A and B vaccines are available (Ambirix®, Twinrix®).

Interchangeability of HAV vaccines

Another practical problem we face on occasion is when the previous dose was given with one vaccine, but that vaccine then becomes unavailable to us for whatever reason (e.g. lack of availability due to manufacturing problems, the purchase of an alternative vaccine etc.). We can use a different HAV vaccine to complete the course or as a booster provided the available vaccine follows the same schedule of immunisation. All available vaccines in the UK, with the exception of Epaxal, are licensed to be administered as a booster in subjects previously immunised with any inactivated hepatitis A vaccine.

Seroconversion

Seroconversion is defined as achievement of anti-HAV levels greater than 20 mIU/mL, which can be determined by an enzyme-linked immunosorbent assay (ELISA) in previously seronegative vaccinees. However, the lower limit of antibody level required to prevent HAV infection has not yet been defined. In addition, HAV vaccination may also stimulate other immune mechanisms that confer further protection against HAV.

Adults aged 20–39 years have a faster rate of seroconversion within 15 days (90%) than older individuals aged 40–62 years (77%). However, all

HAV vaccination may also stimulate other immune mechanisms that confer further protection against HAV.

immunocompetent individuals become seropositive after the reinforcing booster dose of the vaccine.

Immunocompromised patients

Patients who are immunocompromised as a consequence of disease or concomitant treatment, may not always seroconvert to the vaccine. For example, the success of hepatitis A vaccination in human immunodeficiency virus (HIV)-positive subjects is dependent on their CD4+ lymphocyte count. About 15–20% of these cases do not seroconvert, and of those that do, patients may have lower antibody levels. Therefore, closer monitoring of long-term protection is necessary in such groups, and additional doses of the vaccine may be necessary.

Patients with chronic liver disease

Patients with liver disease as a result of hepatitis B or C, or non-viral causes, in addition to those who have received liver or kidney transplants have a reduced response to HAV vaccination compared with healthy individuals. Therefore, in these patients it is essential that the full course of vaccination is administered and seroconversion is routinely tested as part of their clinical management.

Pregnancy and lactation

The effects of the hepatitis A vaccines on foetal development and breast-fed infants have not yet been fully assessed. However, as with all inactivated viral vaccines, the risks to the foetus are considered to be negligible. Therefore, the risk of vaccination should be weighed against the risk of hepatitis A in pregnant women travellers who might be at high risk for exposure to HAV. The HAV vaccine can be considered during pregnancy only when needed because of high risk of infection of a non-immune pregnant woman, and should be used with caution in breast-feeding mothers if they are considered to be at high risk of infection. If possible, the vaccination should be postponed until after a mother has stopped breast feeding. Human normal immunoglobulin is an alternative to HAV vaccination as it is not contraindicated in pregnancy.

Passively transferred maternal antibody can reduce or abolish the response of very young infants to HAV vaccination. Maternal antibody will normally have disappeared from the circulation by 1 year of age, after which the initiation of vaccination can be recommended. Of the three paediatric HAV vaccines available in the UK, Havrix is licensed for administration from the age of 1 year while Vaqta Paediatric and Epaxal are licensed from the age of 2 years.

Duration of immunity

The length of immunity conferred after a full primary immunisation with an HAV vaccine (i.e. the initial dose and the reinforcing booster dose) is 10 years for Avaxim, Havrix and Vaqta, and 20 years for Epaxal according to their UK licences. All HAV vaccines are estimated, based on mathematical modelling, to confer long-term immunity, probably in the order of 18–25 years and beyond. Moreover, even if the antibodies were to disappear, the 'immunological memory' to the vaccine antigen could protect the individual well beyond the time that the antibody to HAV is no longer detectable in the circulation. It is known that the first dose of HAV vaccine is sufficient to induce immunological memory, and a robust anamnestic response follows the reinforcing booster dose in immunocompetent individuals.

There is no universal agreement between manufacturers and/or national authorities on how long protection will last after the two-dose primary course, or indeed whether there will be a need for future long-term HAV booster vaccinations to provide continued protection.

The International Consensus Group on HAV immunity (2003) has concluded that reliance should be placed on immunological memory rather than the long-term booster dose to protect against future symptomatic infection. Based on current knowledge, there are no data to support the need for HAV booster vaccinations in healthy, immunocompetent individuals who have received a primary vaccination course (the first two doses of the vaccine).

Serotesting before HAV vaccination

Serological testing for susceptibility may be useful for adult travellers who are likely to have had prior HAV infection. However, such testing is only indicated if the cost of screening (including laboratory costs and consultations) is less than the cost of vaccination. Generally, about one in five adults in the UK over the age of 40 years have antibodies to HAV. Very few children (less than 4% of those up to the age of 4 years) have such antibodies.

The last UK recommendations regarding serotesting prior to HAV vaccination were made in 1996 in the Department of Health publication *Immunisation Against Infectious Disease* (the 'Green Book'). They

> All HAV vaccines are estimated to confer long-term immunity, probably in the order of 18–25 years and beyond.

recommend that when practicable, testing for antibodies to HAV prior to immunisation may be beneficial in those:

- aged 50 years or over
- born in areas of high or moderate hepatitis A endemicity
- with a history of jaundice.

Post-vaccination testing for serological response is not indicated other than for immunosuppressed patients.

Patients with bleeding diathesis

Patients that are at risk of bleeding (e.g. those with thrombocytopenia or haemophilia) may receive the vaccine subcutaneously. Avaxim is the only vaccine currently licensed for this purpose.

Contraindications to HAV vaccine

As with any therapeutic intervention, it is essential that anyone tasked with giving the HAV vaccine is aware of contraindications to HAV vaccination. These include:

- acute febrile illness (vaccination should be postponed)
- severe reaction to a previously administered dose of the vaccine
- severe hypersensitivity (anaphylactic reaction) to any of the vaccine excipients
- severe hypersensitivity (anaphylactic reaction) to latex (e.g. in the needle shield, stopper etc.)
- children under 1 year of age (none of the vaccines are licensed for this age group)
- pregnancy and lactation, unless there is a definite high risk of HAV infection to the mother.

Adverse reactions to HAV vaccine

The following adverse reactions have been noted for the various HAV vaccines:

- local reactions including mild, transient soreness, redness, and rarely induration at the site of the injection
- general reactions including headaches, fever, malaise, fatigue ('flu-like' symptoms), nausea, diarrhoea, loss of appetite and rash
- rarely reported adverse events include arthralgia, myalgia, convulsions and allergic reactions including anaphylactic reactions
- occasionally we see a transient elevation of liver enzymes; however, a causal relationship with the vaccine has not been confirmed

- neurological manifestations have been very rarely reported and include transverse myelitis, Guillain–Barré syndrome and neuralgic amyotrophy; however, a causal relationship with the vaccine has not been confirmed.

Human normal immunoglobulin for hepatitis A prevention

With the advent of HAV vaccination, human normal immunoglobulin is no longer recommended for travellers as a short-term passive prophylaxis in the UK. On the basis of the available evidence, the HAV vaccine should be used for active immunisation against HAV infection, even in travellers whose departure is imminent. This is because HAV vaccines elicit protective antibodies after 2–3 weeks (which is within the incubation period of the disease) and because the availability of human normal immunoglobulin is limited in many European countries and in the UK, following the Department of Health's decision to stop using British-sourced plasma. Nonetheless, travellers who receive the first dose of their HAV vaccine less than 2 weeks before travelling to an endemic area need to realise that they can still be at risk of hepatitis A infection.

However, there are three indications for the use of human normal immunoglobulin in the UK.

- For protection against hepatitis A amongst household and other close contacts, where there is a delay in identifying cases of more than 1 week from onset of symptoms in the index case. If the delay is less than a week, the vaccine is preferable.
- As part of the control of disease outbreaks, where there is a clear history of exposure and a delay of over 1 week from onset of symptoms in the index case, particularly in those aged 5 years and over (increased morbidity).
- Human normal immunoglobulin should be considered for contacts at high risk because of pre-existing liver disease.

In all other situations the vaccine is preferred.

The dose for human normal immunoglobulin is 250 mg for children under 10 years of age, and 500 mg for all other individuals, given by intramuscular injection. Immunoglobulins are no longer injected into the buttock, and should be administered in the deltoid muscle (at an alternative site than the one used for the HAV vaccine if used concurrently). We can obtain human normal immunoglobulin from the Health Protection Agency or the Scottish Centre for Infection and Environmental Health (SCIEH).

Given the wider availability of human normal immunoglobulin in the US, the Centres for Disease Control and Prevention (CDC) continues to recommend hepatitis A vaccination and concurrently administered human normal immunoglobulin (0.02 mL/kg) at a different injection site, for persons travelling to countries with high rates of hepatitis A, if travel is to occur within 4 weeks of vaccination.

Halting outbreaks of HAV infection in the community

Hepatitis A outbreaks can be difficult to control despite enhanced awareness of preventive measures. The use of human normal immunoglobulin may decrease HAV transmission, but will not stop the outbreak. A single dose of HAV vaccine can halt community outbreaks of hepatitis A, but only if enough susceptible individuals are vaccinated. HAV vaccination can also prevent an epidemic from becoming established in communities where only few cases of HAV infection have occurred.

In general terms, the higher the vaccination coverage of susceptible individuals in a disease outbreak, the better. For example, in a large community in Alaska where fewer than 50% of the estimated eligible population were vaccinated during an outbreak of hepatitis A, the epidemic persisted for more than 50 weeks. In contrast, where more than 80% of susceptible individuals were vaccinated, the outbreak ceased in 4–8 weeks.

Recognition, diagnosis and treatment of hepatitis A in travellers

Recognition of hepatitis A in travellers

Clinicians should remain suspicious of hepatitis A infection in cases where the patient presents with a history of travel abroad or homosexual contact during the past 1–2 months. The *prodromal phase* follows with pyrexia, headache, nausea, vomiting, fatigue, anorexia, abdominal discomfort especially in the right upper quadrant, occasional diarrhoea and arthralgia, which can last for 2–7 days, and possibly a transient erythemato-macular rash. Cigarette smoke and other strong odours are often offensive to the patient. The urine darkens and the stools may be noticeably pale during this period.

The *icteric phase* then follows with jaundice first apparent in the sclerae and later in the skin. The fever resolves, virus excretion ceases and the patient is no longer infectious. Jaundice begins to resolve within a few days but recovery may take several months. Spider angiomas and palmar erythema may be transiently present. In childhood, hepatitis A infection can be a typically minor illness, with more than 80% of cases being asymptomatic. About one in four adults do not develop jaundice.

Hepatitis A outbreaks can be difficult to control despite enhanced awareness of preventive measures.

In childhood, hepatitis A infection can be a typically minor illness, with more than 80% of cases being asymptomatic. About one in four adults do not develop jaundice.

Hepatomegaly is also present. The presence of a small liver predicts a poor outcome; fulminant hepatitis A and extensive necrosis, or acute hepatitis superimposed on pre-existing cirrhosis. Abdominal ultrasound typically shows hepatomegaly and a thickened gall-bladder wall.

Splenomegaly and lymphadenopathy occur in 5% of cases.

The case-fatality rate of hepatitis A according to the World Health Organization (WHO) exceeds 2% amongst those aged over 40 years rising to 4% in those aged 60 years and over. Patients do not become carriers of the virus.

Hepatitis A is highly contagious as a result of large numbers of viruses being excreted in the faeces during the incubation period of the disease (15–50 days, mean 30 days), particularly during the last 2 weeks prior to the onset of symptoms, and for at least 1 week afterwards. During this time, food handlers should be excluded from work. However, faecal excretion for several months has been reported in a few infected neonates and adults. In addition, the source of infection (particularly children) may not develop symptoms and, thus, may not be identified.

A number of authorities do not recommend active immunisation of young travellers to endemic areas as the disease is often asymptomatic in children. Personally, I do not agree with this management approach. Whilst the course of hepatitis A in children may be mild (although this is not always the case), the public health problem that can be generated from an index infection in a child can be enormous. Children can infect young friends and staff in nurseries and other educational establishments, as well as other families in their neighbourhood. In my view, where the adults are vaccinated we should not 'ignore' the children.

How to make a laboratory diagnosis of hepatitis A

Alanine aminotransferase (ALT) levels are markedly elevated in HAV infection, and are greater than the aspartate aminotransferase (AST) elevations. Bilirubin begins to rise several days following the elevation in ALT and AST and usually peaks within 10–14 days. Alkaline phosphatase is usually normal or mildly elevated.

The diagnosis can be confirmed by serology and the presence of IgM antibody to HAV – a highly sensitive and specific test as IgM persists in the serum for 3–12 months, making it possible to retrospectively diagnose acute hepatitis A in patients who present following the resolution of biochemical hepatitis. IgM levels decline during the convalescent phase, at which time serum IgG anti-HAV levels increase. The presence of IgG antibody is indicative of a prior infection and immunity because of past HAV infection, or vaccination, or recent receipt of human normal immunoglobulin. After a natural infection with HAV, IgG remains detectable for life.

Other laboratory features that may be present are mild anaemia, mild leukopenia with relative lymphocytosis, and rarely thrombocytopenia. Occasionally, haemolytic anaemia occurs, usually in association with glucose-6-phosphate dehydrogenase deficiency. Serum proteins are usually normal, but hypoalbuminaemia and increased γ-globulin may be seen in more severe cases. Any prolongation of prothrombin time is potentially serious.

It is important to exclude hepatitis B or C infection with appropriate serology. A hepatitis screen is, therefore, indicated in any case where we suspect infectious hepatitis.

The treatment and outcome of infection

Management of hepatitis A is supportive. It should include bed-rest (whilst ALT is raised) and alcohol avoidance, with regular monitoring of the patient's clinical state and liver function tests. Antipruritic drugs may also help convalescence. For severe pruritus, colestyramine may be considered. Prolonged severe cholestasis responds well to treatment with oral corticosteroids.

Most patients show complete clinical and biochemical recovery within 3–6 months of the onset of the illness. However, complications do occur and include cholestasis, fulminant hepatitis with liver failure (up to 1%) and possible death. Cholestatic viral hepatitis is characterised by a prolonged illness with persistent, profound jaundice and pruritus. In such cases we need to exclude extrahepatic biliary obstruction, especially gallstones. Fulminant hepatitis A is associated with massive hepatic necrosis, coagulopathy, jaundice and renal failure. Patients typically present within 8 weeks of symptoms or within 2 weeks of the onset of jaundice.

Underlying liver disease may predispose infected patients to a more severe outcome. Hepatitis A is more severe in patients with chronic liver disease, especially amongst carriers of hepatitis B or C viruses. In these patients the use of the HAV vaccine should be considered with care.

Patients on the combined oral contraceptive pill should be advised to use other forms of contraception until the liver function tests are back to normal.

Uncomplicated infection in pregnancy is not harmful to the foetus unless maternal infection occurs around the time of delivery.

Differential diagnosis of hepatitis A

When we are faced with a suspected HAV infection, we must always exclude other causes of hepatitis. These include:

- infection occurring in or around the biliary system (e.g. acute cholecystitis, acute descending cholangitis, acute pancreatitis)
- infection with other viruses such as hepatitis B or C or E, leptospirosis, cytomegalovirus, Epstein–Barr virus
- obstructive jaundice resulting from impacted gallstones or cancer of the head or the pancreas
- haemolysis in the case of malarial infection or glucose-6-phosphate dehydrogenase deficiency
- jaundice caused by drugs such as paracetamol or phenothiazines, or by alcohol.

The risk of hepatitis A infection in non-immune British travellers

As the HAV infection spreads predominantly via the faecal–oral route, avoidance of suspect food or drink, in conjunction with good hygiene, especially hand-washing, remain the most important elements in the control of hepatitis A. Young children travellers are not able to fully comply with this. It is, therefore, vitally important in my opinion that they are vaccinated before travel so that they do not run the risk of spreading the infection to others on their return, especially as HAV infection is largely asymptomatic in this age group.

The risk of HAV infection amongst travellers from industrialised countries visiting developing countries is approximately 3/1000 per month of stay for the average non-immune tourist or business traveller. The attack rate increases significantly to 20/1000 per month of travel for backpackers and budget travellers to highly endemic countries.

The risk of a non-immune British traveller contracting hepatitis A abroad has been calculated by Behrens and co-workers (Table 4). The basic risk is given as one, in those who travel to Scandinavia and France. The risk in other countries will be multiples of one. This table demonstrates that it is not just the destination that is important, but also the age of the travellers and whether or not they come in contact with the local population.

Immigrants visiting their country of origin and their families are perhaps at the greatest risk of contracting hepatitis A, especially children who, as we have seen, may contract the disease, remain asymptomatic and then spread the disease to other children at school and people in the community on their return. Immunisation is therefore recommended for children of

Table 4. Relative risk of a British traveller contracting hepatitis A compared with the risk of an individual traveller in France and Scandinavia (taken as one; adapted from Behrens *et al. BMJ* 1995; **311**: 193).	
Destination	**Relative risk of hepatitis A infection**
France	1
Scandinavia	1
Greece	4
Spain	5
Turkey	42
Mexico	612
Region	
European Union	3
Other European countries	4
Eastern Europe	20
Australia and New Zealand	20
Middle East	85
Far East	102
North Africa	110
Rest of Africa	235
South America and Caribbean	243
Indian subcontinent (Bangladesh, India, Pakistan, Nepal, Sri Lanka)	
All travellers	1835
Age <15 years:	
• visiting friends and relatives	2347
• tourists/purpose of visit unknown	295
Age >15 years	
• visiting friends and relatives	1083
• tourists/purpose of visit unknown	1111

immigrant parents born in western Europe (an area of low endemicity) who visit their parents' country of origin in high-endemicity areas.

Failure to vaccinate, rather than failure of the HAV vaccine itself, is the main issue facing travellers and their contacts.

Department of Health recommendations for hepatitis A immunisation

The *Immunisation Against Infectious Disease* (the 'Green Book') makes several specific recommendations for hepatitis A immunisation in the following groups:

- travellers to areas of moderate or high endemicity
- patients with chronic liver disease

Immunisation is recommended for children of immigrant parents born in western Europe (an area of low endemicity) who visit their parents' country of origin in highly endemic areas.

- haemophiliacs
- those at risk of occupational exposure (i.e. laboratory workers who are working with the virus or workers at risk of exposure to untreated sewage)
- staff and residents of institutions with persons with learning disability
- male homosexuals whose sexual behaviour is likely to put them at risk
- to interrupt ongoing community outbreaks of hepatitis A when given to a defined population.

The government's *Statement of Fees and Allowances for GPs – the Red Book* has been superseded by the new General Medical Services (GMS) contract for GPs (discussed in detail below), but recommends hepatitis A immunisation for travellers to all countries except northern Europe and Australasia.

Preventing hepatitis A infection in travellers

Hepatitis A is preventable by good sanitation and personal hygiene. This is particularly important in nurseries and schools where spread of the disease is more likely.

It is important that we remember how HAV infection is acquired in order to give the best possible advice to travellers on disease prevention. Drinking water that has been contaminated at its source or during storage, or consumption of contaminated ice or other products exposed to contaminated water, is a major source of infection. Another leading source of infection is ingestion of food contaminated during or after preparation (e.g. seafood [shellfish should be steamed for at least 90 seconds or heated at 85–90 ºC for 4 minutes before eating], or fruit and vegetables grown in soil contaminated with human waste or contaminated water). Tables 5 and 6 provide general advice that should be given to travellers with regards to water and food precautions.

Travellers to religious festivals or other events, as well as those who are going to stay or work with locals in developing countries need to take particular care and they need our particular attention, especially as regards to immunisation.

Clinical audit in primary care

Clinical audit is a systematic way of critically evaluating the work in which we are involved to ascertain whether any changes in our approach could lead to an improvement in patient care. It is a useful tool to allow us to check that what we are doing is what we think we ought to be doing, and what improvements can be made.

Table 5. General advice to travellers for safe water (adapted from Kassianos G. *Immunization Childhood and Travel Health*, 4th Edition. Oxford: Blackwell Science, 2001).

- Wash hands after using the toilet and before handling/eating food. Use paper towels or hot air to dry hands. Avoid used damp cloth towels – better to drip dry hands.
- Drink plenty, avoid tap water. Uncontaminated rain, spring or deep well water is usually safe.
- Unless confident about the safety of the local water do not use it. Make water safe by:
  - boiling at 100 °C for 10 minutes
  - chemical disinfection using iodine tablets etc.
  - filtration using commercially available water filters.
- Use bottled water from a reputable source. The seal must be intact and opened in your presence. Carbonated water is preferable – it is unlikely to have been filled from the tap.
- As a last resort use tap water that is uncomfortably hot to touch and allow to cool.
- Avoid ice in drinks as it may have been made using tap water.
- It is usually safe to drink wine, beer and minerals (cans and bottles) providing the seal is intact.
- Wipe clean surfaces that may come in contact with mouth. If possible use sterile, individually wrapped straws. Avoid using straws unless they are individually wrapped.
- Hot coffee or tea is safe if water has been boiled for 5 minutes.
- Use 'safe' or pre-boiled water to clean teeth.
- Drink only pasteurised milk, or boil at 55 °C for 30 minutes or 65 °C for 1 minute.
- Always carry a 'safe' drink with you.
- Avoid excessive alcohol as it can exacerbate dehydration.
- Do not open your mouth while taking a shower or swimming. Prepare a bath with very hot water and allow it to cool before using.
- Do not swim in rivers or ponds. Seawater may also be contaminated with sewage.

In the case of hepatitis A immunisation, an excellent application of audit is to examine the number of travellers who have received only one dose of the vaccine but have not returned for their second dose. Another indicator is the number of travellers who have received the full primary course (two doses) of the vaccine and who are due for a booster dose, 10 or more years having elapsed from the primary course. Once patients are identified, steps can be taken to recall these patients.

A number of clinical computer systems that are in use in UK general practice can be programmed appropriately to search for those patients who are due further doses of the vaccine. A number of practices operate with card systems. Recalling these patients for completion of their hepatitis A immunisation is a worthwhile exercise and audit, as a tool, can help in achieving this.

Recalling patients for completion of their hepatitis A immunisation is a worthwhile exercise and audit, as a tool, can help in achieving this.

Table 6. General advice to travellers for safe food (adapted from Kassianos G. *Immunization Childhood and Travel Health*, 4th Edition. Oxford: Blackwell Science, 2001).

- Eat freshly prepared food that is piping hot and thoroughly cooked. Pink meat should be avoided.
- All raw food is subject to contamination.
- Avoid cooked food that has been kept at room temperature.
- Avoid leftovers or reheated food.
- Soft cheeses may be a source of listeriosis or brucellosis.
- Ensure the yolk in an egg is cooked until solid.
- Avoid food, sauces, relishes etc. that have been left out and exposed to flies.
- Spicy foods do not have a lower risk of contamination.
- Avoid shellfish (e.g. clams, mussels, oysters, prawns etc.) or raw fish.
- Avoid cold cuts, salads, raw vegetables, watermelons (sometimes injected with water to increase their weight).
- Avoid dairy products (e.g. puddings and ice creams) unless pasteurised milk has been used.
- Only eat fruit that you can peel personally.
- Eat food from sealed packs or cans but not if package appears swollen.
- Avoid food from street vendors.
- Eat in busy, clean restaurants.
- Ensure the plates and cutlery have been washed with detergent and clean water and have been protected from flies.
- Wash hands before handling/eating food – dry under hand-dryer or with disposable hand-towels.
- Avoid nibbles at the bar – you cannot be sure of the personal hygiene of other customers.
- Never forget the golden rule : "Boil it, cook it, peel it…or forget it!"

Sources of information for travel clinics' clinicians

There are numerous sources of reputable information for clinicians interested in travel health. These sources are outlined in Table 7.

UK GPs' income from hepatitis A immunisation

The new GMS contract for GPs came into force in April 2004. The provision of travel vaccinations is governed by the regulations on *Additional Services*. Practices are able to opt out of these services with the agreement of their Primary Care Organisations (PCOs).

GPs no longer need to claim an item-of-service fee for NHS-approved travel vaccinations. The whole estimated amount that would have been earned by a practice from providing NHS-approved travel vaccinations has been built into the Global Sum, of which vaccinations make up 2%. GPs only have such an obligation to their registered patients (including registered temporary residents).

If a practice opts out of providing NHS-approved travel vaccinations, they lose 2% of their Global Sum. Opt-out GPs are not able to provide

Table 7. Sources of information for travel healthcare professionals.

TRAVAX (subscription only) – *www.travax.scot.nhs.uk*

Fit for Travel – a public access website provided by the NHS (Scotland). It gives travel health information for people travelling abroad from the UK and can be recommended to travellers: *www.fitfortravel.scot.nhs.uk*

Aventis Pasteur MSD – *www.apmsd.co.uk*

Chiron Vaccines Evans – *www.chiron.com*

GlaxoSmithKline – *www.worldwidevaccines.com*

Medical Advisory Services for Travellers Abroad – *www.masta.org*

Centres for Disease Control and Prevention, US – *www.cdc.gov/travel/diseases/hav.htm*

Health Protection Agency – *www.hpa.org.uk/infections/topics_az/topics.asp*

British Liver Trust – *www.britishlivertrust.org.uk/content/diseases/hepatitis_a.asp*

Blood Care Foundation – an organisation that can deliver screened and safe blood and blood products to subscriber travellers around the world – *www.bloodcare.org.uk*; telephone 01293 425 485.

British Travel Health Association – *www.btha.org*; telephone 0141 300 1132

National Travel Health Network and Centre – *www.nathnac.org*

NHS-approved vaccinations and charge the patient traveller. If they provide such vaccinations, it has to be at no cost to the patient traveller.

NHS patients travelling abroad can obtain hepatitis A vaccination paid for by the NHS from their registered GPs provided they are travelling outside northern Europe or Australasia. We are able to make a charge to our registered NHS patients for the administration and cost of the hepatitis A vaccine, which we must purchase privately, only if the travel is to northern Europe or Australasia.

On occasions, we are called to administer the hepatitis A vaccine to patients who are not travelling abroad. If this call is from the Medical Officer of Environmental Health and it is for 'persons in institutions who are exposed to high risk of infection', then the vaccination is not charged to the patient or the PCO. This income has already being accounted for in the Global Sum.

Personal dispensing of hepatitis A vaccine

Non-dispensing GPs in England and Wales can claim a fee for purchasing and dispensing the hepatitis A vaccine (this is also the case for other vaccines for childhood immunisation that are not supplied 'centrally' by the government). The vaccine can be administered by the GP or a nurse. They can be purchased in bulk directly from the manufacturer or any other source and administered to the NHS-registered patients of the practice.

Almost all vaccine suppliers operate discount schemes for GPs. The greater the discount, the greater the practice profit. The largest discounts tend to be in the most competitive areas or when a large number of vaccines are purchased.

Overall, the government reimburses the GP the following:
- the basic price of the hepatitis A vaccine (as defined in Part 2, Clause 8 and 11, of the Drug Tariff, less a government discount calculated in accordance with Part 1 of Annex I)
- an on-cost allowance of 10.5% of the basic price before deduction of the discount referred to above
- a container allowance of 3.8 pence per prescription
- a dispensing fee
- an allowance in respect of VAT, calculated as a percentage (17.5%) both of the basic price less any government discount (see above), and of the container allowance.

The patient does not (and should not be asked to) pay a prescription charge. We do not need to raise a prescription for each NHS-approved hepatitis A vaccine we give. In common with some other 'high-volume' vaccines, we can claim this vaccine as a bulk entry using Form FP34D (Appendix), which is then sent to the Prescription Pricing Authority (PPA) together with the invoice showing the purchase of the vaccine.

If we administer the hepatitis A vaccine to a NHS-registered patient traveller to Australasia or northern Europe, no reimbursement of the vaccine can be claimed, and a NHS prescription should not be issued. The vaccine must be purchased privately and any costs should be borne by the traveller and not the NHS. The same applies for private patients.

Good practice in administering the hepatitis A vaccine

The new GMS contract requires any GP or nurse who administers the hepatitis A vaccine under NHS contract to comply with the following:
- offer the hepatitis A vaccine to all NHS patients that are eligible for it
- provide appropriate advice and information
- record any refusal of the offer of hepatitis A vaccination
- where the offer of hepatitis A vaccination is accepted, administer the vaccine and include in the patient's records the following information:
  - the patient's consent to the administration of the vaccine or the name of the person who gave consent to the vaccination and their relationship to the patient
  - the batch number, expiry date and title of the vaccine
  - the date of administration

- if another vaccine is administered in close succession, the route of administration and the injection site of each vaccine
- any contraindications to the vaccination
- any adverse reactions to this immunisation.

The NHS contractor shall ensure that all staff involved in administering vaccines are trained in the recognition and initial treatment of anaphylaxis.

Conclusion

The hepatitis A vaccines available in the UK have proved to be very effective, well tolerated and cost-effective. As such, we have an effective means of protecting our travellers against hepatitis A infection. In countries where childhood immunisation has been introduced (e.g. across most states in the US) we have the means to eradicate, or at least control hepatitis A, provided governments are willing to spend the resources necessary for mass immunisation.

The best strategy to adopt would involve universal mass vaccination in childhood with catch-up for non-immune adolescents and adults. However, this approach is both financially and organisationally demanding and to date has only been adopted in Israel. Nevertheless, universal vaccination of children is the most effective way to reduce disease incidence in regions of intermediate endemicity. In highly endemic areas, almost all individuals are infected with HAV during childhood, which effectively prevents clinical hepatitis A in adolescents and adults. As such, the WHO does not recommend large-scale vaccination programmes in highly endemic regions.

Vaccination is the key to success in the control of hepatitis A, particularly when it forms part of a wider public health programme that provides safe food and clean water to its population.

Vaccination is the key to success in the control of hepatitis A, particularly when it forms part of a wider public health programme that provides safe food and clean water to its population.

Key points

- Hepatitis A is a widespread and common disease. Infection is endemic in certain regions of the world, and UK travellers visiting these regions are at risk of infection.

- Outbreaks of hepatitis A can be caused by the consumption of contaminated food and water and can be imported and exported between countries.

- The incidence of imported cases of hepatitis A has declined recently following improved sanitation, availability of HAV vaccines on the NHS and improved access to high-quality travel clinics.

- The practice of serotesting patients for HAV antibodies prior to immunisation is only advocated if the cost of vaccination exceeds the cost of screening.

- In the UK, HAV vaccines are recommended over immunisation with human immunoglobulin, although immunoglobulin may be useful in controlling disease outbreaks and treating patients with pre-existing liver disease.

- Although the active immunisation of young travellers to endemic areas is not always recommended by every healthcare professional, this may be advisable considering the potentially serious public health implications arising from a single infected child.

- The risk of hepatitis A infection to non-immune British travellers is dependent on their age, the destination to which they are travelling and the level of contact they have with the local population whilst abroad.

- Clinical audit in primary care may help to identify and recall those patients who are due to complete their hepatitis A vaccination schedule.

19. Hypertension and cardiovascular disease

Dr Mark Davis, MB, ChB, MRCGP, DRCOG, DOcc Med
General Practitioner, Leeds, Secretary, Primary Care Cardiovascular Society

Summary

Hypertension is a significant problem both in the UK and globally, and its management is a major part of GPs' daily workload. However, in spite of the fact that uncontrolled hypertension places patients at a greater risk of cardiovascular disease (CVD) and death, its management in primary care is still suboptimal, despite some improvements in recent years. A number of initiatives have been instigated which, it is hoped, will improve the management of the condition in the UK. These include the National Service Frameworks (NSFs) in England and the new General Medical Services (GMS) contract for GPs. In addition, the availability of new guidelines from the British Hypertension Society (BHS) for the management of hypertension in the UK offers us clear, simple and practical advice to improve the care of our patients. The BHS guidelines call for treatment initiation at certain thresholds determined by the magnitude of blood pressure elevation, the level of cardiovascular risk and the presence or absence of other comorbidities such as diabetes. In order for patients to achieve new and more stringent blood pressure targets, these guidelines indicate that multiple drug treatment (based on the ABCD treatment algorithm) is likely to be necessary. The availability of the new GMS contract has driven the need for effective clinical audit, particularly with regard to our performance in the control of hypertension.

Disease burden

The World Health Organization (WHO) has identified hypertension as one of the most important preventable causes of premature morbidity and mortality in developed and developing countries. It affects about one billion people worldwide and is the most common treatable risk factor for CVD in patients over 50 years of age. If we accept that a blood pressure above 140/90 mmHg requires cardiovascular risk calculation as a minimum requirement, which may necessitate the initiation of treatment, there are an estimated 42% of people aged 35–64 with a blood pressure above this level.

By 2020, CHD and stroke will respectively rank the first and fourth major causes of death and disability worldwide.

When we consider patients over 60 years then 70% will have hypertension. The majority of this latter group of patients will have isolated systolic hypertension.

The ageing of the population in developing countries and the growing 'epidemic' of CVD in developing countries will ensure that by 2020, coronary heart disease (CHD) and stroke will respectively rank the first and fourth major causes of death and disability worldwide.

It is well recognised that people with hypertension frequently have a clustering of additional risk factors for CVD. These include dyslipidaemia, impaired glucose tolerance and central obesity which, in common with hypertension, are all features of the metabolic syndrome. As a result of this clustering of risk factors, the treatment of blood pressure in isolation will leave patients at an unacceptably high risk of cardiovascular complications and death. Consequently, we are now encouraged to calculate overall cardiovascular risk in patients with hypertension by identifying multiple risk factors and then intervening appropriately.

Meta-analyses of large-scale randomised controlled clinical trials have demonstrated that reductions in systolic blood pressure (SBP) of 10–14 mmHg and in diastolic blood pressure (DBP) of 5–6 mmHg lower the incidence of stroke by two-fifths and CHD by one-fifth. The evidence base for the benefits of intervention in patients with high blood pressure gives us an obligation to improve our management of hypertension, although the number of patients involved represents a continuing and significant challenge for primary-care professionals.

National surveys continue to expose the fact that there is still substantial under-diagnosis, under-treatment and poor rates of blood pressure control within the UK, although there are some signs that the situation is slowly improving.

The challenges facing primary care

We are in the fortunate position of having access to a number of clear and practical guidelines for the management of hypertension. The BHS has recently published its fourth set of guidelines (Guidelines for Management of Hypertension: The Report of the Fourth Working Party of the British Hypertension Society 2004 [BHS IV]. *Journal of Human Hypertension* 2004; **18**: 139–85). A user-friendly version of these guidelines was also published in the *British Medical Journal* (*BMJ* 2004; **328**: 634–40). These guidelines are intended for GPs, practice nurses and generalists in hospital and I would commend them to you.

The principal objectives of these guidelines are:

- to promote the primary prevention of hypertension and cardiovascular disease by advocating changes to the diet and lifestyle of the whole population
- to increase the detection and treatment of undiagnosed hypertension by routine screening and to increase the awareness of hypertension amongst the public
- to ensure that patients taking antihypertensive drugs have their blood pressure controlled, as far as is possible, to optimal targets
- to reduce the risk of CVD in treated hypertensive patients by non-pharmacological methods and by the appropriate use of statins and aspirin
- to increase the identification and treatment of patients with mild hypertension who are at high risk of CVD (e.g. elderly patients, patients with ischaemic heart disease, people with diabetes, people with target organ damage or people with multiple risk factors)
- to promote continued adherence to drug treatment by optimising the use of drugs, minimising side-effects and increasing the information and choice given to patients.

New systems of healthcare delivery will be needed to ensure that these new guidelines are implemented effectively in primary care. We will not be successful unless multidisciplinary teams work in a systematic and structured way to advise, educate and support our patients. There will also need to be a move away from rigid clinic-based care towards greater use of remote centres such as pharmacies. There is clearly also a need for the extended role provided by nurse practitioners, pharmacists and other healthcare professionals if we are to build the foundations for a service that enables widespread and effective detection, monitoring and treatment of high blood pressure and its associated increased risk of CVD.

> New systems of healthcare delivery will be needed to ensure that these new guidelines are implemented effectively in primary care.

Initiatives to improve hypertension management

Primary Care Trusts (PCTs) have an important role in supporting and enhancing primary care. They will also take the lead in the development of the new types of service delivery, as discussed in the previous section.

The Department of Health has provided the lead in the prevention of CVD through its NSFs in England (in particular the NSFs for CHD, diabetes and older people). There are also comparable initiatives in Scotland and Wales. The NSFs suggest that we prioritise our efforts by optimally treating hypertension in those at greatest risk. This includes those people with existing occlusive vascular disease and diabetes. They also support our efforts to identify those who have yet to exhibit manifest occlusive vascular disease but who, because of multiple risk factors, are at high risk of CVD.

The National Institute for Clinical Excellence (NICE) is preparing guidance for the management of essential hypertension which will be published during 2004. The latest guidelines from the Joint British Societies on the prevention of CVD are also expected to be published in 2004. It is to be hoped that the NICE guidance will be broadly supportive of the BHS guidelines. However, it is important to note that the NICE guidance will focus solely on the treatment of essential hypertension in uncomplicated patients and will not provide guidance on blood pressure management in the many important subgroups outlined in the BHS guidelines. Also, the NICE guidance will not provide advice on when to use aspirin and statin therapy to reduce the CVD burden in people with high blood pressure. Given this return to single risk factor management, the BHS have argued that such guidance represents a retrogressive step.

> The new GMS contract, published in 2003, is an important step towards the development of primary care in the UK. Of the 550 clinical points available in the GMS contract, 129 relate directly to hypertension.

The new GMS contract, published in 2003, is an important step towards the development of primary care in the UK. The quality framework has a significant leaning towards CVD prevention and management and, as such, the detection and management of hypertension features strongly. The payment consequent upon achieving the quality indicators should encourage practices to improve hypertension management and will reward them for delivering quality care. Of the 550 clinical points available in the GMS contract, 129 relate directly to hypertension. A further 15 points out of the 184 organisational points available also relate to hypertension.

Practical advice to meet these challenges

Nobody working in primary care will underestimate the size of the challenge that we have been set. Practices will be able to identify those patients in whom blood pressure control is desirable by using the disease registers. Patients with existing CVD should be identifiable by using our CHD and stroke registers. They should be subject to regular review, and by using practice protocols and the templates that are readily available on our IT systems, it should be possible to Read-code all the actions that we take. Once these are Read-coded it is relatively straightforward to undertake a search and identify those whose blood pressure is not to target.

Patients with diabetes should also be added to our 'secondary prevention' remit. Evidence clearly suggests that diabetics are at particular risk from raised blood pressure and as such, the targets that are set for diabetics are particularly challenging. The thresholds and targets for intervention in hypertension taken from the BHS guidelines are set out in Table 1.

> **Table 1.** Thresholds and treatment targets for antihypertensive drug treatment. Adapted from Williams *et al. BMJ* 2004; **328**: 634–40.
>
> - Antihypertensive treatment should be initiated in patients with sustained SBP ≥160 mmHg or sustained DBP ≥100 mmHg despite non-pharmacological measures.
> - Antihypertensive treatment should be initiated in patients with SBP 140–159 mmHg or sustained DBP 90–99 mmHg if target organ damage is present, or there is evidence of CVD or diabetes, or where the 10-year CVD risk is ≥20%.
> - For most patients, the recommended blood pressure target is ≤140/85 mmHg. In those with diabetes, renal impairment or established CVD, a lower target of ≤130/80 mmHg is recommended.
> - When using ambulatory blood pressure readings, mean daytime pressures are preferable (this value should be approximately 10/5 mmHg lower than office blood pressure equivalent for thresholds and targets). Similar adjustments are required for averages of home blood pressure readings.
>
> CVD, cardiovascular disease; DBP, diastolic blood pressure; SBP, systolic blood pressure.

Many of our patients with hypertension will not yet be known to us. The new GMS contract encourages us to record blood pressure in patients aged over 45 years at a minimum of 5-year intervals. This is good practice and can be done opportunistically either by GPs or by nursing staff. It is also likely that an increasing number of pharmacists will offer blood pressure screening as part of their service, and if this information is transmitted to the practices, this will help us enormously in our task.

A management algorithm supported by the new BHS guidelines for patients with different levels of blood pressure is presented in Figure 1. This algorithm indicates that patients with a sustained blood pressure above 160/100 mmHg should receive treatment no matter what other risk factors are present. An SBP of 140–160 mmHg and a DBP of 90–100 mmHg warrant further risk assessment. A sustained blood pressure within these parameters would necessitate treatment if there is target organ damage or CVD complications, or if the patient has diabetes or a 10-year risk of CVD above 20%. CVD complications or target organ damage include:

- stroke, transient ischaemic attack, dementia, carotid bruits
- left ventricular hypertrophy or left ventricular strain on electrocardiogram (ECG)
- heart failure
- myocardial infarction, angina, coronary artery bypass graft or angioplasty
- fundal haemorrhages or exudates, papilloedema
- proteinuria
- renal impairment (raised creatinine).

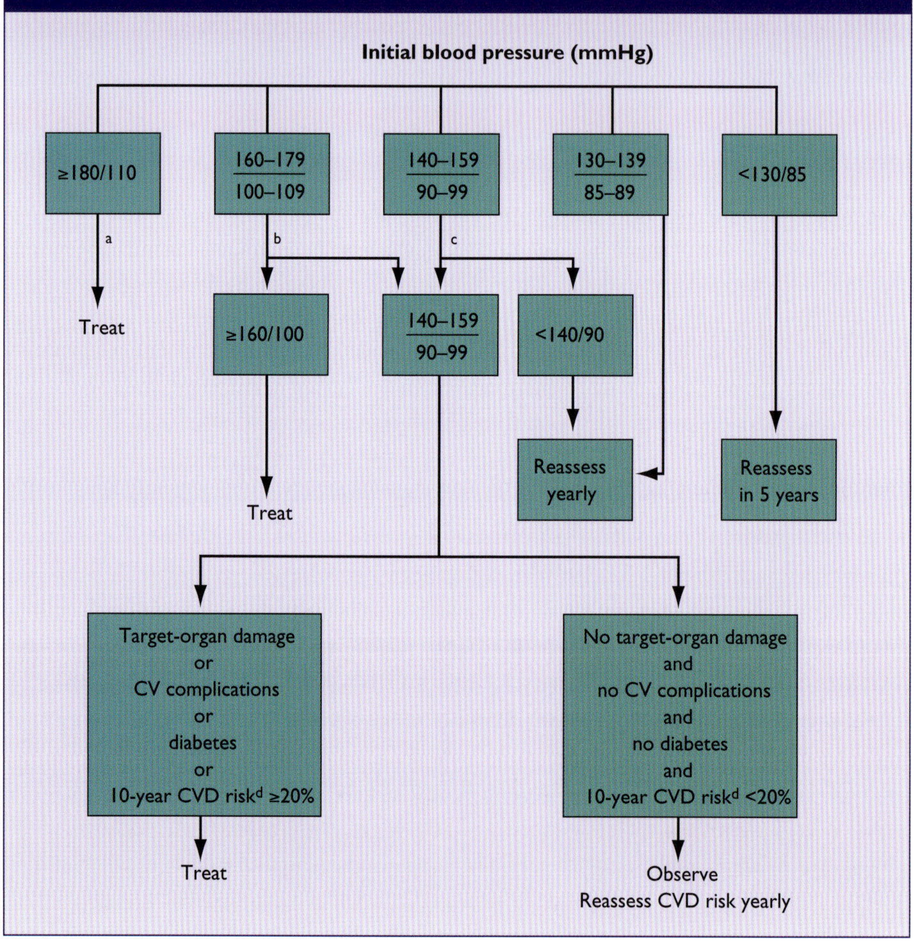

Figure 1. British Hypertension Society guidelines for the management of hypertension. Adapted from Williams *et al. BMJ* 2004; **328**: 634–40.
[a]Unless malignant phase of hypertensive emergency, confirm over 1–2 weeks then treat.
[b]If CV complications, target organ damage, or diabetes are present, confirm over 3–4 weeks then treat; if absent remeasure weekly and treat if blood pressure persists at this level over 4–12 weeks.
[c]If CV complications, target organ damage, or diabetes are present, confirm over 3–4 weeks then treat; if absent remeasure monthly and treat if this level is maintained and if estimated 10-year CVD risk is ≥20%.
[d]Assessed with risk chart for CVD.
CV, cardiovascular; CVD, cardiovascular disease.

There are various validated ways of calculating cardiovascular risk but the most commonly used are those recommended in the Joint British Societies' guidelines. These have been updated and simplified and allow for calculation of CVD, rather than CHD risk, to reflect the importance of stroke prevention as well as CHD prevention. The BHS has published these new tables in its guidelines and it is hoped that they will soon be published in the form of a 'Factfile' by the British Heart Foundation. If patients with this level of mild-to-moderate hypertension do not fulfil the above criteria then it is adequate to reassess their blood pressure and CVD risk annually. Blood pressures below 140/90 mmHg do not require intervention.

In our hypertensive patients we should also undertake the following routine investigations:

- urine strip tests for protein and blood
- serum creatinine and electrolytes
- blood glucose levels (ideally fasting blood glucose)
- serum lipid profile (high density lipoprotein cholesterol [HDL-C] and total cholesterol at the very least; fasted for triglycerides)
- ECG.

As shown in Table 1, the target blood pressure for most of our patients is below 140/85 mmHg. For patients with diabetes, renal impairment or established CVD, a lower target of below 130/80 mmHg is recommended. It is accepted that even with optimal treatment, some patients will not be able to achieve these targets. Because of this, a minimum audit standard has been set which is under 150/90 mmHg in most patients and below 140/80 mmHg in those at the highest risk.

It is accepted that even with optimal treatment, some patients will not be able to reach these targets.

Disease management

Advice on lifestyle modification should be provided to all patients who are being considered for pharmacological interventions. There is some evidence that lifestyle modification can prevent those with borderline or high–normal blood pressures becoming hypertensive and needing treatment. The lifestyle measures that have been shown to lower blood pressure and reduce the rise of blood pressure with age are shown in Table 2.

We know that certain lifestyle measures reduce the risk of CVD and these include smoking cessation and reducing the intake of total and saturated fats and their replacement with monounsaturated fats such as olive oil. To succeed with lifestyle modification some members of the practice team will need to acquire the skills and enthusiasm that are required to achieve behaviour modification. Considerable time will need to be spent with patients and other family members in order to give them the best advice as to how lifestyle change can be achieved.

To succeed with lifestyle modification some members of the practice team will need to acquire the skills and enthusiasm that are required to achieve behaviour modification.

Table 2. Lifestyle measures to lower blood pressure. Adapted from Williams *et al. BMJ* 2004; **328**: 634–40.

- Maintenance of normal body weight (BMI 20–25 kg/m^2)
- Reduce salt intake to <100 mmol/day (equivalent to <6 g of NaCl or <2.4g of Na+ per day)
- Limit alcohol consumption (males: ≤3 units/day; females: ≤2 units/day)
- Engage in regular aerobic physical exercise (e.g. brisk walking) for at least 30 minutes per day on most days of the week, and at least 3 days of the week
- Consume at least five portions of fresh fruit and vegetables daily
- Reduce the intake of total and saturated fat

BMI, body mass index.

Pharmacological interventions

Meta-analyses of blood pressure lowering trials have confirmed that, in general, the main determinant of benefit from antihypertensive drugs is the magnitude of the blood pressure reduction that is achieved rather than the choice of therapy. Although there is only minimal evidence for differences between classes of drugs with regard to cardiovascular outcomes, there are a number of important caveats to this. For example, calcium-channel blocker-based therapy may be less protective than other agents with regard to the development of heart failure, although some small benefits for these agents have been reported with regard to stroke prevention. The Losartan Intervention For Endpoint Reduction in Hypertension (LIFE) study has demonstrated even larger benefits for angiotensin II antagonist therapy over β-blocker therapy with regard to stroke prevention, despite broadly similar blood pressure reductions being achieved with both agents. Finally, in specific groups of patients, there can be compelling indications and compelling contraindications to different drugs (Table 3).

Should none of these special considerations apply, I feel that our choice of drug therapy should follow the ABCD algorithm suggested by the BHS. The theory underpinning this algorithm is that hypertension can be broadly classified as high renin or low renin, and is therefore best treated initially with one of the two categories of hypertensive drugs. This tends to be age and race dependent.

The classes of drugs within the ABCD algorithm are:-

- (A) angiotensin-converting enzyme (ACE) inhibitors or angiotensin II receptor antagonists
- (B) β-blockers
- (C) calcium-channel blockers
- (D) diuretics.

Table 3. Indications, cautions and contraindications for the major classes of antihypertensive agents. Adapted from Williams et al. BMJ 2004; 328: 634–40.

Drug class	Compelling indications	Possible indications	Cautions	Contraindications
α-blockers	BPH	–	Postural hypertension Heart failure[a]	Urinary incontinence
ACE inhibitors	Heart failure Left ventricular dysfunction post-MI or established CHD Type 1 diabetic nephropathy Secondary stroke prevention[b]	Chronic renal disease[c] Type 2 diabetic nephropathy Proteinuric renal disease	Renal impairment[c] Peripheral vascular disease[d]	Pregnancy Renovascular disease[e]
AIIRAs	ACE inhibitor intolerance Type 2 diabetic nephropathy Hypertension with left ventricular hypertrophy Heart failure in ACE inhibitor-intolerant patients Post-MI	Left ventricular dysfunction post-MI Intolerance of other antihypertensives Proteinuric renal disease, chronic renal disease[c] Heart failure	Renal impairment[c] Peripheral vascular disease[d]	Pregnancy Renovascular disease[e]
β-blockers	MI, angina	Heart failure[f] Peripheral vascular	Heart failure[f] Heart block disease Diabetes (except with CHD)	Asthma or COPD
Calcium-channel blockers (dihydropyridine)	Elderly, ISH	Angina	–	–
Calcium-channel blockers (rate limiting)	Angina	Elderly	Combination with β-blockers	Heart block Heart failure
Thiazides/thiazide-like diuretics	Elderly, ISH Heart failure Secondary stroke prevention	–	–	Gout[g]

[a]In heart failure when used as monotherapy.

[b]In combination with a thiazide or thiazide-like diuretic.

[c]ACE inhibitor or AIIRAs may be beneficial in chronic renal failure but should only be used with caution, close supervision and specialist advice when there is established and significant renal impairment.

[d]Caution with ACE inhibitor and AIIRAs in peripheral vascular disease because of its association with renovascular disease.

[e]ACE inhibitors and AIIRAs are sometimes used in patients with renovascular disease under specialist supervision.

[f]β-blockers are used increasingly to treat stable heart failure, but may worsen heart failure.

[g]Thiazides or thiazide-like diuretics may sometimes be necessary to control blood pressure in those with a history of gout, ideally in combination with allopurinol.

ACE, angiotensin-converting enzyme; AIIRA, angiotensin II receptor antagonist; BPH, benign prostatic hyperplasia; CHD, coronary heart disease; COPD, chronic obstructive pulmonary disease; ISH, isolated systolic hypertension; MI, myocardial infarction.

Drugs in the A and B class inhibit the renin–angiotensin system, whilst those in the C and D classes do not. As you can see from the algorithm in Figure 2 those patients who are younger than 55 years and Caucasian should be started on A or B drugs. Patients over 55 years or of Afro-Caribbean origin should start on C or D drugs. As most people require more than one drug to control blood pressure it is usual that step 2 will be reached and this will involve the combination of an A or B drug with a C or D drug. The BHS recommends caution when using a B and D combination in patients at especially high risk of developing diabetes. This caution is justified given the availability of trial evidence which indicates that this combination results in an increased incidence of new onset diabetes.

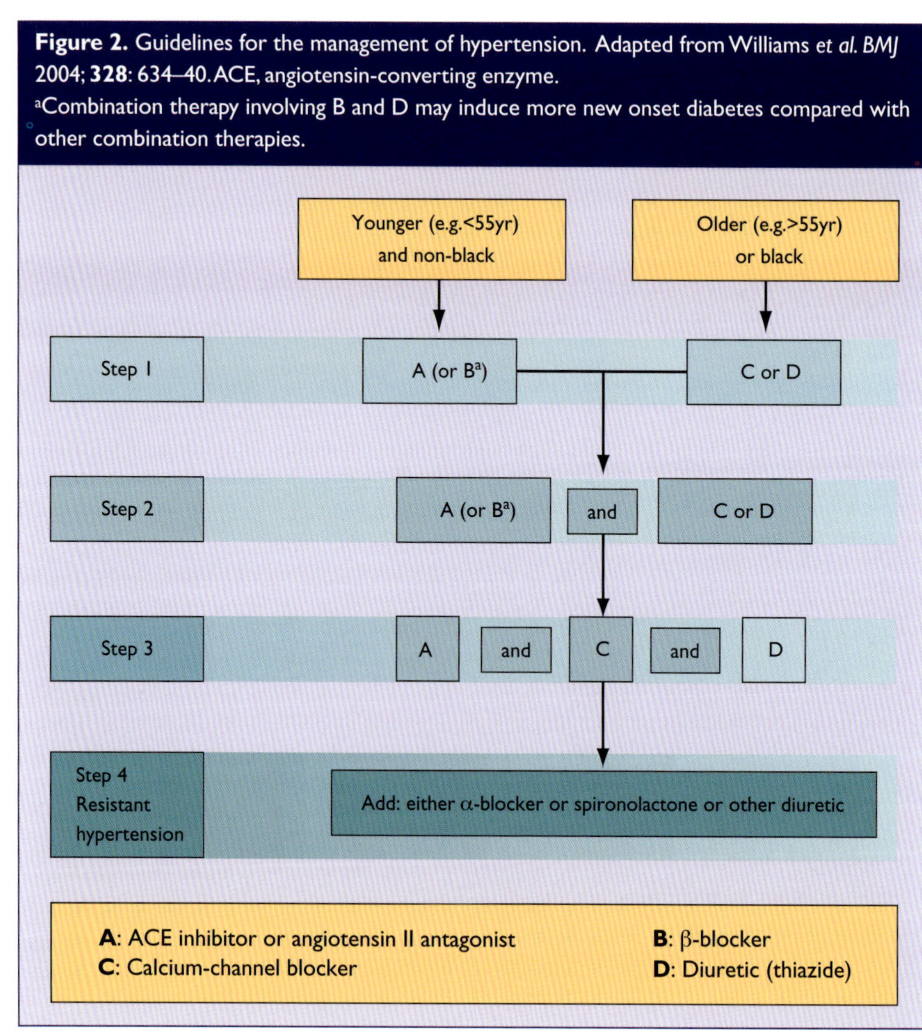

Figure 2. Guidelines for the management of hypertension. Adapted from Williams *et al. BMJ* 2004; **328**: 634–40. ACE, angiotensin-converting enzyme.
ªCombination therapy involving B and D may induce more new onset diabetes compared with other combination therapies.

There is general agreement that the agent used ideally should be effective for 24 hours when taken as a once-daily dose. Unless it is necessary to lower blood pressure urgently, an interval of at least 4 weeks should be allowed to observe a full response before altering the treatment regimen.

Most drugs provide similar blood pressure reductions. The placebo-adjusted reductions for patients with blood pressures of about 160/95 mmHg are approximately 10/5 mmHg. Thus, to reach the revised targets, the vast majority of patients will require combination therapy.

It is likely that most of the management of hypertension within a practice setting will be carried out by nurses working to a practice protocol which should make it clear when patients need to be referred to a GP. Similarly GPs should be clear as to when they should consider referral for a specialist opinion. The BHS indications for specialist referral are summarised in Table 4.

As hypertension is only one of a number of risk factors that can co-exist in this patient population, the BHS also provides guidance on the use of statins and aspirin in both primary and secondary prevention patient populations.

Table 4. Indications for specialist referral. Adapted from Williams *et al. BMJ* 2004; **328**: 634–40.

Urgent treatment required
- Accelerated hypertension (severe hypertension and retinopathy [grade III-IV])
- Severe hypertension (>220/120 mmHg)
- Impending complications (e.g. transient ischaemic attack, left ventricular failure)
  Possible underlying cause
- Any clue in history or examination of a secondary cause (e.g. hypokalaemia with increased or high–normal plasma sodium [Conn's syndrome])
- Elevated creatinine
- Proteinuria or haematuria
- Sudden onset or worsening of hypertension
- Resistance to multidrug regimen (at least three drugs)
- Young age (<20 years: any hypertension; <30 years: needing treatment)

Therapeutic problems
- Multiple drug intolerance
- Multiple drug contraindications
- Persistent non-adherence or non-compliance

Special situations
- Unusual blood pressure variability
- White coat hypertension
- Hypertension in pregnancy

Patient involvement

An essential component of successful blood pressure management is to obtain the active participation of each individual. Patients with high blood pressure should be involved in the decision as to what lifestyle changes they need to take and whether drug therapy is appropriate. The likely risk reduction obtained as a consequence of antihypertensive treatment should be understood. They should also be aware of the likelihood that they will need to take two or three drugs to achieve sufficient reductions and be conscious of the possible side-effects that they may encounter. Wherever possible a written treatment plan should be drawn up and given to the patient.

With modern semi-automated blood pressure machines, it is possible to involve more patients in the measurement of their own blood pressure, which can save visits to a primary healthcare team. However, it is important to remember that the targets are based on 'clinic' blood pressures and home measurements will usually be lower. A correction factor of 10/5 mmHg should be used when considering home results. Individual patients can obtain information directly from the Blood Pressure Association (*www.bpassoc.org.uk*).

Clinical audit

It is now essential that interventions relating to blood pressure control are recorded electronically. The survival of practices in the age of performance management means that electronic audit is no longer optional. We need to ensure that the templates that we use are correctly Read-coded, thereby enabling the information to be retrieved easily from our systems. It seems likely that many practices will use the quality indicators as detailed in the new GMS contract as a basis for their audit. Programmes which interrogate our databases, such as the Population Manager in the EMIS system, will enable us to monitor our progress towards quality points whenever we wish to. Correct Read-coding will also enable individual practices to undertake more sophisticated searches should they so wish.

With regard to blood pressure control, it is important that we should try to achieve the targets as suggested by the BHS and not to use the audit standard as our therapeutic target. Self-evidently, should we attempt to hit the more challenging clinical targets, success in the GMS audit will be more likely and our patients will achieve greater benefit. Hypertension indicators in the GMS contract are outlined in Table 5. In due course, the results of comparable audits carried out by different practices within the PCT will be published and will form the basis of 'league tables'.

Table 5. Hypertension quality indicators in the new General Medical Services contract. Adapted from Williams *et al.* *J Hum Hypertens* 2004; **18**: 139–85.

	Points	Maximum threshold
Secondary prevention in CHD		
Ongoing management		
Percentage of patients with CHD whose notes have a record of BP in previous 15 months	7	90%
Percentage of patients with CHD in whom last BP reading (within the last 15 months) is ≤150/90 mmHg	19	70%
Stroke or TIAs		
Ongoing management		
Percentage of patients with TIA or stroke who have a record of BP in previous 15 months	2	90%
Percentage of patients with a history of TIA or stroke in whom last BP reading (within the last 15 months) is ≤150/90 mmHg	5	70%
Hypertension		
Records		
The practice can produce a register of patients with established hypertension	9	–
Diagnosis and management		
Percentage of patients with hypertension whose notes record smoking status at least once	10	90%
Percentage of patients with hypertension who smoke, whose notes contain a record that smoking cessation advice has been offered at least once	10	90%
Ongoing management		
Percentage of patients with hypertension in whom there is a record of BP in the past 9 months	20	90%
Percentage of patients with hypertension in whom last BP reading (within the last 9 months) is ≤150/90 mmHg	56	70%
Diabetes mellitus		
Ongoing management		
Percentage of patients with diabetes in whom there is a record of BP in the past 15 months	3	90%
Percentage of patients with diabetes in whom last BP reading is ≤145/85 mmHg	17	55%
Records and information about patients		
The BP of patients aged 45 years and over is recorded in the preceding 5 years for at least 55% of patients	10	–
The BP of patients aged 45 years and over is recorded in the preceding 5 years for at least 75% of patients	5	–

BP, blood pressure; CHD, coronary heart disease; TIA, transient ischaemic attack.

Conclusion

It is in the interests of each practice, as well as in the interest of the population that it serves, that we make real progress in reducing blood pressure in our patient population and thereby reduce their cardiovascular risk. As more trial evidence emerges, it is likely that the current guidance will be modified further.

The detection and treatment of high blood pressure and its associated CVD risk will continue to be a key focus of healthcare policy in the UK. We should continue to assess the need for treatment on the basis of absolute risk. The ongoing reorganisation of healthcare within the UK and the emphasis on clinical audit, quality of care and improvements in the systems of care provides us with an excellent opportunity to deliver improved hypertension management and thereby reduce the burden of CVD for the population we serve.

Key points

- Hypertension is one of the most important and preventable causes of morbidity and mortality globally. Large numbers of patients are considered to be hypertensive in the UK.

- Individuals with hypertension are likely to have multiple risk factors for CVD, necessitating an assessment of overall cardiovascular risk and multiple drug intervention where indicated.

- Hypertension is suboptimally managed in primary care in the UK, although there are signs of improvement. Consequently, primary care faces a major challenge in improving the care of hypertensive patients.

- The new guidelines from the BHS provide us with clear and practical advice for the management of hypertension. However, new systems of healthcare delivery will be needed to allow this guidance to be implemented effectively. The entire community healthcare team including nurses and pharmacists will be at the forefront of this strategy.

- A number of other initiatives provide the lead in CVD disease management and emphasise the importance of effective hypertension management. These include the NSFs for CHD, diabetes and for Older People, and the new GMS contract.

- A major proportion of clinical points in the new GMS contract are related directly to the effective management of hypertension.

- Treatment is indicated when a patient has sustained and elevated blood pressure above 160/100 mmHg. This threshold is lower in patients with diabetes and evidence of vascular disease. Patients with milder hypertension require risk assessment, which will drive the decision to treat.

- The BHS guidelines adopt the ABCD algorithm for treatment, and indicate that multiple-drug therapy is likely to achieve the more stringent blood pressure targets that have been set.

- Patients should be actively involved in the decisions regarding lifestyle changes and drug intervention.

- Clinical audit is now an essential part of primary care, driven by the quality standards in the new GMS contract. It is likely that the quality indicators in this framework will be adopted as the basis for clinical audit in practices across the UK.

20. Hypertension and cardiovascular disease

Dr Jonathan Morrell MB BChir. FRCGP DCH DRCOG
General Practitioner, Hastings, East Sussex

Summary

The management of patients with hypertension comprises a significant part of the GP's workload, and an ageing population and increasing prevalence of cardiovascular disease (CVD) means that hypertension will remain a significant burden. Recent surveys have shown that in the UK about 30% of people aged between 35 and 74 years are candidates for anti-hypertensive therapy, and yet only 15% of these receive treatment. Therefore, hypertension represents a current and growing challenge for primary care. Current recommendations indicate antihypertensive therapy for patients with a blood pressure of 140–159/90–99 mmHg, assuming there is no evidence of diabetes or target-organ damage, with the goal being to reduce blood pressure to normal levels. GPs should also encourage lifestyle modifications, such as improved diet and exercise. The majority of hypertensive patients have abnormal lipid profiles and patients should be set targets of <5 and <3 mmol/L for total and LDL cholesterol respectively. Most antihypertensive drugs provide similar blood pressure reductions of about 7–13/4–8 mmHg, but greater reductions can be achieved by combinations of these drugs. Recent data indicate that 63% of patients require combination therapy to achieve their target blood pressure and guidelines have been published to enable GPs to determine the best anti-hypertensive strategy. Patient compliance is a recognised problem when treating hypertension. Patient buy in through improving education and their involvement in treatment is important.

The challenge in primary care

A significant part of a GP's daily routine involves the management of patients with hypertension, principally in the hope that treatment will prevent or delay the onset of coronary heart disease (CHD), stroke and renal impairment. Thirty-seven per cent of adults in England are hypertensive, with systolic blood pressure (SBP) of 140 mmHg or higher or diastolic blood pressure (DBP) of 90 mmHg or higher. Furthermore, there is an increasing likelihood of developing hypertension as age increases, such that the lifetime probability for individuals aged 55–65 years is 90%. The ageing population in developed countries and the 'epidemic' of CVD in developing countries and the former socialist republics of Eastern Europe will ensure that by 2020, death and disability from CHD and stroke will, respectively, rank the first and fourth major causes of the burden of disease worldwide.

Meta-analyses of large-scale, randomised, controlled clinical trials, have demonstrated that reductions in SBP of 10–14 mmHg and in DBP of 5–6 mmHg lower the incidence of stroke by two-fifths and of CHD by one-sixth. Given the pivotal role for hypertension in the pathogenesis of CHD and stroke, the numbers of patients involved and the evidence base for the benefits of interventions, the management of hypertension represents a continuing and growing challenge for primary-care professionals.

Sadly, surveys of current practice reveal woeful discrepancies in the detection, treatment and control of hypertension. Whilst this is a global problem, it is particularly acute in the UK. Using data from the 1998 Health Survey for England, researchers calculated that 29.8% of individuals aged 35–74 years were candidates for antihypertensive therapy, of whom 15.3% were receiving treatment but only 5.4% had adequate blood pressure control.

In addition, even when contemporary treatment is deemed optimal, the survival of treated hypertensives remains significantly reduced compared with matched normotensives. The Gothenburg Multifactor Primary Prevention Trial followed 686 hypertensive men aged 47–55 years and 6810 normotensive control individuals for over 20 years. Despite a carefully structured treatment programme which provided good mean blood pressure control (145/89 mmHg), a reduction in smoking from 34 to 17% and a reduction in mean serum cholesterol from 6.6 to 6.1 mmol/L, the hypertensive group showed increased mortality, with a predominance of deaths from CHD. This observation is not new. CHD outcomes in randomised, controlled clinical trials have consistently failed to match the epidemiological expectations of an equivalent fall in blood pressure. This shortfall is important because, numerically, CHD events remain the most important outcome of hypertension. Two explanations for this discrepancy have key implications for the management of hypertension in primary care.

- CVD is multifactorial; therefore, only a global risk-factor perspective for assessment and treatment will optimise outcome. In the Gothenburg study, the cardiovascular risk profile of the hypertensive group at entry was less acceptable than that of controls. Some individuals already had evidence of target-organ damage, such as left ventricular hypertrophy (LVH) and, in common with other surveys of hypertensive patients, clustering of risk factors (particularly those associated with the insulin-resistance syndrome) was also more evident.

- Blood-pressure reduction in early randomised, controlled clinical trials may have been inadequate to maximise the reduction in cardiovascular events. Recent evidence of the benefits of tighter blood pressure control has now led to a lowering of blood pressure targets, whilst it is likely that these targets will be reduced further in the future.

Thus, the incorporation of global risk strategies, treatment to new blood pressure targets and the development of organisational structures to implement them represent the major challenges in the management of hypertension facing primary-care professionals today.

Global risk strategies

Acknowledgement of the contribution of other risk factors to overall cardiovascular risk, and the endorsement of global risk assessment using Framingham-based risk-factor calculators represent major advances, and are now recommended in the guidelines of the Joint British Societies and the British Hypertension Society (BHS). Use of the risk-profiling charts or the corresponding computer software should become routine for every clinician making decisions about the initiation of antihypertensive and lipid-lowering therapies and aspirin prophylaxis in primary prevention. For patients whose blood pressure is in the range 140–159/90–99 mmHg without evidence of target-organ damage or diabetes, antihypertensive initiation is indicated when the 10-year absolute CHD risk reaches 15% or higher. However, the BHS guidelines are anomalous in that they recommend initiation of treatment at the 160/100 mmHg threshold, a point at which, for some patients, the 15% risk level will not have been reached.

Although there is no direct evidence that reducing blood pressure through lifestyle modification reduces the risk of CVD, it is generally recommended to all patients on the basis that the benefits in terms of CVD risk reduction of any antihypertensive treatment employed are determined *per se* by the blood pressure reduction itself. Table 1 gives a summary of the trials of such lifestyle interventions; it should be noted, however, that these trials are of only short duration.

Smoking cessation is without doubt the single most important lifestyle intervention. However, its benefits are independent of any effect on blood pressure. Similarly, although more than 60 population studies have demonstrated the virtually linear relationship between alcohol consumption and blood pressure levels, these effects are negligible below a threshold

Table 1. Effectiveness of lifestyle interventions for lowering blood pressure.

Intervention	Mean reduction in in SBP/DBP (mmHg)	Number of RCTs	Mean change in risk factor
Weight loss	3/3	18	3–9% of body weight (ideally increments of 5 kg)
Diet low in fat and high in fruit and vegetables	5.5/3	1	
Exercise	5/3	29	50 minutes' aerobic exercise, three times a week
Salt restriction	4/2	58	118 mmol/day
	2.0/0.5	28	60 mmol/day
Potassium supplementation	4.4/2.5	21	60–100 mmol/day (equivalent to five bananas)
Fish-oil supplementation	4.5/2.5	7	3 g/day

RCT, randomised controlled trial; SBP, systolic blood pressure; DBP, diastolic blood pressure.

of 2–3 units per day. Trials of alcohol reduction in heavier drinkers (25–50 units/week) have also been inconclusive.

The majority of hypertensive patients also have abnormal lipid profiles. Although the evidence of benefit from initiating statin therapy extends to a 10-year absolute CHD risk as low as 6%, the current British treatment recommendations only endorse a threshold in primary prevention of 30% over 10 years. Pending guideline revision is addressing this anomaly and the recommended 10-year CHD intervention threshold for lipid-lowering medication is expected to drop to 15%, the same as antihypertensive drugs. The new guidelines are likely to abandon 10-year CHD risk in favour of the broader 10-year cardiovascular risk and this is likely to be expressed as a 10-year intervention threshold of 20%. For those patients currently treated, target levels of <5.0 mmol/L for total cholesterol and <3.0 mmol/L for LDL cholesterol are appropriate but again these targets are also likely to fall. It is a criticism of the new General Medical Services (GMS) contract that it does not specify cholesterol as a quality indicator in the management of patients with hypertension.

Finally, aspirin, 75 mg/day, is recommended for hypertensive patients over 50 years of age whose blood pressure is well controlled (<150/90 mmHg) and who have target-organ damage, type 2 diabetes or a 10-year CHD risk in excess of 15%.

New treatment strategies

Treatment to new targets

The relationship between cardiovascular risk and blood pressure is continuous and does not appear to have a lower 'threshold'. Logically, therefore, the goal of antihypertensive therapy should be to reduce blood pressure to levels defined as 'normal'.

Expert international panels continually distil clinical, scientific and statistical evidence into consensus recommendations. Unsurprisingly, there are a number of discrepancies in target values in these guidelines (Table 2).

It is important to recognise that recommendations are essentially consensus statements and are not supported by individual trial evidence. Data from the Hypertension Optimal Treatment (HOT) study largely underpin the latest wave of reductions in blood pressure targets. However, it should be noted that in this study there were no significant differences in the risk of cardiovascular events between the adjacent target groups (DBP <90, 85 or 80 mmHg). Nevertheless, there was no increase in cardiovascular risk in the lower target group and optimal event reduction was achieved at a DBP of 82.6 mmHg. In patients with diabetes, reducing DBP to less than 80 mmHg dramatically reduced cardiovascular events, resulting in more aggressive targets being set for such individuals. An aggressive approach to hypertension management in patients with diabetes is supported by findings from UK Prospective Diabetes Study (UKPDS 38) where tight blood pressure control (144/82 *vs* 154/87 mmHg) was associated with significant risk reductions in both macro- and microvascular disease.

> The goal of antihypertensive therapy should be to reduce blood pressure to levels defined as 'normal'.

Principles of drug treatment

There is general agreement on several broad principles governing the use of antihypertensive agents.

- The use of long-acting drugs that provide 24-hour efficacy with once-daily dosing will provide more consistent control of blood pressure and thus may offer greater protection against the risk of cardiovascular events and target-organ damage.
- Low drug doses should be used when initiating therapy. If the blood pressure target is not achieved, the dose can be increased if the drug is well tolerated.

Table 2. Blood pressure targets in hypertensive patients with and without diabetes.

Guideline	SBP (mmHg)	DBP (mmHg)	Target in diabetics (mmHg)
British Hypertension Society	<140	<85	<140/80
World Health Organization–	<140 (<130 if	<90 (<85 if	<130/80
International Society of Hypertension	<60 years)	<60 years)	

DBP, diastolic blood pressure; SBP, systolic blood pressure.

- As an alternative, a low dose of an additional drug may be added. Low-dose combinations of both drugs are more likely to be free of side-effects.
- Where there is no clinical response or if a patient does not tolerate the initial agent, they should be switched to a different drug class.

Most drugs from the main classes provide very similar blood pressure reductions. The placebo-adjusted reductions for patients with blood pressure of about 160/95 mmHg are not large in magnitude (SBP 7–13 mmHg; DBP 4–8 mmHg). For many patients, such reductions would not allow guideline blood pressure targets to be met.

In contrast, combinations of drugs with additive effects typically achieve reductions of the order of 12–22 mmHg in SBP and 7–14 mmHg in DBP from a baseline of 160/95 mmHg. In the HOT study, 63% of patients achieving DBP of 90 mmHg or lower and 74% achieving DBP of 80 mmHg or lower required combination treatment. In the Antihypertensive and Lipid-Lowering Treatment to Prevent Heart Attack Trial (ALLHAT), 63% of patients needed combination treatment to achieve blood pressure below 140/90 mmHg. An important feature of the trials is that patient acceptability and concordance with combination treatment is high.

Irrespective of the observations made in clinical trials, in the real world many patients remain difficult to treat and fail to achieve treatment targets. The GP needs to be aware of measurement issues, the progression of hypertension with age, 'white-coat hypertension', secondary causes of hypertension, other medication (particularly non-steroidal anti-inflammatory drugs) and compliance issues, including unreported side-effects.

Antihypertensives have now been available for 50 years, with incremental benefits being claimed for each successive drug class and product. There has been considerable debate on the relative merits of the 'older' antihypertensives, (e.g. diuretics and β-blockers) and 'newer' drugs (e.g. calcium antagonists, ACE inhibitors and angiotensin [AT]-II-receptor antagonists). For example, diuretics and β-blockers have both been shown to reduce the incidence of stroke, but only low-dose diuretics have been shown to reduce the risk of CHD. In addition, agents from 'newer' classes were shown to reduce cardiovascular morbidity and mortality to a similar extent as β-blockers or thiazide diuretics. Data from ALLHAT showed no significant differences in the primary endpoint (fatal and non-fatal myocardial infarction [MI]) between regimens based on a thiazide (chlorthalidone), a calcium antagonist (amlodipine) or an ACE inhibitor (lisinopril). The ACE inhibitor was significantly less effective than the thiazide in reducing the secondary endpoints of stroke and combined CVD. In addition, the incidence of heart failure was significantly greater in the ACE inhibitor and calcium antagonist groups. However, the diagnoses of heart failure were not rigorously validated. In addition, the study included a high proportion of black Americans (35%), who do not respond well to ACE inhibitors because, like older people, their renin–angiotensin systems are relatively suppressed. More recently, the Second Australian National Blood Pressure (ANBP-2) study showed evidence that initiation of antihypertensive treatment involving ACE inhibitors in older subjects, particularly in men with hypertension, lead to better outcomes than treatment with diuretic agents, despite similar reductions of blood pressure. With the lack of difference between these drug classes, the findings of the Losartan Intervention for Endpoint Reduction in Hypertension (LIFE) trial are interesting. In a direct comparison of antihypertensive treatments based on an AT-II-receptor antagonist (losartan) and a β-blocker (atenolol) in patients with LVH, the composite primary endpoint was significantly positive in favour of the AT-II-receptor antagonist, but was largely driven by a 25% reduction in fatal/non-fatal stroke. The data were even more impressive in diabetic subjects, with a 39% reduction in total mortality.

Whilst monotherapy with antihypertensives may produce only relatively modest reductions in blood pressure, there is growing evidence to suggest that some of the benefits of antihypertensive agents in terms of cardiovascular outcomes may be derived independently of the reduction in blood pressure that they provide. For example, in the Heart Outcomes Prevention Evaluation (HOPE) study, an ACE inhibitor (ramipril) was shown to be effective in decreasing ischaemic events and lowering the incidence of MI in a high-risk patient population with vascular disease. Recently, the EUROPA study has provided further support for the use of chronic ACE inhibitor therapy (in this case with perindopril) in lower-risk patients with established but stable coronary artery disease. EUROPA involved over 12,000 patients with documented CHD and demonstrated a highly significant 20% reduction in cardiovascular death, MI and resuscitated cardiac arrest. Like the HOPE study, this reduction in vascular events was associated with only rather modest changes in blood pressure (5/2 mmHg). The benefits of ACE inhibition related to vascular effects appeared to occur in addition to those associated with reduction of blood pressure and in addition to other standard treatments that patients were receiving. Whether the benefits of ACE inhibition can be extended to patients at even lower risk of cardiovascular events remains to be confirmed, but this is an active area of research and may shortly be answered.

Whatever the treatment strategy employed, the bottom line is that what matters most is getting blood pressure controlled, and that most patients will probably need more than one drug to achieve this. Identifying the ideal combination of drugs is the next big question in hypertension, but it is already clear that most combination regimens should involve a thiazide diuretic, even in patients with diabetes. The BHS has recently published recommendations on selecting the best antihypertensive combination – a modification of the AB/CD rule where 'A' represents an ACE inhibitor/AT-II-receptor antagonist, 'B' a β-blocker, 'C' a calcium-channel antagonist and 'D' a diuretic (Figure 1).

If all antihypertensives are equal, then the choice of agent will be related to factors such as cost, side-effects and the presence of co-existing disorders. All guidelines include useful tables identifying compelling and possible

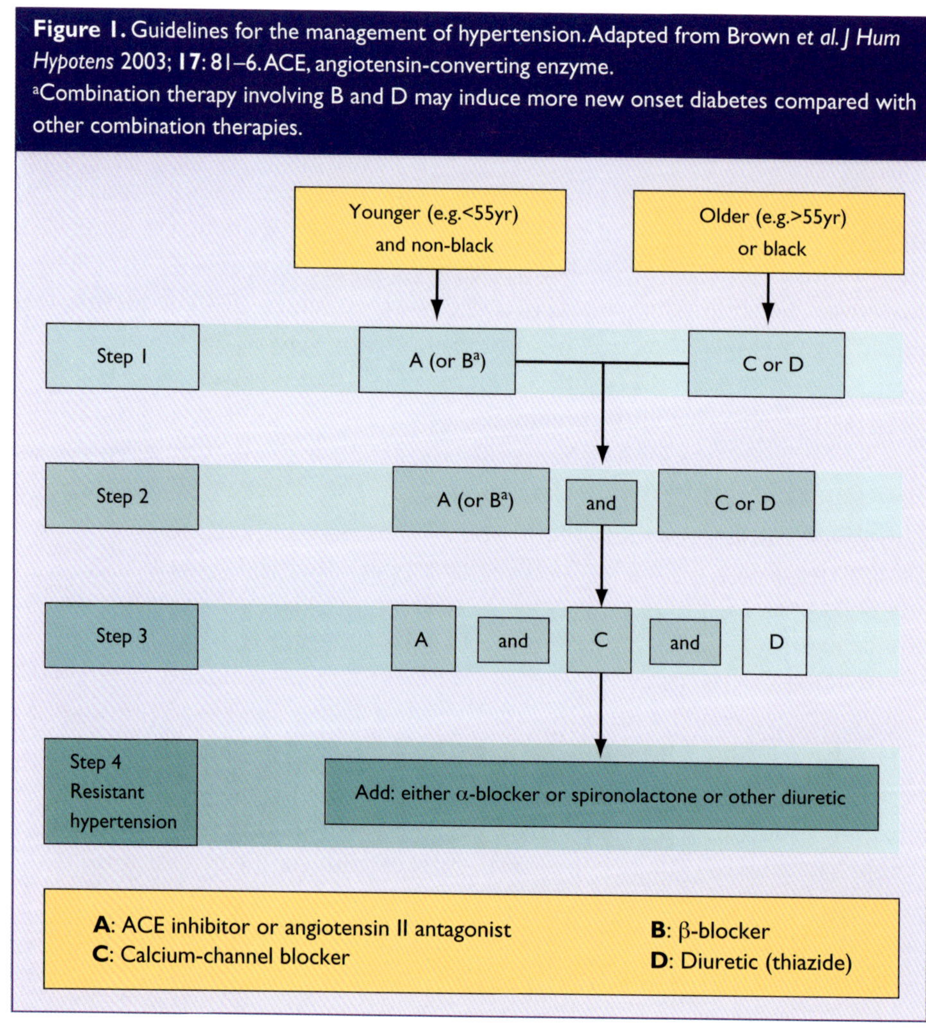

Figure 1. Guidelines for the management of hypertension. Adapted from Brown *et al. J Hum Hypotens* 2003; 17: 81–6. ACE, angiotensin-converting enzyme.
[a]Combination therapy involving B and D may induce more new onset diabetes compared with other combination therapies.

indications, contraindications and cautions for the major classes of antihypertensive drugs.

Priority patients

Absolute risk assessment has highlighted the increased cardiovascular risk of patients with diabetes and in the elderly. In addition, there is accumulating evidence that antihypertensive therapy reduces the likelihood of disease progression in patients with existing cerebrovascular disease, CHD and renal disease. Some ethnic groups such as Afro-Caribbeans and South Asians are also at increased risk.

Hypertension is extremely common in the elderly, with more than 50% of individuals over 60 years of age having isolated systolic hypertension (SBP ≥160 mmHg; DBP ≤90 mmHg). New evidence shows that treatment of hypertension also reduces the risk of developing heart failure and preserves cognitive function. The evidence base for treatment decisions in patients over 80 years of age is inadequate, but a meta-analysis of seven studies indicated benefit from antihypertensive treatment in 1670 patients over 80 years of age (Table 3).

Organisational changes

Case finding has traditionally been the most effective method of detecting hypertensive patients in general practice but is influenced by the GP's enthusiasm and, of course, time constraints. Increasing awareness of hypertension amongst the public, and imaginative schemes (e.g. blood pressure checks at 'flu clinics) could increase the numbers diagnosed.

Once diagnosed, the number of patients with uncontrolled hypertension highlights the problem of implementing the evidence base from tightly controlled clinical trials and meticulously debated consensus advice. Continuation rates of only 40–50% were reported after 6 months' treatment with diuretics, β-blockers, calcium antagonists and ACE inhibitors. Evidence suggests that barriers to treatment persistence occur

> Primary-care professionals should form a therapeutic alliance with their patients to maximise the acceptance of treatment regimens.

Table 3. Reduction in cardiovascular morbidity in patients over 80 years of age in a meta-analysis of seven randomised controlled trials.

	Percentage of cases prevented (95% confidence intervals)
Cardiovascular events	22 (2–60)
Stroke	34 (10–52)
Heart failure	39 (10–60)

early in the therapeutic course. Therefore, primary-care professionals should form a therapeutic alliance with their patients to maximise the acceptance of treatment regimens. GPs also need to optimise the use of drugs, set agreed targets, review adverse effects and maximise information and choice for their patients.

The new GMS contract moves the realm of clinical audit to the forefront of management practice, defining explicitly the audits required to demonstrate good quality hypertension care. The new contract significantly rewards good hypertension management, as over 13% of the quality points available relate to the recording of blood pressure values and the demonstration of tight control (Table 4). Although audit standards are accepted as measures of control, the exercise represents a considerable challenge for the primary care team, given the magnitude of the organisational restructuring required and the problems of polypharmacy and patient compliance. Nurses will have an increasing role in patient management and data recording and it has already been demonstrated that nurse specialists can provide significant improvements in the control of blood pressure and compliance with medication and lifestyle advice.

The demands of the new GMS contract will be met only by good data recording. Increasing use of computers in primary care will facilitate the construction and use of disease registers, improve protocol adherence and

Table 4. Blood pressure indicators, thresholds and points in the new General Medical Services contract.

	Maximum threshold (%)	Points
CHD secondary prevention		
BP last 15m	90	7
BP 150/90 or less last 15m	70	19
Stroke/TIA		
BP last 15m	90	2
BP 150/90 or less last 15m	70	5
Hypertension		
BP last 9m	90	20
BP 150/90 or less last 9m	70	56
Diabetes mellitus		
BP last 15m	90	3
BP 145/85 or less last reading	55	17

BP, blood pressure; CHD, coronary heart disease; TIA, transient ischaemic attack.
Minimum threshold 25%

information capture and allow the use of customised templates for multidisciplinary hypertension management.

Patient involvement and education is a critical issue for the future. Already, in many countries the availability of simple electronic equipment has increased interest in home monitoring. There is good evidence for high degrees of interest, satisfaction, compliance and reliability amongst patients using such devices. The monitors function well and cost a fraction of ambulatory monitoring devices. Both methods of home monitoring facilitate the recognition of 'white-coat hypertension' but even when this is excluded, recordings for SBP and DBP are consistently 10–15 mmHg and 5–10 mmHg lower than office readings. Unfortunately, there is little prospective data relating home readings to events, and consequently, initiation and treatment guidelines are extrapolations of office-based recommendations. Ongoing studies are forthcoming, but with the European Union's intention to withdraw mercury-containing manometers, GPs will also need to convert to electronic devices.

Conclusion

Despite the progressive ageing of the population and recommendations to adopt yet more aggressive initiation thresholds and treatment targets, surveys of blood pressure control are critical of the management of hypertension in primary care.

Primary care still bears the responsibility for implementing best practice and must respond by developing new strategies to deliver enhanced, focused and appropriate care for our hypertensive patients.

Surveys of blood pressure control are critical of the management of hypertension. Primary care must respond by developing new strategies to deliver enhanced, focused and appropriate care.

Key points

- Hypertension is routinely managed in primary care, and forms a sizeable part of a GP's daily routine.

- Hypertension plays a pivotal role in the development of cardiovascular disease and its management represents an ongoing and growing challenge for primary healthcare professionals.

- Currently, the management of hypertension is suboptimal, such that only about half the patients eligible for treatment are receiving antihypertensive therapy. Moreover, even when patients are treated, targets are not frequently met, with patients often requiring combination therapy to reach their blood pressure goals.

- Control of blood pressure should form part of an overall global cardiovascular risk strategy, which takes into account other risk factors such as hypercholesterolaemia, diabetes and lifestyle factors such as smoking and diet.

- The use of risk-profiling charts provides invaluable information for practitioners when making decisions about the initiation of antihypertensive and lipid-lowering therapy and aspirin prophylaxis.

- The selection of an appropriate antihypertensive agent is governed by a number of broad principles. However, what is most critical is that elevated blood pressure is controlled, with most patients requiring a combination of different drugs.

- Compliance to antihypertensive therapy is a critical determinant of patient outcome. By providing education and encouraging active involvement in their own care, overall treatment outcomes can be expected to be improved.

- Appropriate strategies of care and organisational structures need to be implemented to deliver enhanced and focused care for hypertensive patients.

21. Influenza

Nigel Higson MA BM BCh DRCOG
General Practitioner
Chairman of the Primary Care Virology Group

Summary

Despite the fact that there has been an absence of influenza epidemics or global pandemics over recent years, influenza is still responsible for a substantial morbidity and mortality burden, not to mention being a major disrupter of the economy. As a consequence of this impact, government policy now focuses on controlling the spread of infection with influenza vaccination targeted at those aged over 65 years and to younger patients considered to be at high risk of serious complications post-infection. Indeed, the new General Medical Services (GMS) contract provides financial incentives to deliver vaccination to all these groups of patients. Furthermore, given that children are major sources of the spread of infection, it can be hoped that one day vaccination will also be routinely extended to this population. Despite the prevalence of influenza, discriminating influenza infections from other viral and bacterial upper respiratory tract infections which persist in the winter-time can be challenging. Effective training of all practice staff together with establishing a written policy on how to manage a local outbreak of influenza infections will ensure that our resources are appropriately targeted to those who need them most. We can also apply the principles of clinical audit that can identify areas for improvement in future years, and may place us in a stronger position when we face the next inevitable, influenza epidemic, or worse, pandemic.

Introduction

Influenza is an efficient virus of mass destruction – one which has killed more people in the last century than all political conflicts, including two world wars, combined. It is able to wreak havoc across all age groups and seriously disrupts the industrial and service sectors of the UK economy more efficiently than any trade unionist! It is no wonder that Governments are finally realising that there is political expediency in attempting to limit the impact of influenza by implementing mass vaccination campaigns

Influenza policy now features strongly in the new GMS Quality and Outcome Framework, with some 30 points available spread across a number of clinical areas.

supplemented by financial incentives to GPs. For example, influenza policy now features strongly in the new GMS Quality and Outcome Framework (QOF), with some 30 points available spread across a number of clinical areas.

Burden of influenza and policy

In the UK, influenza peaks in the early months of the year although the virus does persist throughout the year. An increasing incidence of influenza has a knock-on effect on other infections spread by droplet. For example, meningococcal- and pneumococcal-induced disease rises in parallel to the increasing incidence of influenza infections, owing to the increase in the number of patients coughing and sneezing. The highest attack rates are in children, and school-aged children in particular play a pivotal role in the spread of influenza, both within their own household and within the local community. An American study has illustrated this by demonstrating that 33% of the children evaluated had developed influenza in the first year of life, with the majority of influenza infections occurring from 6 months of age.

Influenza is a highly infectious disease with a transmission rate of 20–90%. Even when an epidemic is not evident, some 3000–4000 deaths can be directly attributed to influenza infections each winter. The majority of the mortality or deteriorating morbidity burden is secondary to complicating infection following influenza. In the UK, epidemics between 1975 and 1990 resulted in up to 29,000 extra deaths during each epidemic.

In the UK, the current national government policy is to offer blanket influenza vaccination to everyone aged 65 years and over on the 31st December, with direct payment made to the GP for each such vaccine administered. GPs are also encouraged to seek out and offer vaccination to others in higher risk groups who are under the age of 65 years (Table 1).

Virology of influenza infection

The influenza viruses are part of the *Orthomyxoviridae* family and comprise three main types – A, B and C – each with many different subtypes. The influenza A and B viruses have two main surface proteins –haemagglutinin (H) and neuraminidase (N) – which allow the virus to enter and emerge from the host cells. In contrast, influenza C only has a single surface protein. The virus has the ability to alter its antigenic activity, as a result of either minor changes in these surface proteins (antigenic drift), as can occur from year to year, or through major changes (antigenic shift) resulting from intermingling of gene segments between different influenza A subtypes. Antigenic shift often leads to epidemics as a consequence of the absence of

Table 1. High-risk groups eligible for influenza vaccination, including the relevant quality indicator points from the General Medical Services (GMS) contract.

Risk group	Quality and outcomes framework (QOF)	Points
Chronic respiratory disease (including asthma and COPD)	ASTHMA 7	12 points
	COPD 8	6 points
Chronic heart disease (including heart failure)	CHD 12	7 points
Chronic renal disease	–	–
Diabetes mellitus	DM18	3 points
Immunosuppression due to disease or treatment[a]	–	–
The elderly (particularly those aged over 75 years)	–	–
Those in residential institutions (e.g. nursing homes, rest homes, barracks, residential schools etc.)	–	–
Stroke/Transient ischaemic attack	STROKE 10	2 points

[a]including those without spleens or those with splenic dysfunction.
COPD, chronic obstructive pulmonay disease.

natural immunity to the emerging novel subtypes in the affected community. The viruses are classified by their type, their origin, their strain, their year of identification and the H and N subtypes that are present on the viral envelope. Fifteen different subtypes of haemagglutinin and nine different subtypes of neuraminidase have been isolated.

Influenza A has been isolated from birds and, more occasionally from other animals, suggesting that birds are a natural host for influenza A. In contrast, influenza B has only been isolated from humans, whilst influenza C has been found in humans and some domestic animals.

The influenza virus invades the respiratory epithelium and rapidly destroys the ciliated nasal and tracheal epithelial cells causing impairment of the mucociliary clearance. This predisposes the infected individual to bacterial super infection. The virus gains entry through the epithelial endothelium by chemical attachment of the haemagglutinin particles to sialic acid-containing receptors on the cell surface. Replication of the viral genome within the host cell allows the creation of new viral particles, which are released by the action of neuraminidase which cleaves the haemagglutinin–sialic acid complex. The site of viral replication remains in the respiratory tract. The clinical symptoms of influenza do not occur primarily as result of viraemia – although this can occur – but rather a result of the host's immune response.

Viral particles can be found in the exhaled air of infected individuals for up to 48 hours before symptoms develop and for about 7 days afterwards.

In young children, prolonged virus shedding can continue for up to 6 days before symptoms appear and for 13 days after symptoms resolve.

Meeting the practical challenges of influenza infection

Influenza presents a complex and most interesting challenge to every GP, public health physician, occupational health physician and virologist. Millions are spent by the UK Government annually on controlling and treating influenza infection, and yet we still become confused over exactly what to do when presented with an influenza-like illness.

An editorial in the *BMJ* (Jefferson T. How to deal with influenza? *BMJ* 2004; **329**: 633–4) considered the difficulties that governments and practitioners face when presented with respiratory tract illnesses which were 'influenza like'. In his editorial, Jefferson proposed that developments in laboratory diagnosis were needed in order both to rationalise the statistical analyses which mislead and also to ensure that correct treatment is offered when true influenza is present. The current means of influenza surveillance – although innovative and revolutionary for its time – is too slow and totally inadequate for a disease that is easily transmittable and which, with the speed of international transport, can be acquired on one side of the world, with patients only becoming symptomatic when they reach their final destination. The Spanish 'flu pandemic of 1917 illustrated the ability of a new influenza virus to make use of international troop dispersal after the First World War in the days of steam trains and coal-fired steamers. What would be the impact of the emergence of a new influenza virus in the era of cheap aviation and long-haul travel? Vaccine manufacturing – a process that takes months – may have kept pace with the relatively slow spread of the disease in the days of the steam train and steamer, but it is apparent that it would not now be possible to control any major epidemic or pandemic with vaccination alone. So why vaccinate?

Vaccination of the risk groups outlined previously is fundamental to the Government's determination to prevent the blockage of hospital beds by those who are likely to be at highest risk of the complications of influenza. The current vaccination policy, however, does nothing to prevent disruption to industry. We should recall that 'flu is not spread by little old ladies sat in nursing homes or their own homes, it is spread by children coughing and spluttering in the faces of their siblings, parents or schoolmates across open-plan, round-table classrooms. It is then spread further by adults sneezing in crowded trains and in public gatherings. As such, we can only hope that government policy may shift over the coming years to encourage the routine vaccination of more children and adults.

Diagnosis and management

There is a wide overlap of symptoms and signs between different viral and bacterial illnesses that are active over the winter months (Table 2). Rapid onset is a classical feature of viral disease, with very little production of mucous or phlegm, aligned with considerable muscle aching and fatigue. Headache often arises with viral illnesses and this is derived from meningeal inflammation, which may cause concern when attempting to differentially diagnose such infections from meningitis. With influenza-like infections, respiratory rates increase and there is a feeling of discomfort in the 'tubes' where most of the viral damage is occurring.

Colonisation of the respiratory tract with bacteria – mainly *Staphylococcus* or *Streptococcus* – can arise as a primary infection or as an opportunistic event following initial viral damage to the ciliated epithelial cells – their normal function being to clear infected mucous from the respiratory tract. Bacterial infection produces a more toxic picture with expectoration of profuse infected mucous from the lower respiratory tract, a feeling of heaviness and inability to expand the lungs. In such cases,

Table 2. Comparison of influenza with other viral upper respiratory tract infections and the complications of influenza.

Influenza	Colds or 'flu-like illnesses
Severe malaise	Mild malaise
Rapid onset	Slow onset over days
Profound muscular aches and pains	Minimal aches and pain
Marked fever	Mild intermittent fever
Severe and early headache	Mild dull headache
Minimal nasal secretions	Prominent nasal secretions
Poor or limited appetite	Normal appetite

Complications of influenza
Influenza pneumonitis
Secondary bacterial pneumonia
Otitis Media
Excerbation of chronic lung diseases
Croup and bronchiolitis in children
Febrile convulsions
Guillain–Barre paralysis
Secondary meningococcal infection
Post-viral fatigue
Myocarditis

cyanosis may be apparent and pO_2 will decline. Decreased immunity in those at risk of pneumonia will increase the chance of bacteraemia and secondary organ damage elsewhere in the body when 'strep pneumoniae' takes a hold.

Differentiating between mild self-limiting upper respiratory tract infections and those signifying more important infections is easy when the patient is in front of the doctor in a surgery. It is perhaps less easy when a relative is phoning on behalf of the patient, as a second-hand description of any disease can be exaggerated or understated. Indeed, many GPs will have experience of being caught out by the patient who complains of mild indigestion only to have a myocardial infarction, or the one with severe acute abdominal agony who only has a touch of diarrhoea.

With all the pressures on primary care at the moment, it is essential that the practice consider ways in which to cope should there be an outbreak of 'flu, influenza, severe acute respiratory syndrome (SARS) or other respiratory disease. Influenza vaccination, when community uptake is at low levels, will not prevent the spread of influenza. Vaccination against *Pneumococcus* of those in high-risk groups will have benefits to the individual and has been shown to diminish the morbidity associated with 'strep pneumoniae' infection. Certainly, it is worthwhile expending a little extra effort in promoting both pneumococcal and influenza vaccines to at-risk groups, perhaps by using local media as a mechanism for raising awareness, and not just concentrating on the groups for which payment is given.

There are now three effective treatments licensed for use in the UK against influenza: amantadine is licensed to treat influenza A infections whilst zanamivir and oseltamivir are both licensed for influenza A and B infections. There is currently no effective treatment available for SARS. Respect amongst practitioners for the National Institute for Clinical Excellence (NICE) guidance on the management of influenza is scant, but there have been a number of declarations from NICE regarding appropriate use of drugs both in the prophylaxis and in the treatment of influenza infection. Personally, I believe that there should be no difficulty in using any of these drugs, provided that the diagnosis of influenza is made with reasonable conviction and that the type of influenza circulating in the community is known. The Health Protection Authority (*www.hpa.org.uk*) provides weekly influenza reports, and these should perhaps be indexed for viewing on a weekly basis by one of the GPs in the practice in order that action is taken and appropriate policies implemented. The NICE guidance for the use of these agents can be read on their website at *www.nice.org.uk.*

Training reception staff to differentiate between patients with self-limiting mild upper respiratory tract infections and those with significant disease is a matter of training in common sense. Patients who present to the surgery sounding blocked-up and with a constantly dripping nose or feeling a 'little below par' are most likely to be suffering a mild 'cold', which will respond to time and simple analgesia. In such cases, referral to self-help or a local pharmacy is appropriate. Those who present with difficulty in breathing, profuse sweating, severe headache and on the verge of collapse are more likely to be suffering from influenza or a more serious respiratory infection, and require immediate and appropriate assessment. Receptionists, however, should be discouraged from trying to triage by telephone. Calls from patients complaining of respiratory disease should be screened by a nurse or doctor who can attempt to determine the extent and degree of their symptoms (Figure 1). Simple written policies or 'in-house' education sessions involving both practitioners and practice staff can help to decrease the workload arising from outbreaks of respiratory disease. Changes in working patterns may be necessary, perhaps by appointing one practitioner to be responsible for dealing with all such cases while the others get on with other routine work.

A major source of workload at this time of year comes from residential and nursing homes who would not only prefer to have their patients

Simple written policies or 'in-house' education sessions involving both practitioners and practice staff can help to decrease the workload arising from outbreaks of respiratory disease.

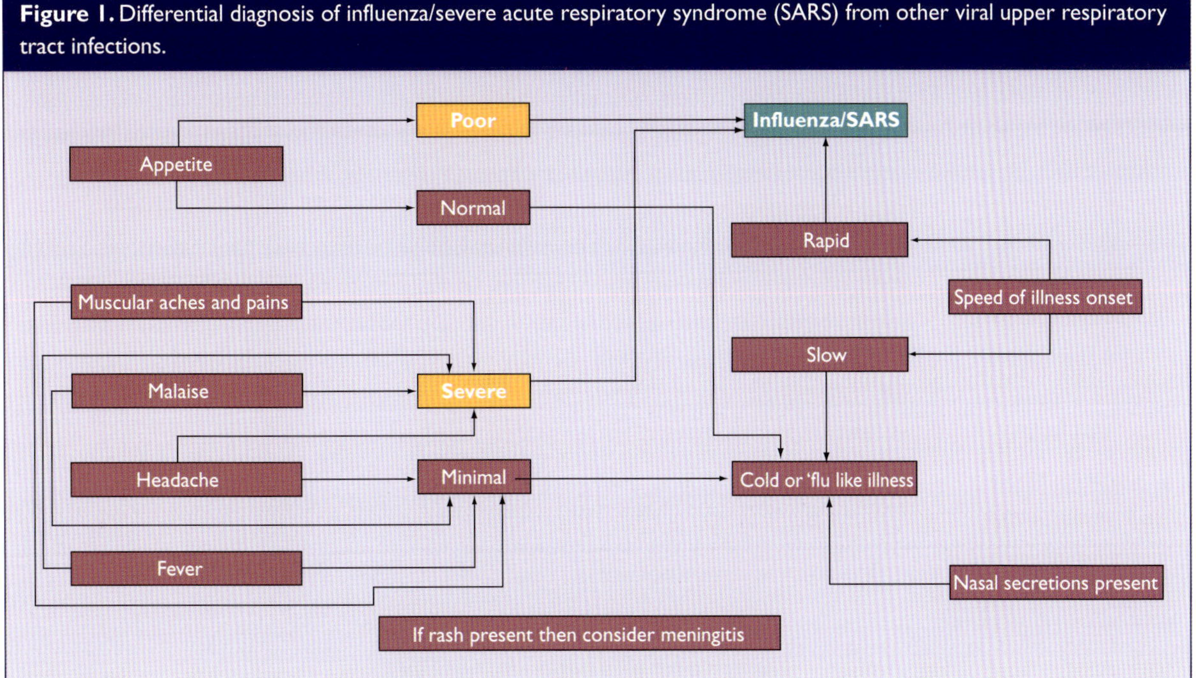

Figure 1. Differential diagnosis of influenza/severe acute respiratory syndrome (SARS) from other viral upper respiratory tract infections.

assessed by a doctor in order to minimise their responsibility, but would also prefer that their patients did not catch any form of respiratory infection, in order to reduce the risk of a rapidly spreading infection amongst other residents and staff in the home. Priority should be given to this group for both vaccination and appropriate post-vaccine prophylaxis, not only for the residents but also for all the staff in the home. All hospital and healthcare workers should also ensure that they are vaccinated against influenza annually at the earliest possible date that vaccine becomes available. Remember, influenza can strike at any time between October and March with very little warning.

In summary, I would recommend the following approach to patient management.

- Vaccinate all patients at risk of complications (Armstrong and colleagues have published a 5-year study demonstrating a significant protective effect of vaccination on mortality. *BMJ* 2004; **329**: 660–3).
- Vaccinate all healthcare workers.
- Vaccinate yourself.
- Carry a supply of one of the three antiviral treatments known to be effective in influenza infections (amantadine for influenza A infections only, and zanamivir or oseltamivir for influenza A and B infections).
- Be prepared to check serology or obtain nasal swabs to determine the presence of influenza virus.

How do we measure our performance in preventing morbidity in influenza?

Arguments have been raised in this article about the inadequacy of current diagnostic and epidemiological information about the spread of influenza. There have also been a number of years recently when influenza has not risen to epidemic proportions. As such, a 'laissez-faire' attitude has developed not only amongst patients but also amongst practitioners. Simple audit of the reasons behind a failure to vaccinate can identify areas for improvement in future years. Such an approach may highlight that patients have moved address and hence not received an invitation, or that they have misunderstood the need for annual vaccination. Additional clinical audit possibilities, other than those directly linked to payment in the QOF, may involve the accuracy of a diagnosis of patients coded as suffering influenza on the practice database (Read code: H27), and perhaps may also identify whether attempts have been made to confirm diagnosis by serology or viral swab.

What should we be hoping to change?

Influenza is used by many – and regrettably not just by the lay person – as a term to describe any upper respiratory tract infection. It is also commonly used to justify absence from work as influenza is a much stronger noun than the 'common cold'. Such misuse of the name influenza diminishes the seriousness of true influenza infection. Influenza has been, is, and will remain, a major indiscriminate killer with chameleonic ability to change for the worse. As a profession we should discourage abuse of the term influenza and restrict its use purely to describe the disease caused by influenza virus.

Use of antivirals is considered by many as an 'expensive' option, which, according to those who measure quantitative outcomes, merely decreases the duration of the illness by 1 day. However, qualitatively, antivirals have been shown in clinical studies to improve dramatically the return to normal function, which can often take days after the acute feverish illness has subsided in the absence of antiviral intervention. Considering the millions that are invested in administering the influenza vaccine on an annual basis, the rational use of antivirals can be more than justified.

In the future, we can hope for the development of a more effective and encompassing influenza vaccine which will allow periodic rather than annual vaccination. Such a vaccine may then be incorporated into the childhood schedule to diminish the spread of this disease. In the meantime, antivirals should play an important additional role in the control of influenza infection.

> Influenza has been, is, and will remain, a major indiscriminate killer with chameleonic ability to change for the worse.

Key points

- Influenza has a major impact on winter mortality and morbidity and also profoundly disrupts the UK economy.

- Mass influenza vaccination programmes form the major component of government influenza policy, whilst the new GMS contract offers financial incentives to GPs delivering vaccination, with 30 QOF points available.

- In the UK, influenza vaccination is targeted at everyone aged over 65 years. Other high-risk groups are also recommended for vaccination. Changes to government vaccination policy should be encouraged in future years, focusing on routine vaccination of children in order to diminish the spread of infection.

- Differentially diagnosing influenza infection from other viral and bacterial illness can be challenging. A series of clinical features provide a high index of suspicion for an influenza-related infection: rapid onset of symptoms, minimal production of mucous, severe headache, muscle pain and malaise.

- It is essential that the primary-care practice formulates a plan to cope with outbreaks of 'flu, SARS and other respiratory disease.

- Training and education sessions involving all members of the practice will more readily allow us to differentiate between self-limiting mild upper respiratory tract infections and more severe illness, allowing us to target our resources to those who need them most.

- All GPs and other healthcare workers should be vaccinated against influenza, as should all patients at risk of complications of influenza infection. It is also important to have stocks available of antiviral treatments such as oseltamivir and zanamivir to control outbreaks and to advance resolution of the disease. The rational use of such agents would appear to be more than justified.

- We can audit our performance in reducing the impact of influenza infection in a relatively simple fashion. For example, we can evaluate reasons why there was a failure to vaccinate in an eligible individual, together with assessing the accuracy of diagnosis of patients coded as suffering from influenza.

- It is important to educate patients and others about the nature and use of the term 'influenza', restricting its use purely to describe disease caused by influenza virus infection.

22. Lipid disorders

Dr Jonathan Morrell MB BChir. FRCGP DCH DRCOG
General Practitioner, Hastings, East Sussex

Summary

The extent of hypercholesterolaemia in the UK means that the burden of its
management now falls principally on primary care. However, given the holistic and
multidisciplinary nature of primary care, it is well placed to meet this challenge,
although new structures of care need to be established in order to support
the process.

In order to optimise patient management in this setting, primary care must:
identify and treat patients with a high global cardiovascular risk according to national
guidelines; achieve target low density lipoprotein cholesterol (LDL-C) goals; develop
systems of care to ensure targets are delivered and long-term compliance is
achieved; develop associated quality assurance via appropriate clinical audit.

The challenge in primary care

It is remarkable how the treatment of lipid disorders has moved in just a
decade from the domain of a few interested secondary-care specialists to
become a mainstream activity for all primary-care professionals. Clearly
this represents an appreciation of the burden of atherosclerotic disease
in society, the realisation of the central, causative role of abnormal lipid
levels and the emergence of incontrovertible evidence of benefit from
lipid-modifying trials.

The burden of cardiovascular disease in the UK is large and is likely to
increase as the population ages. At current rates, nearly half the population
will die from a cardiovascular cause and so the problem impacts on all
healthcare professionals. By virtue of different patterns of ethnicity,
geography (there is a North–South divide) and socioeconomic status,
different practices are exposed to different rates of cardiovascular morbidity
and mortality. Table 1 shows the percentages of the Scottish population, an
area of high risk in the UK, aged 35–64 years, requiring lipid-lowering
treatment for different levels of absolute risk.

> The treatment of
> lipid disorders
> has become
> a mainstream
> activity for all
> primary-care
> professionals.

Table 1. Population burden: patients from a Scottish population, aged 35–64 years, requiring lipid-lowering treatments for different levels of absolute coronary heart disease (CHD) risk. (From Haq *et al.* Heart 2001; **86**: 289–95.)

	10-year CHD risk (%)	Patients requiring lipid-lowering medication (%)
Secondary prevention	–	8.5
Primary prevention	6	32.9
	15	9.7
	20	5.4
	30	1.5

Although trial evidence clearly demonstrates benefit from a level of 6% coronary heart disease (CHD) risk over 10 years, current UK guidelines for primary prevention have, until recently, only endorsed intervention at the 30% 10-year level. The fiscal and workload implications for treatment to the lowest level of the evidence base are enormous and beyond the resources of most societies. Even treating to standards such as the National Service Framework (NSF) for CHD in England places a huge workload on primary care. In a theoretical practice of 10,000 patients, it has been estimated that 2221 'disease control measures' will have to be performed to satisfy the requirements of the NSF for CHD in secondary prevention and high-risk patients at the 30% 10-year risk level. When you consider that a 'disease control measure' such as achieving target blood pressure or cholesterol level might take several consultations, the workload implications are enormous. Despite this challenge, new recommendations identify a lower drug intervention threshold of a 20% 10-year cardiovascular risk (equivalent to a 15% 10-year CHD risk) and the government is set to commit financially to the implications of full implementation.

Despite the public health importance of preventing cardiovascular disease (CVD), there is much evidence for an implementation gap between potential interventions suggested by the evidence base and what happens in practice. European Action on Secondary and Primary Prevention by Intervention to Reduce Events (EUROASPIRE II), a survey of CHD secondary prevention undertaken in 15 European countries between 1999 and 2000, showed that 58% of patients in this high-risk group failed to reach the target for total cholesterol (<5.0 mmol/L). Many practices in the UK have subsequently worked hard at secondary prevention but considerable heterogeneity remains in achievement; it is this inequality that national initiatives are formulated to address. The challenge to primary care is therefore to maximise cardiovascular prevention interventions at a level that is evidence based, pragmatic and affordable, within the direction of a national 'blueprint'.

Lessons from the evidence base

Treating to global cardiovascular risk

During the last decade a series of landmark trials has established the evidence base for lipid-lowering in patients across a spectrum of cardiovascular risk. The early trial designs followed the clinical dichotomy of primary and secondary prevention but gradually the concept of a global cardiovascular risk continuum began to emerge. An individual's cardiovascular risk is determined not by isolated levels of single risk factors but the composite interaction of them all. This was classically illustrated by Haffner's work in Finland, where he showed that the 7-year CHD event rate in type 2 diabetics without prior myocardial infaction (MI) was the equivalent of that in non-diabetic subjects who had already suffered an event. In other words, the risk in a primary-prevention population can be as high as in those patients requiring secondary prevention. It took the findings of the Heart Protection Study (HPS) to confirm that lipid-lowering therapy (in this case with a statin) should be targeted to a patient's global cardiovascular risk. In this study of high-risk individuals, not only did patients with entry cholesterol levels below 5.0 mmol/L (or LDL-C levels below 3.0 or even 2.6 mmol/L) benefit from a statin, but they also benefited to the same degree as patients with higher entry values.

Extending the range of intervention

In addition to the concept of targeting patients according to their level of cardiovascular risk irrespective of their cholesterol, the HPS also confirmed the value of lipid lowering in various patient groups hitherto not covered by the evidence base. Benefits were shown for women, patients over 75 years of age, those with atherosclerotic disease elsewhere (peripheral arterial disease and non-haemorrhagic stroke) and those with diabetes and metabolic syndrome. The findings thus extend the range of patients who will benefit from treatment.

Lowering LDL-C

It is becoming increasingly apparent that the primary goal of lipid-lowering therapy with statins is reduction of LDL-C. Trials that demonstrate sufficient between-group LDL-C reduction show the most positive outcomes. By maintaining an average 0.96 mmol/L difference between the

The primary goal of lipid-lowering therapy with statins is reduction of LDL-C.

study groups in the HPS over 5 years, the outcomes were positive. In contrast, erosion of the LDL-C differential between groups in the lipid-lowering arm of the recently published Antihypertensive and Lipid-Lowering Treatment to Prevent Heart Attack Trial (ALLHAT) meant that it failed to achieve a positive outcome. Analysis of one Greek hospital's CHD secondary prevention activity showed that reducing LDL-C by 46%, by treating to the National Cholesterol Education Program (NCEP) LDL-C target level of less than 2.6 mmol/L, halved the subsequent cardiovascular event rate in just 3 years, compared with usual care. Aggressive LDL-C reduction observed in recent trials such as REVERSAL (Reversal of Atherosclerosis with Aggressive Lipid Lowering), PROVE-IT (Pravastatin or Atorvastatin Evaluation and Infection Therapy) and ALLIANCE (Aggressive Lipid-Lowering Initiation Abates New Cardiac Events) confirms an enhanced clinical benefit at low target levels and underlines the decision of guideline committees to lower lipid targets to new values.

Lifestyle

It must be remembered that all clinical trials using lipid-lowering drugs are performed with patients in whom lifestyle interventions have been addressed. The benefits of optimising weight, stopping smoking, increasing physical activity and eating a healthy diet are manifest. Diet alone often reduces LDL-C by more than 10% (in addition to the reduction achieved by drugs) and probably confers benefit through other mechanisms beyond lipid modification. Using a 'portfolio' of dietary measures (plant sterols, soy protein and viscous fibre) LDL-C has been reported to fall by 29%. Unfortunately, however, lifestyle measures are poorly implemented in practice through lack of expertise, time and conviction.

The atherogenic lipoprotein profile

Many patients with cardiovascular disease do not display obviously elevated LDL-C. The atherogenic lipoprotein phenotype is a term given to the dyslipidaemia characterised by low levels of high density lipoprotein cholesterol (HDL-C), raised triglycerides and a change in LDL-C structure towards a smaller, denser and more atherogenic version of the normal particle. This pattern of dyslipidaemia is often seen in individuals with diabetes, insulin resistance or the metabolic syndrome. With the increasing prevalence of obesity and physical inactivity in our society, metabolic syndrome already has a prevalence of 20–25%, and the future cardiovascular consequences of this are of enormous concern. When triglycerides are raised, statins will effect significant reductions, but they are not very effective in raising HDL-C. As such, additional roles for fibrates and nicotinic acid, particularly in combination with statins, need to be defined by appropriate outcome trials.

Drugs

Treating to global cardiovascular risk means applying the range of cardiovascular prevention interventions appropriate for each individual. Clearly, this means optimising blood pressure and glycaemic control, as well as the lipid profile, and using antiplatelet drugs if appropriate. Prescribing analyses show that most practitioners will use statins.

The growing evidence base for the statins has allowed a more rigorous assessment of their cost-effectiveness; data looking at different CHD risk thresholds are shown in Table 2.

In comparison with many other valued healthcare interventions, the cost-effectiveness of statins is clearly well within the National Institute for Clinical Excellence (NICE) 'benchmark' for cost per life-years gained and this explains the commitment of central government to fund their use. The trials show that, to be effective, statins need to be continued for several years before affecting outcomes; the challenge of ensuring appropriate follow-up and compliance is another task for primary care.

In comparison with many other valued healthcare interventions, the cost-effectiveness of statins is clearly demonstrated.

Meeting the challenges in primary care

Patient identification

Reacting to both best practice and national initiatives, primary-care teams have already begun to identify patients with established CVD for intervention. Most GPs have concentrated on patients with established CHD but this strategy should be extended to include patients with peripheral arterial disease, ischaemic stroke and diabetes, whose absolute risk

Table 2. Implications of targeting statin treatment at four coronary heart disease (CHD) risk levels, showing the number needed to treat (NNT), cost-effectiveness and implications for the UK population. (From Pickin *et al.* Heart 1999; **82**: 325–32.)

	1-year CHD risk level			
	4.5%	3.0%	2.0%	1.5%
NNT (over 5 years)	13	20	30	40
Cost per life-year gained (£)	5100	8200	10,700	12,500
UK adults above threshold (%)	5.1	8.2	15.8	24.7
Annual cost (£ million)	549	885	1712	2673

of a further cardiovascular event is also high. The huge numbers of people requiring primary prevention assessment poses a major challenge to the primary care workload but a pragmatic start would be to offer risk assessment to those patients with metabolic syndrome, hypertension or a family history of premature vascular disease.

Patient assessment

In secondary prevention, the decision to treat is straightforward. Diabetes should be treated as a CHD risk-equivalent. In some cases, life expectancy and comorbidity enter the equation, and this is particularly relevant when assessing the elderly. In primary prevention, the 10-year cardiovascular event risk can be calculated using Framingham-based risk function charts, such as those produced by the Joint British Societies and the British Hypertension Society (BHS). A computerised version of the mathematical function allows more precise calculation. Intervention is recommended at the 20% 10-year CVD threshold (equivalent to 15% 10-year CHD risk). Patients whose 10-year CHD risk is 10–15% remain at increased risk, and because the evidence base suggests treatment benefit, the UK government has recently sanctioned the sale of simvastatin direct to consumers under pharmacist control.

An important feature of the assessment of abnormal lipid levels is to exclude the causes of secondary hyperlipidaemia. Commonly these include obesity, diabetes and excessive alcohol intake. Fasting blood glucose, liver function tests and measurement of thyroid stimulating hormone are useful investigations before initiating treatment.

Developing structured care

The existence of the implementation gap between expectation and reality underlines the failure, in many practices, to develop systematic care pathways for patients needing CVD prevention interventions. The computer is central to the efforts of most successful practices, and appropriate coding, database construction, and the use of templates and call and recall systems all enhance the delivery of care. Much research has focused on the role of the primary-care nurse, and data from the Grampian region in Scotland show significant improvements in the level of interventions and even the death rate at 4.7 years in CHD patients attending nurse-led clinics.

Nurses already have established roles in chronic disease management in asthma and diabetes in primary care. As the aims are so similar, a logical step would be to expand practice diabetes clinics to become CVD prevention clinics. Clearly, extra resources will be needed, but revenue from new contractual arrangements for GPs might facilitate this. Primary-care organisations will coordinate local activities and facilitate integration with secondary-care services. The role of intermediate-care GP 'specialists' is likely to expand.

Lipid targets

The NSF CHD targets suggest that total cholesterol should be reduced to less than 5.0 mmol/L (or by 25%, whichever is greater) and LDL-C to less than 3.0 mmol/L (or by 30%, whichever is greater). Despite their relative simplicity, these targets are still poorly interpreted, to the disadvantage of some patients.

The majority of practitioners aim to achieve the headline total cholesterol target and pay little attention to LDL-C, the concept of percentage reduction or the subtleties of the lipoprotein profile. This approach is likely to be perpetuated by the new General Medical Services (GMS) contract which only rewards total cholesterol achievements.

Until direct LDL-C measurement becomes widely available, LDL-C must be calculated mathematically using the Friedewald equation. As this requires the additional measurement of both HDL-C and triglycerides, the fasting profile is required, with attendant inconvenience to both patient and practice. In addition, many GPs are denied access to full fasting lipid profiles by their laboratories. Nevertheless, as LDL-C is the major lipoprotein involved in atherosclerotic plaque formation, a better predictor of CHD and the major target of statins, it is logical to have this as the major target. Situations exist, particularly in patients with low HDL-C, where target cholesterol may be reached but not target LDL-C. In the US, NCEP guidelines are couched in terms of LDL-C and do not refer to total cholesterol levels.

Percentage reduction was introduced as a concept to ensure satisfactory reductions of total cholesterol and LDL-C in treated patients. The lessons from the trials show us, for example, that treating a patient with an initial cholesterol of 5.1 mmol/L and achieving a result of 4.9 mmol/L is unlikely to produce benefit. For such a patient, the percentage-reduction strategy would be more beneficial and more in keeping with the evidence base. Using percentage reduction in target setting is difficult to audit, however, and is rarely undertaken in primary care.

New recommendations from the Joint British Societies and the BHS identify lower targets for total cholesterol (less than 4.0 mmol/L) and LDL-C (less than 2.0 mmol/L) but retain 5.0 mmol/L and 3.0 mmol/L respectively as audit standards.

With the current fixation on achieving lipid targets, it should be borne in mind that the targets are derived by consensus panels and have little evidence from clinical outcome trials *per se*. Many patients in the clinical trials failed to achieve target levels, yet, presumably, derived benefit from treatment. Prescribers must therefore weigh up the benefit from the specific settings of randomised trials with the extrapolated benefit derived from the relative surrogate of achieving target lipid values.

Strategies to achieve target lipid levels

Most commonly, GPs are choosing a target-based strategy. Although their efficacy varies, statins are all highly effective in reducing total cholesterol and LDL-C. The more potent statins reduce cholesterol more and therefore more patients reach target concentrations at starter doses. Many GPs prefer the ease of this approach over dose titration, which may involve more patient visits.

Whatever strategy is chosen, all practitioners will encounter patients in whom target lipid levels are not being achieved. Possible solutions include:

- checking compliance
- checking dietary adherence
- titrating statin (each dose-doubling reduces LDL-C by 6%)
- switching statin
- adding a plant sterol or stanol product to the diet
- adding a cholesterol absorption inhibitor
- combination therapy (usually ezetimibe, sometimes a fibrate or nicotinic acid)
- referral to a lipid specialist.

Quality assurance

The importance and ease of clinical audit of cholesterol measurements make them ideal quality indicators within the new contractual frameworks for primary care. In the secondary prevention of CHD, seven quality points are available for ensuring that 90% of CHD patients have a cholesterol recording over the preceding 15 months, and 19 quality points are available if 60% achieve the total cholesterol target of 5.0 mmol/L or below over the same time period. The same standards and time frames apply to cerebrovascular disease and diabetes, with two and three points available, respectively, for measurement, and five and six points, respectively, for target achievement.

Primary healthcare professionals need to develop appropriately structured care to facilitate easy recording of data, and built-in audits can update automatically when chronologically programmed to ensure that the quality standards are met.

Key points

- The scale of CVD in the UK means that tackling it is a primary care problem.

- Although new structures of care need to be developed, primary care, with its holistic and multidisciplinary approach, is well placed to meet the challenge.

- In essence, primary care needs to:

  - identify and treat patients at high global CVD risk in accordance with national initiatives

  - achieve target lipid levels, preferably LDL-C based

  - develop systems of care to ensure target delivery and foster long-term compliance

  - develop associated quality assurance.

23. Migraine

Dr Kevin Gruffydd-Jones MA MRCGP DRCOG Dip Sports Med Dip Occ Health
General Practitioner, Box, Wiltshire
Honorary Lecturer, University of Bath and University of Aberdeen

Summary

Despite the huge impact of migraine on quality of life, only half of sufferers consult their GP about it. This is partly due to a perception that their condition will not be taken seriously and a belief that there are no effective treatments available to them. The formulation of a patient management plan can assist doctors in the diagnosis and management of migraine. The key steps of such a strategy are to establish an accurate diagnosis and to educate patients about the underlying causes and treatment options for migraine. It is also important to individualise therapy and to continually review and adjust treatment. Much can be done to alleviate the symptoms of migraine or prevent the onset of individual attacks. Avoidance of trigger factors and non-pharmacological therapies, such as acupuncture, can complement acute and chronic pharmacotherapy.

Introduction

Migraine is a debilitating condition affecting approximately 6% of men and 15% of women in the UK, and is most prevalent among the 16–45 year age group. This impact upon individuals in their most productive years, leads to a heavy burden on the economy, with an estimated 18 million working days lost each year due to migraine. The effect on the quality of life of the individual is also devastating. Many patients with migraine fear the effects of the attack itself, and also avoid everyday situations that might trigger off an attack. This can have a profound effect on the sufferer's social life with significant disruption in normal relationships and possibly even marriage breakdowns.

In spite of this huge impact upon quality of life, only 50% of patients with migraine consult their GP. This may be due to low expectations about receiving a sympathetic reception from their GP coupled with low expectations about receiving effective treatment. Some typical comments overheard from patients at self-help group meetings include: "My doctor

Many patients with migraine fear the effects of the attack itself, and also avoid everyday situations that might trigger off an attack.

won't want to be bothered with just a headache" or "I wish that I did have a brain tumour then something could be done!"

This article aims to help the busy GP deal sympathetically and effectively with patients with migraine they see in primary care. Much of the advice is derived from guidelines drawn up by The Migraine in Primary Care Advisors (MIPCA). Readers are referred to the website *www.mipca.org.uk/guidelineword.html* for further information.

Patient management plan

An overall management plan for migraine is outlined in Table 1. However, many hard-pressed GPs will quite rightly point out that such a strategy would be impossible to carry out in a single, 10 minute consultation. However the suggested steps can be carried out over a series of appointments and will lead to an improvement in diagnosis and treatment.

Diagnosis

The diagnosis of migraine is largely based on a characteristic patient history, but also on the presence of a negative physical examination. This reassures the patient that the GP or nurse practitioner has taken their situation seriously and boosts the patient's confidence in the subsequent management plan. In addition it provides added reassurance to the examiner that the diagnosis is correct. For example, I have had the surprising experience in finding papilloedema in a patient with "barn door" migraine! In fact, the patient had benign intracranial hypertension.

The characteristic features of migraine headaches are outlined in Table 2, and are derived from the International Headache Society criteria for migraine. Most commonly, our patients will tell us that they are

> The diagnosis of migraine is largely based on a characteristic patient history, but also on the presence of a negative physical examination.

Table 1. Overall primary care management plan for migraine.
1. Establish diagnosis
2. Explanation and education
3. Assess the pattern and impact of the individual's migraine
4. Devise an individual management plan incorporating:
– control of trigger factors
– complementary management
– acute pharmacological treatment
– chronic pharmacological treatment
5. Review and adjust treatment

> **Table 2.** Diagnostic features of migraine headache.
>
> ---
>
> - Duration (when untreated): 4–72 hours[a]
> - Symptom free between attacks
> - Headache is moderate-to-severe in intensity, aggravated by and causing disruption to routine activities
> - Usually unilateral and throbbing in nature
> - Associated symptoms of nausea/vomiting, photophobia and phonophobia (fear of loud sound)
>
> ---
>
> [a]Duration may be shorter in children.

experiencing "sickly headaches which come and go (completely) and make you want to lie down."

Only about 10–15% of patients experience 'classic' migraine (i.e. migraine with aura). Aura manifestations can be divided into:

- positive phenomena (e.g. enhanced visual images such as zig-zag lights, bright patterns and/or colours)
- negative phenomena (e.g. temporary loss of field of vision, loss of sensation or hemiplegia).

Typically, the aura lasts no more than 60 minutes and the headache usually occurs within 60 minutes of the end of the aura phase. Diagnostic confusion can arise in the relatively rare situation where aura occurs without the headache. In this case, secondary care specialist advice should be sought. Referral to a specialist headache clinic or to a neurologist should also be considered if any of the following 'red flag' symptoms occur:

- first headache occurring in patients over 40 years of age
- severe headache which differs from usual pattern
- persistent or progressive associated symptoms
- neurological symptoms
- headache on awakening, particularly in children (this also occurs in cervical spondylosis).

In practice, the differential diagnosis of headache is usually between tension-type and chronic daily headaches. In the former, the headache tends to be bilateral, 'pressing' or 'band-like' in quality, does not tend to disturb daily activities and occurs without nausea and vomiting. Chronic-daily headache is a common, but under-diagnosed form of headache in primary care. Patients have frequent headaches (typically more than 15 days per month) which are a mixture of migraine-like (unilateral and throbbing) and tension-type (bilateral and pressure) headaches.

The condition is often found in migraine sufferers who have a high, but unsuccessful, exposure to analgesics, particularly opiate-based agents. Treatment in such cases can be difficult and usually consists of:

- gradual withdrawal of over-used analgesic
- the use of amitriptyline regularly at night
- patient counselling
- effective migraine control using triptans.

One other rarer condition of note is cluster headache. Currently, this is not thought of as a migraine variant, but rather a distinct disease entity. Characteristically, sufferers are male and middle aged. The primary experience is of excruciating clusters of unilateral headaches which last between 15 and 180 minutes and are associated with watering eyes and a blocked nose. Acute treatment can be given with subcutaneous sumatriptan or portable oxygen, whilst chronic treatment is usually with serotonin antagonists or sodium valproate.

Patient education

Many patients are often concerned that their headache may be the symptom of an underlying, more sinister condition. An explanation about the condition may relieve the stress of uncertainty, which, paradoxically, may be fuelling the headache. In this respect, it is very important to ask if the patient has any particular concerns about their symptoms. In addition to a simple explanation about the nature of migraine it is useful to outline the management plan (Table 1), in order to pre-empt any false perceptions of a 'quick fix' solution to their problem. The Migraine Action Association, a patient self-help group, offers excellent advice and support for migraine sufferers. Patients can be directed to their web-site at *www.migraine.org.uk*.

Establishing the pattern and impact of migraine

It is of critical importance to emphasise that migraine is not simply a headache. A migraine attack starts with a prodromal phase where the patient is aware of 'something about to happen'. Some 10–15% of patients experience an aura, which is followed by the headache phase and then periods of resolution and recovery. At best, the whole process can last several hours, minimally disrupting activities. At worst, the sufferer may be confined to bed for several days, incapacitated by severe headache, vomiting and exhaustion. However, an individual sufferer may experience different severities of attack at different times. The completion of a headache diary by the patient is a useful tool and can provide a lot of vital information to the doctor/nurse, including:

At worst, the sufferer may be confined to bed for several days, incapacitated by severe headache, vomiting and exhaustion.

- frequency and duration of attacks
- associated symptoms (e.g. nausea) and aura
- impact of a migraine attack (e.g. days lost due to illness,
- impact on social activities)
- possible trigger factors
- medication taken.

A more formal assessment of the impact of migraine upon a patient's life can be carried out using a simple, paper-based questionnaire prior to the patient being seen in the surgery. The Migraine Disability Assessment (MIDAS; which can be found at *www.migraine-disability.net*) uses five disability questions, and classifies patients into four disability grades ranging from minimal to severe disability.

Devise an individualised treatment plan

On the basis of information gleaned from the headache diary and from the disability score (if the MIDAS is administered), an individualised treatment plan can be devised in conjunction with the patient, according to the pattern of migraine and also to the patient's treatment preferences. It should be emphasised to the patient that migraine cannot be cured, as many patients have unrealistic treatment aims and become disillusioned when these aims are not met. However, migraine can be effectively controlled. Several treatment regimens may have to be tried before the right one is found which is suitable for the individual concerned. In addition, the treatment regimen may need to be altered according to the nature of the attack. For example, the majority of a patient's attacks may be treated with an oral triptan, but occasionally the same patient may experience a severe attack with associated vomiting, for which a subcutaneous or intranasal preparation of the drug may be required.

The different elements of an effective treatment plan are outlined below.

> An individualised treatment plan can be devised in conjunction with the patient, according to the pattern of migraine and also to the patient's treatment preferences.

Control of trigger factors

Many patients focus on the avoidance of trigger factors and, in particular, the avoidance of certain foodstuffs as the cornerstone in their management of the condition. However, in reality only 10–20% of migraine attacks are triggered by food, and there is only limited evidence indicating that their avoidance helps control migraine attacks. In addition, the avoidance of certain trigger factors can actually be worse than the disease itself, as avoidance of certain situations where they might be exposed to potential trigger factors can profoundly and negatively impact upon their entire lives. Nevertheless, many patients do have identifiable trigger factors and minimising exposure to them whilst maintaining as normal a life as possible seems a sensible aim. Common trigger factors are presented in Table 3. However, usually there is combination of multiple trigger factors in any one individual and, therefore, an adjustment of lifestyle is usually more practical than complete avoidance of all triggers.

Although between 60 and 80% of women have migraine associated with menstruation, only 10% of women have 'true' menstrual migraine, that is migraine which only occurs within 2–3 days of menstruation. Such patients are often helped by the use of a matrix oestrogen patch from day −3 to day 4 after menstruation.

Correction of neck problems by chiropractic treatment and correction of dental malocclusion can be particularly helpful for appropriate patients.

Complementary therapies

Many patients will have tried complementary therapies before going to their GP. Some therapies such as chiropractic, stress management, biofeedback and acupuncture have proven efficacy. Preparations including feverfew, a garden herb, have been shown to reduce the frequency of attacks in some patients. However, the amount of active ingredient can vary significantly between the various commercial preparations. The Migraine Action Association (*www.migraine.org.uk*) provides a useful leaflet on feverfew. In general, about 40% of patients will have experienced some reduction in the number and severity of attacks with these therapies. However, the evidence for the efficacy of other complementary therapies such as homeopathy and aromatherapy remains less convincing.

Table 3. Trigger factors in migraine attacks.

Foods	Chocolate, dairy products, citrus fruits, red wine, caffeine, monosodium glutamate
Lack of fluid or food	
Neck and jaw problems	Cervical hypomobility, dental malocclusion
Stress or relaxation following stress	A long sleep may be sufficient to provoke an attack
Physical activity	
Environmental factors	Heat, cold, wind, odours
Hormonal factors	Menstrually related or from the oral contraceptive pill

Acute pharmacotherapy

The goal of acute therapy should be to provide rapid and effective relief from headache and any associated migraine symptoms, thereby allowing the patient to resume their normal activities as quickly as possible. The majority of clinical trials look at the therapeutic response at 2 hours post-dosing.

The choice of treatment is dependent on a number of factors including:

- the pattern and impact of attacks (i.e. an oral preparation may be more appropriate for a mild attack whilst a subcutaneous injection or intranasal preparation may be necessary for a severe attack)
- the use of any previous treatments (many patients will have already tried simple over-the-counter analgesics and anti-emetics)
- side-effects and possible interactions with other drugs
- cost (whilst direct costs of a triptan can be relatively high, their success in treating attacks means that general usage is low and, as a consequence, for many practices they do not rank among the high-spend drugs on the quarterly prescription-pricing authority [PPA] statement).

The currently available pharmacological options in the UK for the treatment of migraine attacks are shown in Table 4.

Chronic pharmacotherapy

The decision to start regular prophylactic therapy should be made as a joint decision with the patient. Again, it is important to reiterate to the patient

Table 4. Currently available drug classes in the UK for the treatment of migraine attacks.

Simple analgesics/NSAID (e.g. tolfenamic acid)	Aspirin monotherapy is more effective than paracetamol. Injectable diclofenac is also useful in severe attacks.
Compound analgesics (e.g. co-codamol, Migraleve)	Little evidence for efficacy in large randomised clinical trials. Associated with the development of chronic daily headache.
Analgesic/anti-emetic combinations (e.g. aspirin/metoclopramide and	Caution necessary with aspirin side-effects and other contraindications (e.g. history of asthma and ulcer) paracetamol/domperidone.
Ergotamine preparations	Unpredictable efficacy in combination with undesirable side-effects. Now largely superseded by the triptans.
Triptans Sumatriptan (oral, intranasal, injectable) Naratritan (oral) Zolmitriptan(oral, intranasal) Rizatriptan(oral) Almotriptan (oral) Eletriptan (oral) Frovatriptan (oral)	Proven efficacy with a low incidence of side-effects. However, triptans are contraindicated in ischaemic heart disease, unstable angina, unrecognised cardiac disease and uncontrolled hypertension.

The decision to start regular prophylactic therapy should be made as a joint decision with the patient.

that migraine cannot be cured and that, in general, 50% of patients will have a 50% reduction in migraine attacks with regular therapy.

Prophylaxis should be considered when the patient experiences frequent attacks (four or more attacks per month), high impact attacks or when the patient experiences significant disability despite acute therapy. Set against this backdrop, potential side-effects of regular therapy must also be discussed with the patient. Table 5 outlines the chronic pharmacological options that are currently available to us in primary care.

Review of treatment

After treatment has been initiated, it should be reviewed again after 1 month and changed if there has been no obvious beneficial response. If the patient remains stable, treatment should then be reviewed every 6 months. The pattern of migraine can change over time, possibly necessitating an alteration in the treatment regimen. In particular, prophylactic treatment may be stepped down, rather than stopped abruptly to avoid precipitating an attack, and then stopped.

Table 5. Prophylactic migraine pharmacotherapeutic options.

β-blockers (e.g. propranolol, metoprolol, timolol, nadolol)	Contraindicated in asthma, whilst use may be limited by the side-effects of lethargy and cold peripheries.
Serotonin antagonists (e.g. pizotifen, methysergide)	Titrate the dose slowly upwards over 1 month to minimise drowsiness. May also cause unacceptable weight gain. Methysergide is very effective but is associated with high risk side-effects and therefore should be initiated in hospital.
Antidepressants (e.g Amitriptyline,[a] 25 mg at night)	Associated with anti-cholinergic side-effects
Anti-convulsants (e.g. sodium valproate,[a] 200 mg twice daily)	Used at lower doses than for epilepsy, but dose should be titrate upwards slowly to minimise side-effects of drowsiness, weight gain.
Anti-hypertensives (e.g. clonidine, 25 mg)	Used at lower dose than for hypertension. Caution when used with other anti-hypertensives.

[a]Not licensed for migraine in UK

Referral to neurological specialists in secondary care should take place if:
- there are doubts over the diagnosis, particularly in the presence of the 'red flag' symptoms discussed previously
- there is no response to treatment
- there is an increase in attack severity without obvious cause.

Organisation of care

Unfortunately and unjustifiably, migraine remains low on the government's priority list despite the huge social impact of the condition at both individual and society level. Hence, there are limited resources to formally structure care for migraine in clinical practice. However, at the very least practices should aim to keep a register of patients with migraine and aim to review them every 6 months. Enthusiastic practices have enlisted the help of practice nurses and local pharmacists in migraine management with a great deal of success. There is also scope for developing Primary Care Trust (PCT)-wide headache clinics by GPs with a special interest in the area. However, migraine is still something of a 'cinderella' disease in primary care, but with the aid of a sympathetic ear, realistic expectations and effective therapy tailored to the individual, much more can now be done to alleviate the distress caused by this debilitating condition.

Conclusion

There is a continuing perception among patients with migraine that their condition will not be taken seriously by their GP and that there is very little in the way of effective treatment on offer if it is. However, the introduction of new pharmacological agents, particularly the triptans, and the publication of evidence-based guidelines on the management of migraine empowers GPs to improve the quality of life in those patients. The construction of a patient management plan that focuses on accurate and rapid diagnosis, patient education and tailored treatment forms the basis for an efficient and effective strategy for the management of migraine.

Key points

- Migraine is a condition that needs to be taken seriously in primary care, not least because of its huge impact on quality of life.

- Many patients have very low expectations with regard to migraine treatment and the response they face when they bring their condition to the attention of their GP. As such, only half of patients with migraine actually consult their GP.

- Establishing an accurate diagnosis and offering appropriate education about the causes of migraine and the treatment options available should form the key components of a patient management plan. Such plans should be individualised, regularly reviewed and adjusted accordingly.

- There are a number of characteristic features of migraine which can help when diagnosing the condition in primary care. Differentiating migraine from tension-type and chronic daily headaches is the most common diagnostic challenge in primary care. In certain cases, it will be necessary to refer the patient to a specialist headache clinic.

- Non-pharmacological approaches to the management of migraine include avoidance of migraine triggers and complementary therapies such as acupuncture.

- Pharmacotherapy can be used either to provide rapid relief of the migraine symptoms (acute treatment) or to reduce or prevent attacks in individuals with frequent or high impact attacks (chronic treatment). Treatment should be reviewed regularly as part of the management plan.

- Primary care practices should try to keep a register of migraine patients with the aim of recalling and reviewing these individuals every 6 months. Establishing headache clinics at a PCT level will also serve to improve the management of this debilitating condition.

24. Obesity

Dr Ian Campbell MBChB, MRCGP, DRCOG, DLORCS
General Practitioner, Nottingham
Associate Specialist, University Hospital
Nottingham Chair, National Obesity Forum

Summary

Obesity is a major and growing clinical problem, particularly in the western world, with the condition reaching epidemic proportions in the UK. This has profound consequences for our health service, the economy and indeed the social fabric of our society. However, a number of initiatives have been established which aim to tackle the problem of obesity directly. Much of the clinical burden of the condition falls upon the entire primary healthcare team to manage. One way in which the management of obesity can be improved is through the establishment of regular obesity clinics. However, this demands appropriate resources and also the effective identification of patients who are eligible for intervention. Lifestyle modifications including dietary changes and the introduction of regular exercise are widely acknowledged as the starting point for intervention. Even modest reductions in weight loss can serve to improve patients' quality of life, promote motivation and therefore improve long-term outcome. Good doctor–patient communication can assist in this motivation. When lifestyle changes fail to achieve weight loss of sufficient magnitude, adjunctive drug therapy is at our disposal to manage the condition further.

The need for obesity management

Obesity is described by the World Health Organization (WHO) as one of the fastest growing epidemics in the western world, and is associated with a number of clinical, economic and social repercussions. Conservative estimates suggest that the cost to the NHS of dealing with the consequences of obesity alone is in the order of £0.5 billion per annum. When indirect costs are taken into account, obesity is estimated to contribute a total economic burden of around £2.6 billion per annum. In addition, an estimated 30,000 deaths are directly attributed to the condition each year. Obesity is also one of the primary causes of a number of potentially fatal conditions including coronary heart disease (CHD),

Obesity is one of the fastest growing epidemics in the western world, and is associated with a number of clinical, economic and social repercussions.

congestive heart failure, hypertension, type 2 diabetes, depression and some cancers (including cancers of the colon, rectum, prostate, breast, ovaries, stomach and oesophagus).

This sobering evidence has prompted the NHS to develop a number of obesity-related targets and measures. For example, obesity has been implicated in the Planning and Priorities framework for Primary Care Trusts (PCTs) 2003–2006, the National Service Frameworks (NSFs) for CHD and diabetes, the new General Medical Services (GMS) contract and, most recently, the Chief Medical Officer's 2003 Report.

This should leave GPs in no doubt that obesity is being seriously targeted as a Government health priority, and it is therefore of considerable benefit for Primary Care Organisations (PCOs) to develop and implement weight management and nutrition policies as part of their overall approach to achieving these Department of Health-led goals and targets.

> Obesity is being seriously targeted as a Government health priority.

Overcoming practice scepticism

Many people, including medical professionals, believe that obesity does not warrant serious medical help, not least because of the negative way obese people are perceived. Some practice stakeholders may therefore need some convincing about the merits of establishing an obesity clinic. However, the evidence of the resultant improvements in comorbid disease management and prevention is clinically and economically overwhelming, and this should help to dispel any remaining doubts about the need for prompt action.

Some stakeholders may also be sceptical about the possible cost-effectiveness benefit of obesity management, especially for those patients on adjunctive drug treatment. However, recent National Institute of Clinical Excellence (NICE) guidance on the use of anti-obesity agents, such as orlistat and sibutramine, clearly outlines which patients are suitable for drug treatment, and can therefore help GPs to achieve better weight-management results, with fewer comorbid complications.

Practical primary-care management

Patient identification

The first step towards implementing a proactive weight-management programme is to identify those patients for whom intervention is appropriate.

When identifying a patient with obesity, it is essential to consider other risk/contributory factors. Many obese patients (body mass index [BMI] ≥ 30 kg/m^2) will be presenting regularly to the surgery with other conditions such as type 2 diabetes and hypertension. One favoured option is to approach these patients actively during routine chronic disease monitoring appointments with a view to recruiting them for weight management support and treatment. In my experience the majority of patients will welcome your direct approach. Many obese people genuinely want to lose weight but are at a loss as where to start. This is exemplified by the plethora of dietary information available, which can often be confusing and even conflicting. Your professional intervention may help to reassure the patient that weight loss is realistic and attainable.

An alternative approach is to audit patients with a recorded BMI of at least 30 kg/m², in the absence of comorbid disease, but perhaps with a significant family history or other risk factors for comorbid disease development. A third approach, of course, is to welcome self-referral of already concerned and motivated patients.

Patient types

There are a number of specific types of patients with obesity who should be targeted for weight management.

- **Type one**. This is the 'I want to lose weight' patient. They want to take responsibility for their weight and recognise that weight loss is something they need to address because of the negative effects on their long-term health. They are realistic in their targets and recognise that there are no easy ways to succeed. However, despite this, they may have already undergone previously unsuccessful weight loss attempts and will therefore require careful monitoring.
- **Type two**. This is the 'I must lose weight' patient. They will usually present with a comorbid complication such as type 2 diabetes, and will be aware of the immediate risks of their excessive weight. It is important to them that they succeed.
- **Type three**. This is the 'I'm desperate to lose weight' patient. They tend to be pre-occupied with their weight and will go to any lengths to lose excess weight. They are determined to succeed.

Diagnosis

After taking an appropriate history, a number of general investigations and biochemical tests are appropriate. The results will confirm any underlying comorbidity, serve as a baseline with which to assess future progress and may also serve to reassure the patient that they are theoretically able to lose weight. Such investigations should include:

- height
- weight

- BMI
- waist circumference
- blood pressure
- urinalysis
- full blood count
- thyroid function
- liver function
- lipid profile
- fasting blood sugar.

A BMI of 25 kg/m^2 or greater indicates that a patient is overweight whilst a BMI of 30 kg/m^2 or more is representative of clinical obesity. Similarly, a waist circumference of over 102 cm for men and 88 cm for women equates to the same risk ratio as a BMI of 30 kg/m^2 and indicates a potentially serious health risk.

Patient management

The good news is that even modest weight reduction can improve a patient's quality of life and increase their life expectancy. For example, a 10% loss in weight reduces the likelihood of an obesity-related death by 20%. It may also lead to a 10 mmHg fall in diastolic blood pressure, a 50% reduction in fasting blood glucose levels, a 10% drop in total cholesterol (and a corresponding 8% increase in high density lipoprotein cholesterol [HDL-C]) and a 30% reduction in triglycerides.

Lifestyle modification

The first-line treatment of obesity comprises affirmation of support, with diet and lifestyle advice, coupled with behavioural therapy. A useful target for projected weight loss is 10% over a 3–6 month period, often followed by a period of weight stability, and then, if appropriate, continuation of weight loss with a further 5–10% reduction thereafter. Weight loss rates of 0.5–1 kg/week are usually appropriate and achievable and require an average reduction in calorific intake of 500–600 kcal/day, incorporation of a healthy low-fat diet and 30 minutes of brisk exercise at least five-times weekly.

Many obese patients have a diet that contains an excess of energy but is nutritionally deficient (i.e. low levels of vitamins, micronutrients or fibre). Therefore, it is important that any dietary recommendations facilitate a balanced diet and are not just hypocalorific. A simple solution is for patients to increase their fruit and vegetable intake, and/or increase the proportion of energy derived from complex carbohydrates.

> A waist circumference of over 102 cm for men and 88 cm for women equates to the same risk ratio as a BMI of 30 kg/m^2 and indicates a potentially serious health risk.

> A simple solution is for patients to increase their fruit and vegetable intake, and/or increase the proportion of energy derived from complex carbohydrates.

In primary care, straightforward simple advice delivered by a motivated and informed doctor or nurse is usually appropriate. If necessary, referral to a practice or community-based dietician, where available, can also prove invaluable. However, if such a resource is unavailable, patients can often gain added support and advice from using a reputable local weight loss group.

As discussed previously, patients should be encouraged to increase their daily exercise regimens, and aim for 30–40 minutes of additional activity five days per week. Brisk walking, cycling and swimming are effective 'fat-burning' activities. Local exercise programmes can also be useful. In addition to its effects on promoting weight loss, regular exercise has been shown to reduce insulin resistance, lower blood pressure, reduce low density lipoprotein cholesterol (LDL-C) and triglycerides and increase HDL-C levels.

Modifying eating behaviour is an important part of weight management, and changing eating habits and increasing activity levels will work together to provide improved prospects for long-term weight maintenance. Initial primary-care behavioural therapy should focus on sensible eating advice, such as:

- shop for food after eating a meal (i.e. when you are not hungry)
- store healthy foods where you can see them
- use smaller plates and utensils
- eat smaller portions of food
- stop eating when you feel full
- eat more slowly
- chew food thoroughly before swallowing.

However, it is vital to remember that helping patients change long-established eating behaviour requires empathy and specialised counselling skills, and patients must be encouraged to explore and analyse their own behaviour, whilst making appropriate, gradual and sustainable changes.

It is vital to remember that helping patients change long-established eating behaviour requires empathy and specialised counselling skills.

Adjunctive drug treatment

For a number of patients, diet, exercise and behavioural therapy will not be sufficient, and adjunctive therapy may be required. In these cases, two drugs are commonly used, which have been shown to be effective in the long-term treatment of obesity – sibutramine and orlistat. Adjunctive treatment with these agents should be considered:

- after 2–6 months of compliance to dietary, behavioural and activity advice without an appropriate response
- after failure to achieve 10% weight loss

- to achieve further reduction in symptoms
- to improve markers of comorbidity and to improve control of comorbid disease (e.g. blood glucose)
- to improve exercise tolerance
- in cases of weight-related psychological disturbance
- to assist in weight maintenance.

The doctor can provide invaluable support to the patient, and whilst monitoring weight loss response, can reinforce the lifestyle changes as discussed above. Sibutramine may be best suited to a patient who has difficulty in controlling portion size, or who is unable to adapt to a low-fat diet and who has been unable to demonstrate a 5% body weight loss by lifestyle change alone. Orlistat may be preferred by patients who have adopted a low-fat diet, but who need support to maintain those dietary changes and who have managed to demonstrate weight loss of at least 2.5 kg in a preceding month. With sibutramine, blood pressure and pulse need to be monitored every 2 weeks for the first 3 months, monthly for 3 months and once every 3 months thereafter. Current licensing arrangements allow for 12 months' continuous treatment with sibutramine and up to 24 months with orlistat.

An example of a clinical management algorithm involving both lifestyle modification and adjunctive pharmacological intervention is shown in Figure 1.

Establishing and running an obesity clinic

All patients with a BMI of at least 30 kg/m^2 (or a BMI >27 kg/m^2 with comorbidities [e.g. hypertension, type 2 diabetes, dyslipidaemia or CHD]) should be considered for enrolment into an obesity clinic. However, it is essential that each patient is highly motivated (or can be motivated by your intervention/support) to lose weight.

During an initial presentation, GPs should offer a partnership between themselves and the patients, and should encourage them to attend the clinic for at least 1 year. Achievable goals also need to be established during the first appointment. Many patients have unrealistic expectations of weight loss, and it is vital to stress that even modest weight losses, followed by periods of weight maintenance, can have profound health benefits. All weight loss targets should be staggered, to help monitor gradual progress (e.g. 0.5–1 kg/week on average, with a total of 5–10% weight loss over 6 months).

It is important that all practice-team members are available for ongoing support and follow-up, as patient motivation and compliance is bound to

Figure 1. Clinical management of patients with obesity involving lifestyle modification and adjunctive drug treatment. Adapted from the National Obesity Forum Guidelines. *http://www.nationalobesityforum.org.uk*

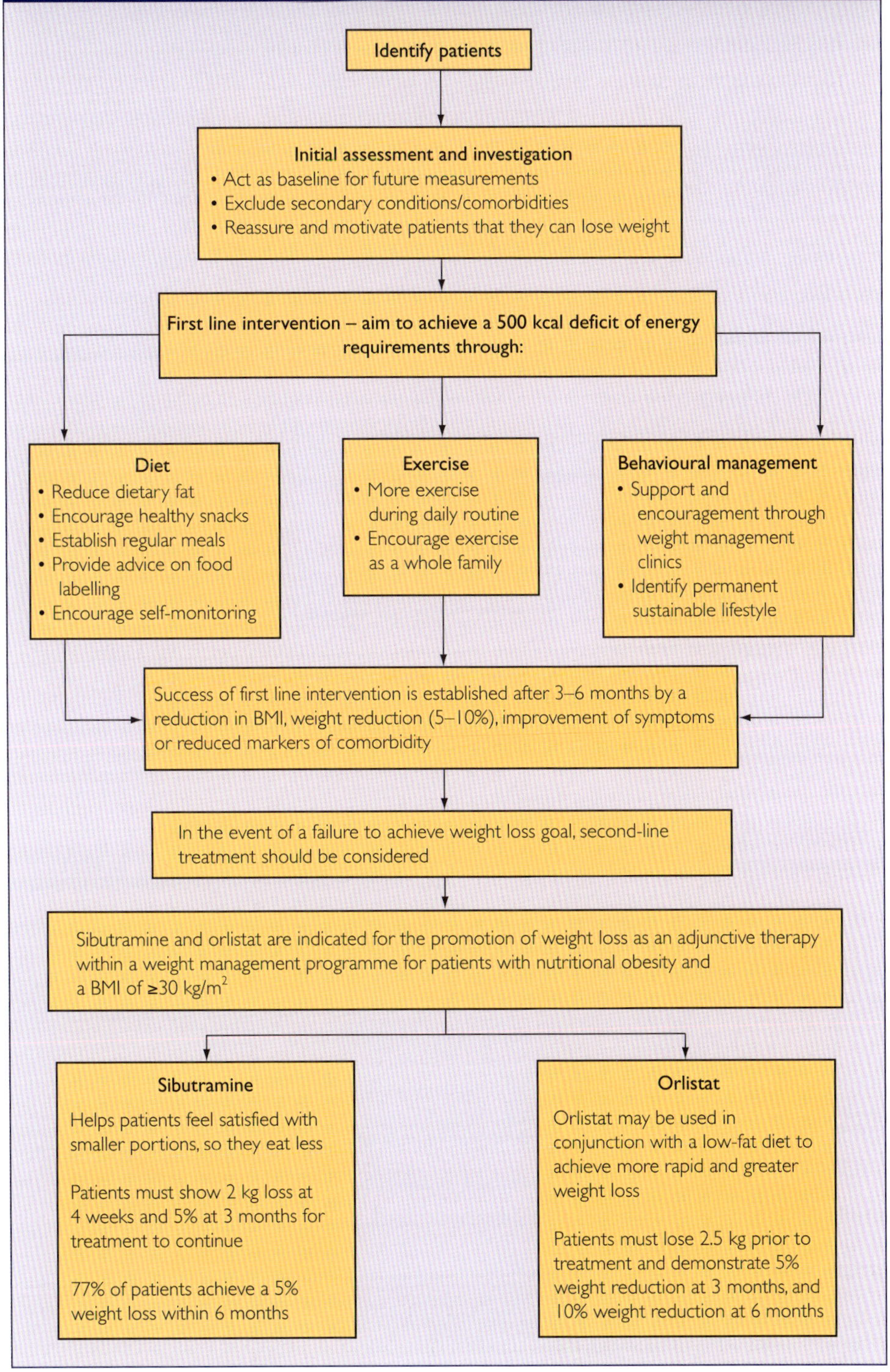

wane from time to time. Appointments to the clinic should be on a monthly basis as a minimum and at each visit the patient should foremost receive encouragement, and a review of progress to date offered. Their new weight can be discussed and food and activity diaries reviewed, to encourage patients to make changes to their diets and lifestyle.

Healthy eating advice should also be provided, and the merits of regular eating patterns, low fat and smaller meal portions and set exercise regimens should be discussed. All recommended changes must be realistic and achievable. As the patient–physician relationship builds, the patient may feel able to discuss obesity-related social problems, and/or any environmental weight-loss barriers. Improvements in communication provide the GP with an opportunity to introduce discussion on some of the following to aid the weight-reduction process:

- hunger scores
- alcohol consumption
- coping with cravings/resisting temptation
- detailed discussions about balanced diets
- food label interpretation.

It should be emphasised that all sustained weight loss, however small, should be recognised by the healthcare professional and the patient congratulated accordingly.

Throughout the course of treatment, and perhaps over a series of consultations in the obesity clinic, patients should be advised to:

- think about the main reasons why they have become overweight
- think about how losing weight will improve their health and quality of life
- monitor food intake by a 1-week food diary (when, what and why?)
- record all physical activity
- reduce fat and sugar content
- increase fruit and vegetable consumption
- reduce portion size
- develop ideas of how to increase physical activity
- reduce alcohol intake
- review their progress to date.

At each appointment the patient's weight should be checked, along with their blood pressure, waist measurement and pre-existing comorbid disease should be regularly monitored.

It is important to stress the long-term benefits of weight loss, and the need for long-term habit change throughout the programme.

An obesity case study

A 56-year-old, unemployed, married man, presented to the surgery complaining of fatigue and polyuria. He was visibly overweight, and his recent medical history revealed that his weight had increased from 83 kg to 105 kg within the last two years.

Initial investigations revealed the following:

- weight 105 kg
- height 182 cm
- BMI 33 kg/m^2
- waist circumference 115 cm
- blood pressure 138/92 mm/Hg
- fasting blood glucose 7.5 mmol/L
- triglycerides 2.2 mmol/L
- existing medication (venlafaxine, 150 mg, omeprazole 10 mg, salbutamol and beclomethasone inhalers).

The patient was diagnosed with co-existing type 2 diabetes, dyslipidaemia, and obesity (i.e. the principal presentation of the metabolic syndrome). The doctor and patient agreed that weight loss was a priority, and consequently the patient was advised about the necessary dietary and lifestyle changes. He agreed to partake in 30 minutes of additional exercise, four times per week, and to decrease his calorific intake by 600 kcal. The practice nurse offered support and encouragement throughout the treatment process.

His fasting glucose levels and blood pressure were monitored at fortnightly intervals, and after two months of this diet and exercise regimen, the following results were observed:

- weight 101 kg
- waist circumference 111 cm
- blood pressure 136/90 mmHg
- fasting blood glucose 7.2 mmol/L
- HbA$_{1C}$ 7.9%.

Nutritional analysis revealed that the patient was still eating a high-fat diet, was still tempted to eat large portions of food, and was still prone to snacking between meals. The patient also admitted that his size was affecting his social confidence, and that he believed his excess weight had been a factor in his failure to find full-time employment. He displayed a real willingness to lose his excess weight, and both the doctor and patient agreed that the best course of action would be to continue with his weight loss programme.

He continued with his diet and exercise routine, but was also prescribed adjunctive drug treatment and advised to use a patient support programme available for patients prescribed pharmacotherapy. Steady weight loss was observed, and during each consultation, the patient revealed that he was not as tempted as before to eat large portions of food or snack between meals. Twelve months after his initial consultation, his results were:

- weight 91 kg (14% weight loss)
- waist circumference 98 cm (16 cm reduction)
- BMI 27 kg/m^2
- blood pressure 130/82 mmHg
- fasting blood glucose 6.6 mmol/L
- HbA_{1C} 6.7%
- triglycerides 1.7 mmol/L.

The patient reported increased mobility, and his breathing felt easier. He has continued with his lifestyle-change programme, and further successes are expected in the future.

Conclusions

There is growing evidence to suggest that the primary-care team is best placed to provide weight management. Achieving a target weight loss of 5–10% will substantially reduce obesity-related health risks and have positive effects on patients' quality of life and self-esteem.

A dedicated weight management clinic can help to maintain patient motivation and compliance, whilst addressing any potential weight-loss barriers along the way. However, all weight-reduction targets should be realistic and possible for patients to achieve success.

Key points

- Obesity has now reached epidemic proportions in many parts of the western world and, as such, has major clinical, economic and social repercussions.

- Consequently, obesity is being targeted as a major health priority in the UK, through a variety of initiatives such as the NSFs for CHD and diabetes and through the new GMS contract for GPs.

- Management of the condition demands that sceptism amongst healthcare professionals about the perceived importance of obesity is tackled promptly.

- Weight management programmes can be effectively implemented in primary care, particularly via the establishment of regular obesity clinics.

- A critical element in patient management is effective identification of patients requiring appropriate intervention, something that can often be done through regular monitoring appointments for those with chronic comorbid disorders.

- Initial management should involve taking a history, and appropriate physical and biochemical investigations.

- Patients with obesity should receive reassurance and support from their doctor that they are able to lose weight, and that even modest reductions in weight provide significant improvements in clinical outcome.

- Appropriate 'fat-burning' exercise should also be encouraged to promote weight loss, whilst eating-behaviour patterns should be examined by both the doctor and the patient.

- When lifestyle modifications have failed to achieve weight loss of sufficient magnitude, adjunctive drug treatment can be considered.

25. Osteoarthritis

Dr Pam Brown BSc MB ChB DFFP MBA Dip Ther Dip Sport Ex Med
General Practitioner, Uplands, Swansea
Tutor, Diploma in Primary Care Rheumatology, University of Bath
Member Scientific Advisory Group, National Osteoporosis Society

Summary

Given the large numbers of patients with musculoskeletal problems in the UK, primary care faces a major challenge to improve care for these individuals. However, there is now a huge amount that GPs and other healthcare professionals can do to control the symptoms associated with these conditions, with the long-term aim of preventing the disability that can occur with the progression of the condition. Active case-finding and screening is not appropriate in the case of osteoarthritis as we are not currently armed with drugs that can halt or reverse the progression of the condition. However, accurate diagnosis of osteoarthritis is essential to ensure that patients are managed appropriately. Establishing management plans based on personal experience and evidence-based medicine can also assist in this regard. In addition, patient education has an important role in clinical management, for example by encouraging them to remain mobile to preserve as much function as possible. Physiotherapy may also help in retaining mobility. The availability of a broad range of anti-inflammatory and analgesic drugs can serve to achieve symptomatic relief and improve patients' impaired quality of life. In certain cases, such as those with inflammatory disease or bony lesions, referral to a specialist for surgical intervention may be necessary.

The challenge in primary care

Musculoskeletal problems are responsible for 15–20% of consultations in primary care, with osteoarthritis accounting for the largest proportion of these. Osteoarthritis is a common disease, affecting 1.3–1.75 million people in England and Wales. Radiographic evidence of osteoarthritis is present in the majority of people over 60 years of age, and osteoarthritis of the knee is twice as common as osteoarthritis of the hip. However, only 10–20% of patients will be symptomatic.

> There is now a huge amount that both we and our patients can do to control the symptoms of osteoarthritis, thereby preserving mobility.

Although it may be tempting to think of osteoarthritis as a natural consequence of ageing and to dismiss it simply as something that people just have to live with, the disability that it causes can largely be prevented and treated. There is now a huge amount that both we and our patients can do to control the symptoms of osteoarthritis, thereby preserving mobility.

Identifying patients

Unlike other common chronic diseases such as coronary heart disease (CHD) or diabetes, which we manage effectively in primary care, screening for osteoarthritis is not appropriate as we do not have therapies that can alter the progression of the disease. Patients present with pain, stiffness and anxiety about what is happening to their joints, and may also experience increasing loss of function and disability. Some individuals seek consultation only when they have severe, uncontrollable pain from end-stage joint destruction.

Usually the diagnosis will be clear after taking a history and examining the affected joints. Examination may reveal joint swelling, deformity, tenderness, crepitus and decreased range of movement. Special tests such as the Thomas test[a] can identify a fixed flexion deformity of the hip, while a waddling gait and positive Trendelenberg test will confirm weakness of hip abductors. These can then be addressed by physiotherapy, shoe raise or, ultimately, surgery.

Since osteoarthritis is associated with ageing, most people who present with osteoarthritis are over 60 years old. However, a few patients will present at a younger age with secondary osteoarthritis in a single joint, usually as a result of previous damage to this joint (e.g. Perthe's disease as a child, mensicectomy, or damage to the joint from competitive sport in early adulthood). Older patients are likely to have comorbid conditions and will thus be taking multiple drugs. These must be taken into consideration when formulating a management plan for individual patients.

Practice factors

The older the demographics of the practice, the more patients you are likely to have with symptomatic osteoarthritis. However, only a very small proportion will present for treatment. As populations survive to older ages, we can expect to see an increase in our osteoarthritis workload and

---

Usually the diagnosis will be clear after taking a history and examining the affected joints.

It is worth investing time and energy in formulating your own personal, evidence-based, cost-effective management plan for osteoarthritis.

---

[a]A Thomas test can detect fixed flexion deformity. The patients lies on their back on the examination couch with their legs extended. As the good hip is passively flexed (normal range is about 135°), a fixed flexion deformity of the contralateral hip causes the thigh on the affected side to rise up off the couch – a positive Thomas test.

consequently osteoarthritis-related costs. It is therefore worth investing time and energy in formulating your own personal, evidence-based, cost-effective management plan for osteoarthritis.

Goals of management

Although there may be a temptation to dismiss osteoarthritis as a natural consequence of ageing and to tell patients that they will just have to live with their symptoms, there is a huge amount that both healthcare professionals and the patient themselves can do to ease the symptoms. Some patients return frequently, complaining of multiple aches and pains; we must take this as a sign that we have underestimated the impact of their symptoms or have failed to provide the necessary education or pain relief to allow them to continue with their lives. Involvement of the whole multidisciplinary primary-care team (i.e. practice nurse, physiotherapist, occupational therapist and pharmacist) in the management of osteoarthritis is very important.

1. Provide patient education and information about self-management of the disease

Although consultation time is short, it is helpful to educate patients about the disease, self-management options and future prognosis. Education can be spread over several consultations or provided by your practice nurse. It reassures patients to know that their symptoms are likely to fluctuate over time, and that only a small percentage of people will require joint-replacement surgery. Explaining to patients that using their joints is unlikely to increase damage may encourage them to remain mobile and preserve as much function as possible, as well as helping with pain relief.

If we can help our patients understand that there is no cure for osteoarthritis, that drugs treat only the symptoms rather than changing the course of the disease, but that usually osteoarthritis is a benign disease that does not cause major disruption to function, they will accept having to live with some discomfort. However, if patients instead believe that continuing symptoms mean that treatment is not working and that the disease is continuing to damage their joints, then the natural response is to return to surgery frequently to seek new drugs until they become symptom free. Realistically, this is an unachievable goal. Therefore, education has an important role in managing patients' expectations.

Some studies have demonstrated the benefits of education and self-help courses. Such courses are available in the UK through Arthritis Care or the Arthritis Research Campaign. These organisations provide a variety of clear,

Education has an important role in managing patients' expectations.

concise leaflets about the whole range of musculoskeletal diseases, whilst participation in a patient group may also be of value to some patients and carers.

2. Identify those with inflammatory arthritis and other diseases

One of our important roles in primary care is to differentiate inflammatory arthritis and other bone and joint diseases from osteoarthritis, so that where appropriate, patients are referred for rheumatological advice early, before irreversible joint destruction occurs. 'Red flags' that may alert us that a patient is not suffering from osteoarthritis include:

- early morning stiffness for more than 1 hour
- joint swelling/effusion
- involvement of a single joint
- atypical pattern of affected joints
- systemic upset
- constant, progressive bone pain
- associated skin rash or bowel symptoms
- previous history of gout.

Blood tests can be helpful in confirming inflammatory joint disease or other conditions such as myeloma, but are not needed routinely in patients with a clinical diagnosis of osteoarthritis, and results should be normal in the absence of concomitant disease in such patients. When examining patients for signs of osteoarthritis, remember that pain from the lumbar spine may be referred to the hip, and from the hip to the knee, so it is essential to examine joints above and below the site of pain.

Osteoarthritis and rheumatoid arthritis can be differentiated by the pattern of joint involvement, joint and soft tissue swelling, early morning stiffness for longer than 1 hour, and systemic upset (pallor, tiredness, raised erythrocyte sedimentation rate [ESR]). In osteoarthritis, the distal and proximal interphalangeal joints of the fingers, the carpometacarpal joint at the base of the thumb, hips, knees, the first metatarsophalangeal joint of the great toe, and the facet joints of the spine are most commonly involved. However, in rheumatoid arthritis, the wrists, metacarpophalangeal and proximal interphalangeal joints in the hands, shoulders and knees and the metatarsophalangeal joints of the feet are more commonly involved. Joints may swell and feel hot and tender in rheumatoid arthritis.

Some of the differential diagnostic challenges between osteoarthritis and other conditions of specific joints are summarised in Table 1.

Table 1. Differential diagnosis in osteoarthritis.

Joint	Condition	Management
'Knee' pain	Peri-articular ligament pain	Careful injection of steroid
Knee	Degenerative meniscal tear	Arthroscopic surgery
Knee or first metatarsophalangeal joint	Gout	NSAIDs/colchicine
Knee, hip or shoulder	Septic arthritis	Admit for intravenous antibiotics
'Hip' pain	Trochanteric bursitis	Injection of steroid
Back and neck pain	Ankylosing spondylitis	NSAID, refer for rheumatologist opinion and physiotherapy for back exercise programme
Multiple joints	Inflammatory arthropathy (e.g. rheumatoid arthritis, psoriatic arthropathy)	Refer for diagnosis and DMARD therapy if appropriate

DMARD, disease-modifying antirheumatic drug; NSAID, non-steroidal anti-inflammatory drug.

3. Achieve symptom relief and improve quality of life

Patients present to us with pain, stiffness ('gelling'), crepitus, decreased mobility or because the disease is interfering with their ability to carry on a normal life. Many are reluctant to take analgesics. It is therefore important to explain that it is better to control the pain, allowing them to remain mobile and continue with their normal lifestyle, than to avoid analgesics and become progressively more immobile. Although heavy manual work is best avoided, there is evidence that gentle exercise such as walking or swimming, and specific exercises for individual joints can strengthen muscles and improve joint pain in osteoarthritis.

There is growing evidence that obesity is a major risk factor for symptomatic osteoarthritis, particularly in the weight-bearing joints. Obesity increases the need for hip-joint replacement, and results in poorer outcomes from surgery.

Treatment options to alleviate pain and stiffness and preserve function in osteoarthritis include:

- oral analgesics (e.g. paracetamol, 1 g four-times daily, or compound analgesics such as co-codamol, 8/500 mg or 30/500 mg, two tablets four-times daily; effervescent paracetamol or co-codamol should not be used in elderly patients given the large sodium load associated with such preparations)
- topical non-steroidal anti-inflammatory drugs (NSAIDs)
- topical capsaicin cream
- oral NSAIDs

It is important to explain that it is better to control the pain, allowing them to remain mobile and continue with their normal lifestyle, than to avoid analgesics and become progressively more immobile.

- cyclo-oxygenase (COX)-2 inhibitors
- glucosamine sulphate
- heat, cold, wax baths
- physiotherapy (e.g. modalities, electrical therapies, exercise programmes)
- transcutaneous nerve stimulation
- unloading of the affected joint (e.g. wearing soft-soled trainer shoes, weight loss, walking aids, splints)
- joint replacement.

A variety of assessment tools can be used to monitor benefits of such treatment, including a simple visual analog score (VAS) used in isolation or as part of the self-administered Western Ontario and McMaster's University Osteoarthritis Index (WOMAC) questionnaires for knee, hip and hand osteoarthritis, which assess pain, stiffness and physical function. However, the majority of patients can tell us directly whether treatment has made any impact on their symptoms.

Before prescribing treatment, it is best to check what over-the-counter therapies have already been tried, and then tailor your prescription accordingly. For example, most patients have tried paracetamol before coming to surgery, but many will not have taken it regularly or at the full dosage. Combination analgesics such as co-codamol, 8/500 mg or 30/500 mg, co-proxamol and co-dydramol would usually be the next agents used. Long-acting products (e.g. sustained-release dihydrocodeine) that are taken twice daily may be better in patients who wake frequently with severe nocturnal joint pain. A 2-week trial of different analgesics or NSAIDs may be useful in such patients.

Often patients need considerable encouragement to take analgesics regularly to overcome the perceptions that efficacy will disappear with regular use, and that they will somehow become addicted to painkillers. Simple explanation can help here. It is also useful to explain that different people may benefit from different painkillers and that it is worth trying several different ones if pain is uncontrolled until the one that suits best is identified. This willingness on the part of the GP to try a variety of different drugs can make a huge difference to the patient's life, as well as helping them to understand that we really do care about their symptoms.

Some patients have inflammatory flares, with one or more swollen, acutely tender joints, or stiffness may be more prominent. In these situations (once other diagnoses have been excluded) an NSAID may be appropriate. Since NSAIDs can cause gastrointestinal and renal side-effects and appear to be no more effective than analgesics in treating osteoarthritis, they should only be used when analgesics have failed to control symptoms.

Topical NSAIDs have also been shown to be effective for the relief of acute and chronic pain.

The National Institute for Clinical Excellence (NICE) recently published guidance on the use of COX-2-selective inhibitors (celecoxib, etodolac, rofecoxib and meloxicam) in the UK, and recommended their use instead of conventional NSAIDs in people at 'high risk' of developing serious gastrointestinal problems (e.g. those aged 65 years or older, those taking other drugs that can cause gastrointestinal problems, those with existing gastrointestinal problems or those requiring long-term therapy). COX-2 inhibitors should be avoided in those with a previous history of peptic ulcers, and are not recommended in those with co-existing cardiovascular disease or in those taking aspirin. Patients taking aspirin should not be given ibuprofen since the combination may be associated with an increased risk of cardiovascular problems. Side-effects of NSAIDs vary and increase with increasing dose. In addition, the efficacy of the same drug may vary between patients. Co-prescribing histamine H_2-receptor antagonists, proton-pump inhibitors or misoprostol is likely to be beneficial in preventing the gastrointestinal side-effects associated with conventional NSAIDs, but co-prescribing with COX-2 inhibitors is not recommended by NICE.

Many patients use complementary therapies for osteoarthritis. This often reflects unsatisfactory consultations with the medical profession, or being told they will just have to live with their pain. Reducing animal fat consumption, taking fish oil supplements and acupuncture have been shown to improve symptoms in some patients. Several randomised controlled trials of glucosamine sulphate, 1500–2000 mg daily, have shown benefits on pain and stiffness. However, not all patients are helped, and glucosamine is not available on prescription in some countries. If patients choose to buy it, a trial of the full therapeutic dose for 2–3 months should be recommended, and should be discontinued if there is no benefit. Glucosamine may slow disease progression but this is not yet confirmed. Glucosamine combined with chondroitin and manganese ascorbate has also been shown to be better than placebo in osteoarthritis.

Intra-articular injection of steroid or hyaluronan into the knee may improve pain and thus mobility. Steroid injection is short acting (1–4 weeks), whilst the effects of hyaluronan may last for up to 6 months. Steroid injections are helpful in other joints such as the carpometacarpal joint of the thumb, and can be safely administered in primary care by experienced practitioners.

Chronic, uncontrolled pain may result in loss of sleep and depression. These effects result in a lowering of the pain threshold, and establish a vicious cycle. Antidepressants used at low doses at night-time (e.g. amitriptyline, 10 mg) can improve sleep and increase pain relief. Conventional doses of tricyclic antidepressants or selective serotonin reuptake inhibitors may be needed in those with established depression.

4. Maintain mobility and function

Maintaining mobility and function depends on adequate symptom relief, and may be helped by physiotherapy. Physiotherapists can assess suitability for walking aids such as walking sticks and Zimmer frames, and teach exercises to maintain muscle function and preserve a range of motion in joints. Taping of the patella and splinting of damaged joints may also help with pain relief.

Occupational therapists can assess the patient's home and provide aids and appliances such as chair or toilet raises, or adaptations to bathroom facilities which make it easier for patients to remain independent despite progressive joint damage.

5. Refer patients for orthopaedic assessment and/or surgery where appropriate

NICE published referral advice statements in 2001 (*www.nice.org.uk*), including advice on referral of osteoarthritis of the hip and knee. The referral advice statements are not formal NICE guidance, but are consensus statements based on the best available evidence, designed to stimulate local discussions on how best to prioritise referrals from primary to secondary care.

A summary of the referral advice for osteoarthritis of the hip and osteoarthritis of the knee is shown in Table 2. NICE recommends that health authorities, trusts and primary care organisations (PCOs) should work to local definitions of maximum waiting times in each of these categories. The multidisciplinary advisory groups consider a maximum waiting time of 2 weeks to be appropriate for the urgent category. GPs may wish to discuss this referral advice with their PCO and local orthopaedic surgeons.

Surgical options include arthroscopic lavage, patellar resurfacing, osteotomy, arthroplasty and arthrodesis. It is important to refer patients early enough to take account of waiting list times, whilst not exacerbating the waiting list situation further by referring all patients with osteoarthritis. It is useful to discuss surgical management options with patients before referral, as it is surprising how many patients have unrealistic expectations about what referral to a specialist can achieve. In addition, many patients

Table 2. Referral advice for osteoarthritis of the hip and knee from the National Institute of Clinical Excellence (NICE).
http://www.nice.org.uk/pdf/Referrlaadvice.pdf

Osteoarthritis of the hip
The majority of patient management can be undertaken in primary care, However, referral to a specialist service is advised if:
• there is evidence of infection in the joint(****)
• symptoms rapidly deteriorate and are causing severe disability (***)
• the symptoms impair quality of life (*)

Osteoarthritis of the knee
The majority of the patient management is undertaken in primary care. However, referral to a specialist service is advised if:
• there is evidence of infection in the joint (****)
• there is evidence of acute inflammation caused by, for example, haemarthrosis, gout or pseudo-gout (***)
• giving way is a problem despite therapy (**)
• symptoms rapidly deteriorate and are causing severe disability (**)
• the symptoms impair quality of life. Referral should be based on an explicit scoring system that should be developed locally in a partnership involving patients together with healthcare professional in primary and secondary care. Referral criteria should take into account the extent to which the condition is causing pain, disability, sleeplessness, loss of independence, inability to undertake normal activities, reduced functional capacity or psychiatric illness (*)

Referral timings
Arrangements should be made so that the patient:
• **** is seen immediately (within a day)
• ***is seen urgently (2 weeks recommended)
• ** is seen soon
• * has a routine appointment

are not willing to contemplate surgery, in which case referral is inappropriate. Patients whose osteoarthritis means they cannot sleep, walk or work because of severe pain unrelieved by medical therapy options clearly require surgical intervention.

Occasionally radiographs are needed to assess suitability for joint replacement, but usually the referral is based on uncontrollable pain. Other situations where a radiograph may be appropriate in osteoarthritis include:
- to exclude bony injury
- when a bony lesion is suspected
- to confirm pseudogout
- to assess need for joint replacement.

Radiographs are not necessary to confirm the diagnosis of osteoarthritis, as they will not significantly alter the management of the disorder. It is important to remember that radiographs of most people over 60 years of age will show some osteoarthritic changes in the hips, knees and spinal facet joints. However, radiograph changes correlate poorly with clinical symptoms, and it is therefore important to treat the patient rather than their radiograph findings. Further information on the appropriate use of radiographs can be found in *Making The Best Use of a Department of Radiology*, published by the Royal College of General Practitioners and Royal College of Radiologists in the UK.

Improving practice

Since guidelines and evidence-based recommendations for the management of patients with osteoarthritis are available, it is useful to compare how our management matches these recommendations.

The first step in improving practice is to review the guidelines and pick out a few recommendations that you believe will lend themselves to formal audit or review. For example, you may look at the NICE guidance on use of COX-2 inhibitors, and decide to review the use of these drugs in your practice. Since the guidance focuses on high-risk groups, including those over 65 years of age and those taking long-term NSAIDs, you could review all patients over 65 years of age who are regularly prescribed any NSAID, and work out what percentage of these patients are taking a COX-2 inhibitor. You may then decide to look at all patients currently prescribed a COX-2 inhibitor, and see if they meet the 'high-risk' criteria. Both of these prescribing reviews can be carried out relatively easily using constructed searches on the practice computer system.

Conclusion

Osteoarthritis is very common, causes considerable pain and impacts greatly on quality of life of many older people. Modifiable risk factors are not yet fully understood, but are likely to include joint injury and obesity. It is important to differentiate between those with osteoarthritis and those with inflammatory joint disease or other bony lesions who may need referral for specialist assessment. The majority of patients with mild-to-moderate osteoarthritis can be managed successfully in primary care. Many treatment options are available, and it is important that both patients and GPs take the time to explore treatment options to optimise symptom control and maintain function in individual patients. Surgery, including joint replacement, can improve symptoms in those with end-stage joint destruction. Consequently, there is no longer any excuse for considering osteoarthritis symptoms and disability as merely inevitable consequences of ageing, or telling patients 'you will just have to live with it as there is nothing we can do'!

Key points

- Musculoskeletal problems represent a significant proportion of a GPs daily workload, accounting for 15–20% of consultations, with osteoarthritis the most common complaint.

- As the demographics of the UK change, we can expect an even greater proportion of our workload taken up with such consultations.

- Screening for osteoarthritis is not appropriate given that there are no interventions which retard or reverse the progression of the disease.

- Accurate diagnosis is essential for appropriate management of the patient, whilst awareness of differential diagnoses is critical as patients with inflammatory disease will need urgent referral for specialist rheumatology advice.

- Establishing personal, evidence-based, cost-effective management plans can assist in improving care for our patients.

- The objectives of clinical management focus on patient education and information, achieving symptomatic relief, thereby improving quality of life and the maintenance of mobility and function.

26. Osteoporosis

Dr Pam Brown, BSc, MB ChB, DFFP, MBA, Dip Ther, Dip Sports Ex Med.
General Practitioner, Uplands, Swansea
Tutor, Diploma in Primary Care Rheumatology, University of Bath
Member Scientific Advisory Group, National Osteoporosis Society

Summary

Osteoporosis is a very common disease which exerts a significant burden of morbidity on the patient. As a consequence, the management of osteoporosis consumes significant healthcare resources, with an estimated annual cost of around £1.7 billion. A sizeable component of this cost relates to the management of osteoporotic fractures, which in many cases can be prevented with the implementation of appropriate systems of care that seek to identify individuals at high risk of fracture and thus who would benefit most from intervention. High-risk individuals can be identified in the community by a selective case-finding strategy in which risk is assessed either opportunistically when a patient presents in the surgery or by actively interrogating computer-based practice records. By targeting appropriate bone-sparing pharmacological interventions to these high-risk patients, we can go a long way to minimising the burden of the condition and also ensure that we use such interventions in a cost-effective fashion.

The burden of osteoporosis in primary care

Osteoporosis is defined as a progressive systemic skeletal disease characterised by low bone mass and micro-architectural deterioration of bone tissue, with a consequent increase in bone fragility and susceptibility to fractures. It is a very common disease, with one woman in three over the age of 50 years affected. Between one-in-eight and one-in-twelve men are also affected. The prevalence increases amongst Caucasian women from 15% in those aged 50 years to more than 70% at age 80.

Osteoporosis is important clinically because of the fractures that it causes. In the UK every year it is estimated that there are more than 310,000 osteoporotic fractures, comprising 70,000 hip fractures, 70,000 Colles fractures, 120,000 vertebral fractures and 50,000 other fractures due

> In the UK every year it is estimated that there are more than 310,000 osteoporotic fractures.

to osteoporosis. Caucasian women at the time of menopause have a 30–40% lifetime risk of fracture, with a 14% risk of hip fracture.

Fractures result in pain, disability, loss of independence, hospitalisation and mortality, yet many osteoporotic fractures are preventable if people at high risk are treated appropriately. The number of fractures continues to increase year on year, out of proportion to the changing demographics of the elderly population. Osteoporotic hip fractures occupy more than 20% of orthopaedic beds each year, and result in more than 14,000 deaths each year in the UK. Estimated costs are around £1.7 billion annually. The burden of fractures and costs for a typical primary care organisation are shown in Table 1.

As well as the annual incident fractures, there is a burden of disease from the pool of previously diagnosed and undiagnosed osteoporotic fractures and people with osteoporosis, all of whom are also at very high risk of future fracture.

Although around 80% of women are able to walk independently prior to a hip fracture, at 1 year post-fracture 20% will have died as a direct result, only 15–20% will be able to walk unaided and less than 10% can climb stairs unaided even though 60% were able to do this prior to the fracture.

We now know that those who have had a previous low trauma or fragility fracture are much more likely to have another, with as many as one-in-five patients who have had a vertebral fracture refracturing within 1 year. Where there is no fracture liaison service in secondary care, GPs and the primary-care team are in the best position to be able to identify and treat these patients to reduce the burden of further fractures. The numbers likely to be at highest risk within an average practice are small enough to be manageable (Figure 1), yet tackling this group can have a dramatic impact on future fracture rates.

> *GPs and the primary care team are in the best position to be able to identify and treat patients who have had a previous fracture to reduce the burden of further fractures.*

Table 1. Fracture incidence and costs of fractures for a typical Primary Care Organisation (PCO).

Fracture type	Number of patients per PCO (100,000)	Hospital costs per fracture (£)	Total costs per fracture (£)	Total costs per PCO (£)
Hip	120	5,300	21,500	2,580,000
Wrist	120	500	500	60,000
Vertebral (diagnosed)	200 (40)	500	500	20,000
Other	100	1,400	1,400	140,600
Total cost				**2,800,600**

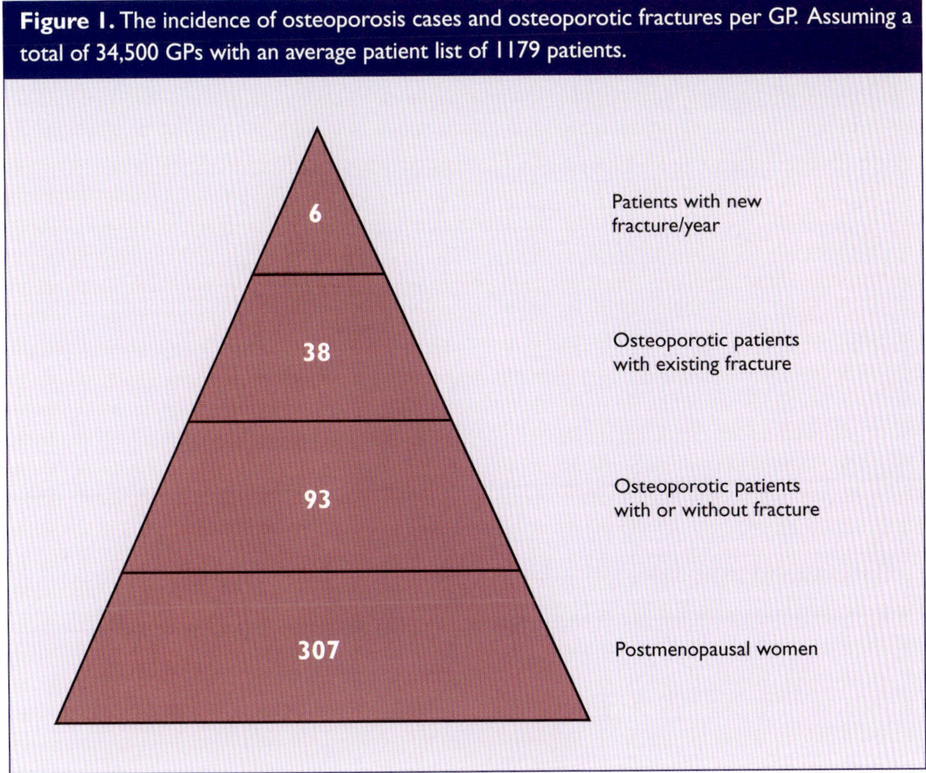

Figure 1. The incidence of osteoporosis cases and osteoporotic fractures per GP. Assuming a total of 34,500 GPs with an average patient list of 1179 patients.

Practical strategies and identifying patients

The goals of osteoporosis management are to prevent initial and subsequent fractures. It is usually most appropriate to begin by tackling secondary prevention and target those who have already had a fracture. Two practical ways to identify this group are discussed later in this article. Once successful, the practice or Primary Care Organisation (PCO) can then move on to primary prevention, which is, of course, more resource intensive.

The key strategies that can be used here are similar to those that can be used for other chronic diseases such as coronary heart disease (CHD) or diabetes – namely population strategies and individual or selective case-finding strategies. These are outlined in Table 2.

Population strategies

A 10% increase in bone mineral density (BMD) across the population would translate into a halving of osteoporotic fractures. However, the lifestyle advice involved (i.e. increasing dietary calcium, weight-bearing exercise and smoking cessation) is time consuming to deliver, and most people are unwilling or unable to make long-term lifestyle changes. In

Table 2. Practical strategies for managing osteoporosis.	
Population strategies	• Improve bone mineral density across the whole population • Population screening
High-risk strategies (selective case-finding)	• Opportunistic identification of high-risk individuals • 'Search and rescue' strategies for high-risk groups

addition, there is little evidence from randomised controlled trials that this approach will actually decrease fractures in reality. Therefore, this approach should not be relied upon as the sole method for fracture prevention. Since this lifestyle advice is similar to that provided to reduce the risk of CHD, stroke and diabetes, it is important to remind patients of the likely benefits such lifestyle changes will have on their skeletons.

The second population strategy involves screening all perimenopausal women with dual energy X-ray absorptiometry (DXA) scans at the time of the menopause, and then encouraging those found to be at high risk to take bone-sparing therapy. This strategy was piloted in Hull and Aberdeen but was not found to be cost-effective. DXA is expensive as a screening tool and has low sensitivity for identifying women who will fracture. Moreover, being aware that they were at risk of osteoporosis did not markedly influence women to take bone-sparing therapy.

Therefore, the recommended strategy that will be discussed in the remainder of this section is an individual and selective case-finding approach. This involves identifying those patients who are most at risk of osteoporosis and fragility fractures, and ensuring that they receive optimal advice and treatment to prevent first or subsequent fractures.

In a primary-care setting, this approach would involve risk factor assessment, such as previous fracture or steroid use, to identify those at increased risk, either opportunistically when they present in surgery, or by searching the practice computer records for those with documented risk factors. Both methods can help to identify the prevalence pool of high-risk patients within the practice.

In secondary care, a separate method of selective case finding – the Fracture Liaison Service – operates in an increasing number of centres across the UK. Based on the premise that those who have already had one low-trauma fracture are at greatly increased risk of subsequent fractures, the Fracture Liaison Services assesses those with incident fractures, and identifies those who need further treatment with bone-sparing agents to reduce the risk of future fractures. Recommendations are then made for continuing drug therapy in primary care.

Goals of clinical management

Osteoporosis is important because of the fractures that it causes, and therefore the goals of management are to prevent first and subsequent fractures. Apart from vertebral fractures which result from normal activities of daily living, other osteoporotic fractures are usually caused by a combination of increased bone fragility and a fall. Therefore, to be most effective, one must identify and manage both the osteoporosis and the falls.

The overarching strategies to achieve this have been discussed earlier in this section. Here we will focus on the practical aspects of how to provide an osteoporosis service in the primary-care setting.

The main goals of osteoporosis prevention and management in primary care are to:

- maximise peak bone mass
- identify patients at highest risk of fracture
- use investigations cost-effectively
- exclude secondary osteoporosis
- provide lifestyle advice to all those at risk
- provide appropriate drug treatment to those at highest risk and encourage concordance
- identify and manage those at increased risk of falls.

Each of these goals will be discussed in detail in the following sections.

To be most effective, one must identify and manage both the osteoporosis and the falls.

Maximise peak bone mass

The risk of osteoporosis and fracture in later life depends on three factors: the peak bone mass achieved in the teens and twenties, the age at which bone loss begins and the rate at which bone loss continues thereafter. It is therefore vital to ensure that children and teenagers optimise their peak bone mass by healthy eating, exercise and avoidance of smoking, anorexia and amenorrhoea. Supplementation with calcium can result in 1–5% increases in BMD, whilst consumption of milk and other dairy produce that also contain protein may be even more effective. The benefits derived from such an approach may be greatest in the pre-pubertal period and during early supplementation. Modest exercise is also beneficial, but excessive exercise that results in amenorrhoea is detrimental.

It is vital to ensure that children and teenagers optimise their peak bone mass by healthy eating, exercise and avoidance of smoking, anorexia and amenorrhoea.

Identify patients at highest risk of fracture

High-risk groups for osteoporotic fracture include:

- a history of previous fragility fracture
- oral steroid use
- housebound, frail elderly individuals

- BMD T-score less than −2.5 on a DXA scan
- a maternal history of hip fracture
- premature menopause/hysterectomy (before 45 years of age)
- prolonged amenorrhoea not due to pregnancy
- Cummings Hip Fracture Risk score of 5 or more
- body mass index below 19 kg/m^2
- fallers.

Although osteoporosis can only be accurately diagnosed by DXA, several other factors can help identify those at high risk of fracture. It is anticipated that eventually a variety of risk factors (including DXA T-scores) will be combined to produce a 10-year prediction of fracture risk, similar to CHD risk scores, which will allow treatment to be targeted to those at highest risk of future fracture.

Peripheral DXA (pDXA) (calcaneum or forearm) or quantitative ultrasound (QUS) can also be helpful in identifying those at highest risk of future fracture. However, pDXA cannot be used for monitoring therapy and QUS cannot be used for diagnosing osteoporosis or monitoring therapy. The National Osteoporosis Society provides guidance on the use and limitations of these investigations – this guidance can be downloaded from the Health Professionals' section of the website at *www.nos.org.uk*. If the forearm T-score is between −1 and −2.5 on pDXA, then axial DXA is recommended, whereas if the T-score is less than −2.5, then treatment can be initiated. Low QUS is an independent risk factor for future osteoporotic fracture in postmenopausal women but is not recommended for use in other groups.

Two commonly used scoring systems, the Cummings Hip Fracture Risk score and the Black Fracture Index are summarised in Tables 3 and 4. Patients with five or more hip fracture risk factors are 25-times more likely to suffer a hip fracture than those with two or less risk factors. These scoring systems can therefore help identify the highest-risk, frail elderly population. The Fracture Index provides an estimate of 5-year risk of osteoporotic fractures and can be calculated with or without DXA scores. Women with scores of six and higher, and four and above, with and without DXA respectively, need further assessment.

The Cummings Hip Fracture Risk score and the Black Fracture Index can help identify the highest-risk, frail elderly population.

Use investigations to confirm the diagnosis when appropriate

Axial DXA of the hip and lumbar spine is the 'gold standard' investigation for diagnosing osteoporosis, and the definition of osteoporosis is based on finding a T-score of −2.5 or less on axial DXA. However, DXA should be used only if it will change the patient's management. Thus, an elderly lady

Table 3. Hip fracture risk factors used in determining the Cummings Risk Factor score.

- Age greater than 80 years
- Fracture since the age of 50 years
- Maternal hip fracture
- Poor or very poor health
- Anticonvulsant treatment
- Long-acting benzodiazepine treatment
- Weight below that at age 25 years
- Height above 168 cm at age 25 years
- Consumption of more than two cups of coffee per day
- On their feet for less than 4 hours per day
- No walking for exercise
- Unable to rise from chair without using arms
- Previous hyperparathyroidism
- Lowest quartile depth perception
- Lowest quartile contrast sensitivity

Table 4. Fracture index questions and scoring.

	Score
1. Current age	
Under 65	0
65–69	1
70–74	2
75–79	3
80–84	4
85 or older	5
2. Fracture after the age of 50	1
3. Maternal hip fracture after age of 50	1
4. Weight 125 pounds or less	1
5. Current smoker	1
6. Uses arms to rise from chair	2
7. Hip BMD result if available	
T- score ≥ -1	0
T-score between -1 and -2	2
T-score between -2 and -2.5	3
T-score < -2.5	4

who has had several low-trauma fractures will need appropriate bone-sparing therapy, and probably will not need a DXA scan prior to starting treatment. Guidance from the National Institute for Clinical Excellence

(NICE) is due to be published later in 2004, which may clarify this and other ssues.

DXA has a high specificity but low sensitivity, which means that those with low BMD are at high risk of fracture, but around 50% of those who go on to fracture will have had a relatively normal BMD. Thus, DXA results should be viewed along with other risk factors in deciding which patients need therapy to prevent or treat osteoporosis.

Exclude secondary osteoporosis

Our patients will not thank us if we treat their osteoporotic fracture but fail to identify an underlying condition that has caused it, or if we fail to diagnose that their vertebral fracture was due to bony secondaries rather than osteoporosis. We need to have a particularly high index of suspicion in patients who have had previous cancer, are elderly or who have evidence of systemic features such as weight loss or night pain. Investigations should be tailored to the particular patient, but may include:

- full blood count (FBC), erythrocyte sedimentation rate (ESR)
- myeloma screen (protein electrophoresis, Bence-Jones protein in urine)
- thyroid profile
- bone profile – calcium, alkaline phosphatase
- cortisol levels.

Provide lifestyle advice to all at risk

Lifestyle advice regarding healthy diet, exercise and smoking cessation to reduce the risks of CHD, stroke and diabetes, is provided routinely in primary care, but we rarely remember to stress the benefits that these interventions provide to the skeleton. These lifestyle messages need to be communicated from the 'cradle to the grave' to maximise peak bone mass, maintain bone mass and reduce loss later in life.

Population-based studies have demonstrated improved BMD and possibly reduced hip fracture rates amongst elderly people who eat a diet rich in fruit and vegetables, which are high in potassium, magnesium and vitamin K. High caffeine intake, particularly if combined with low calcium intake, may result in lower BMD and increased hip fracture rates. Adolescents and elderly patients are most at risk of vitamin D deficiency with 10–16% of teenagers having vitamin D-deficient diets and 37% of institutionalised elderly patients having low blood vitamin D levels.

One to two alcoholic drinks a day may improve BMD. In contrast, consumption of more than 14 units a week is associated with increased fracture risk. Postmenopausal smokers have an increased cumulative hip fracture risk up to the age of 85 (19% in smokers compared with 12% in non-smokers).

High-impact weight-bearing exercise, such as jumping or jogging and slow-lifting of heavy weights (70–85% of personal maximum), can increase BMD in adults by 1–5%, but the benefits reverse once exercise stops. The FICSIT (Frailty and Injuries: Cooperative Studies of Intervention Techniques) meta-analysis demonstrated a significant reduction in falls with individually tailored exercise programmes, including a 50% reduction in falls after a Tai Chi programme.

Drug treatment of those at highest risk

Specific details about pharmacotherapy can be found elsewhere and are beyond the scope of this article, so here we will concentrate on the practical aspects of deciding who needs treatment and how to improve concordance with drug therapy.

Many GPs may be concerned by the impact that they believe tackling osteoporosis will have on their prescribing figures. However, this need not be a concern. As is illustrated in Figure 1, the numbers of patients at the highest risk in each practice, who may require bisphosphonate or other drug therapy, are smaller than GPs might anticipate. Also, some practices may have patients who are currently treated with bisphosphonates but who are at a relatively low risk of future fracture. As with other medical interventions, targeting treatment to those at higher risk of fracture allows drugs to be used more cost-effectively.

Specific patient groups who benefit from bone-sparing pharmacological intervention include those:

- who have had axial DXA (T-score <−2.5; T-score −1 to −2.5 (osteopenia) and previous fracture or other multiple risk factors)
- with a pDXA T-score below −2.5
- over 65 years commencing oral steroids and likely to receive treatment for 3 months or more
- under 65 years on oral steroids whose DXA T-score is −1.5 or less
- with one or more fragility fractures who do not need DXA evaluation, after exclusion of secondary osteoporosis where appropriate
- in nursing or residential homes (high-dose calcium and vitamin D) to prevent hip fractures.

Advice is usually available from local osteoporosis specialists or GPs with a special interest in osteoporosis to help guide treatment decisions in more complex cases, and in many parts of the UK the DXA scan report will include recommendations for treatment.

Whether drug treatment is initiated in primary or secondary care, patients need to be reviewed in primary care, ideally 3–4 months after starting treatment, to ensure they are continuing to take their medication, and, in the case of bisphosphonates, are taking medication in the correct way so that it is likely to be effective.

Monitoring with axial DXA after 18 months to 2 years of treatment will allow confirmation of a treatment effect, but this may not be appropriate in all patients.

Identify and manage those at increased risk of falling

Standard 6 of the National Service Framework (NSF) for Older People confirms that practices have a responsibility to identify fallers and those at risk of falling, and also those with osteoporosis or at high risk of fragility fractures or refracture, and to take appropriate action to manage these patients.

The risk of falling and the likelihood of resulting injuries increases steadily after the age of 60 years, with fall rates about three-times higher in nursing and residential homes than they are in the community. About 35–40% of mobile elderly patients will fall each year, and 5% will be hospitalised as a result. Several risk factors for falls have been identified and incorporated into fall-assessment risk tools. The simplest tool employs only three risk factors: hip weakness, unstable balance and taking four or more medications. Those with no risk factors have a 12% annual falls risk, compared with 100% for those with all three risk factors.

In practice, all older people or their carers should be asked once a year about falls. Those who have fallen should be assessed with the 'get up and go test', where the patient is asked to stand up from a chair without using their arms, to walk several paces and turn round and return to the chair. Those presenting after a fall, those reporting multiple falls, and those with gait or balance difficulties when tested, need referral for formal falls assessment.

There is evidence that multifactorial interventions can decrease risk of future falls when targeted at high risk people. These include:
- medication assessment
- intervention for postural hypotension
- environmental hazard modification
- gait training and advice on the use of walking sticks and zimmer frames
- exercise programmes including balance training and Tai Chi
- treatment of comorbid cardiovascular problems.

Hip protectors may decrease risk of hip fractures in fallers, but are only likely to be acceptable to those in nursing or residential homes, and even in this group compliance is a problem.

Improving osteoporosis management

Unfortunately, there are no quality points for osteoporosis within the new General Medical Services (GMS) contract, and therefore, if we are to make a significant impact on osteoporosis and fractures in Primary Care, it is likely that initiatives and incentives at the level of PCOs such as Primary Care Trusts (PCTs) and Local Health Boards (LHBs) will be needed to encourage widespread action. The National Osteoporosis Society has produced guidance for PCOs in England, Wales and Scotland to simplify the implementation of seamless primary and secondary care services. These can be accessed on the Health Professionals' section of the National Osteoporosis Society website at *www.nos.org.uk*.

A variety of other guidelines are available which can help primary-care teams manage osteoporosis effectively. Two of the most useful are the general osteoporosis guidelines produced by the Scottish Intercollegiate Guidelines Network (SIGN) (*www.sign.ac.uk*) and the Glucocorticoid Induced Osteoporosis Guidelines published in November 2002, by the Royal College of Physicians, the Bone and Tooth Society and the National Osteoporosis Society (*www.rcplondon.ac.uk*).

The impact of information technology and clinical audit

To meet the requirements of the NSF for Older People, it is important that all fallers and those with fractures should be identified and recorded in primary care. It is particularly important for the over 75s (or possibly even over 65s) that falls and osteoporosis risk assessments are carried out.

Datasets containing the necessary Read codes have been produced by Dr Mike Harvey and Dr Jonathan Bayly – members of the Scientific Advisory Group of the National Osteoporosis Society – and these are available on the Health Professionals' section of the National Osteoporosis Society website at *www.nos.org.uk*.

The NSF for Older People recommends clinical audit of the groups shown in Table 5. The fallers should be included in the practice Falls Register and those with previous fractures or diagnosed osteoporosis on a DXA scan can be included in an Osteoporosis Register. It is then very straightforward for practices to audit whether these patients have received appropriate assessments and management.

This will improve levels of care for osteoporosis patients and help reduce fracture risk from falls. Primary-care teams need to work together with

Table 5. Clinical audit in osteoporosis, as recommended by the criteria of the National Service Framework (NSF) for Older People.

- Number of fallers in the last year
- Number with more than two falls or one fall and poor gait/balance as determined by the 'get up and go test' who need formal falls assessment
- Number of fallers who have received a falls assessment
- Number of fragility fractures in the last year by type
- Number of housebound/in residential accommodation who have received falls assessment
- Number of fallers who are prescribed high strength calcium and vitamin D
- Number on steroids who have received osteoporosis assessment

colleagues in secondary care who will be putting in place Fracture Liaison Programmes and working to improve rehabilitation after fractures, as per the recommendations of the *Blue Book* produced by the British Orthopaedic Association in 2003. Together this should provide a seamless service to identify and manage patients with incident and prevalent fractures.

Conclusions

Osteoporosis is preventable and treatable, yet every year in the UK alone it is responsible for more than 310,000 fragility fractures, which in turn result in pain, disability and deaths, with a huge financial cost. Targeting interventions, whether lifestyle or drug therapies, at those with the highest risk of future fracture, will ensure that we make an impact on fracture rates whilst making the most cost-effective use of our resources, in terms of both people and pounds.

Key points

- Osteoporosis is a very common disease affecting up to one woman in three over 50 years but also affecting up to one-in-eight men.

- Osteoporotic fractures result in pain, disability, loss of independence, hospitalisation and mortality, but can be prevented with appropriate systems of care which focus on high-risk individuals.

- The primary aim of management within primary care is to prevent initial and subsequent fractures, although primary prevention of initial fractures is more resource intensive.

- The recommended strategy to identify patients at risk of osteoporotic fractures is an individual, selective case-finding approach, via risk factor assessment either opportunistically or by actively searching computer records.

- In addition to fracture prevention, it is essential to identify and manage patients at an increased risk of falls.

- Other goals of osteoporosis prevention and management include maximisation of peak bone mass via lifestyle intervention and the use of bone-sparing medication where most appropriate.

- No quality points are available for effective osteoporosis management in the new GMS contract, and thus other initiatives are required to encourage widespread action.

27. Psoriasis

Dr Tim Mitchell, MBChB MRCGP DRCOG DPD
General Practitioner, Bristol
Secretary, Primary Care Dermatology Society

Summary

Psoriasis is a relatively common disease but its management in primary care has been hampered by a lack of service provision, a lack of education and a failure to acknowledge the important impact the condition has on patients' quality of life. One way of improving care in the area of chronic inflammatory skin disease is the establishment of dedicated skin clinics, focusing on the care of patients with psoriasis, chronic eczema and acne, and involving the entire multidisciplinary primary healthcare team. Patient and professional education is a critical element of the entire process, and will engender a greater understanding of the impact of psoriasis and ensure that patients' satisfaction with care improves. An essential part of treatment should be the implementation of individual patient management plans in order to align both patients and GPs' expectations of care.

Introduction

In the era of the new General Medical Services (GMS) GP contract with its promises of a greater focus on primary care and the opportunity to develop enhanced local services, it makes sense to take a hard look at a group of patients who suffer a chronic disease but who are not generally well supported and managed in the community.

Over the past 10 years, the All Party Parliamentary Group on Skin has produced several reports highlighting the problems that patients with chronic skin diseases face as a result of a lack of provision of services, a lack of education for the majority of healthcare professionals and a lack of acknowledgement of the impact of skin disease on quality of life.

The extent of the problem

Psoriasis is relatively common, with about 2–3% of the population affected. Whilst we know that there are many good treatments available which can be mixed and matched to suit most patients, there are still many patients who are not receiving any treatment at all and others who are extremely dissatisfied with the care offered to them.

Figures produced by the Psoriasis Association have shown that between 70 and 80% of people with psoriasis do not consult a GP within the course of any single year. Of these, some are receiving no treatment, others – including some who travel to the Dead Sea – are self-treating and a few are trying complementary therapies. Reasons for this are many and varied, but common ones include:

- a perception that 'trivial' psoriasis is not 'worthy' of treatment
- a reluctance on the part of the patient to use 'messy' creams on a daily basis
- a feeling that the condition will always return whatever is done
- a lack of sympathy from the GP.

Of those who are using treatments prescribed by their GP, about two fifths admit to being 'unhappy' or 'very unhappy' with the efficacy of the treatment. I feel that are a large part of this dissatisfaction with their care is due to a lack of general support, monitoring and an overall management plan that should accompany the handing over of a prescription. Indeed, without adopting such an approach the prescription might as well be thrown straight in the bin – at least this would save both the patient and the NHS money!

Psoriasis can be a very stubborn disease to treat and it does have a remarkable and disheartening tendency to return even after the skin has been clear for some time. Many patients will cite this as the worst thing about the disease, and it also means that patients begin any new treatment with quite a negative outlook. As psychology and stress play such an important part in triggering and exacerbating psoriasis, a negative frame of mind will impact even more detrimentally on the chances of success from even the best of our available treatments. If we look ahead to the new treatments becoming available over the next few years, some of them are so expensive that we must implement better systems of care in order that our patients gain maximum value from them.

Understanding this propensity of psoriasis to relapse and the impact it can have on quality of life, means that management of psoriasis in primary care must be much more than the simple prescribing of creams. It must, as is much of primary-care work, be truly holistic and look at the disease in the context of the patient's life, experiences and beliefs.

Perceptions about psoriasis

Many people with psoriasis, and those without it, often react with horror when confronted with extensive disease. This is principally because of the lack of awareness about the condition and numerous prevailing misconceptions. These include:

- 'psoriasis is infectious'
- 'psoriasis is an allergy'
- 'it's to do with the blood'
- 'it will never get better'.

Of course, not one of these ideas is correct, but as psoriasis will often relapse and remit regardless of treatment it is very tempting to attribute an exacerbation to preceding life events. This leads to a whole litany of mythology and false information about what works and what doesn't work for the disease, what makes it worse and why this or that expensive herbal or 'alternative' remedy is worth the money. Just a brief search on the internet will illustrate the problem of misinformation much better than I can in these pages!

It is of vital importance that anyone managing patients with psoriasis has a good understanding of the disease and an ability to listen in order to understand the impact it has on an individual's life. In my opinion, every primary healthcare team should have at least one individual who is well educated with a specific interest in the disease area and the time available to deal with patients' concerns and worries. Primary care suffers as much as the rest of the NHS from target setting and it can be all too easy to find that the time to simply talk to patients is lost.

Practical strategies to improve care

Psoriasis clinics

Over a decade ago, one of the many changes imposed on the way GP's work involved the setting up of chronic skin disease management clinics. These were designed to improve the care of patients with asthma and diabetes and very quickly became an established part of almost every GP practice across the country. It occurred to me at the time that such a clinic could also make a great difference to the quality of life of patients with chronic inflammatory skin disease such as psoriasis, eczema and acne. However, this was not recognised by those with the power to make the decision! After many more changes in the NHS, the need for such an approach is even more important today, not least because of the inclusion of skin cancer in the '2-week wait' referral process. The failure to adopt such an approach has consumed a huge amount of dermatologists' time and has resulted in longer waits for patients whose lives are made a misery by extensive inflammatory skin disease.

Luckily, however, this situation brought dermatology to the attention of the decision makers as a waiting list issue and prompted an *Action On* programme which examined a variety of different service provision ideas. Many Primary Care Trusts are now looking at different models of service provision as well as demand management. I am more optimistic now that positive changes will be happening over the next few years.

Of course, many of the referrals to the '2-week wait' clinics would be totally unnecessary if dermatology were to be recognised as an essential part of GP and community nurse training as has been recommended on several occasions in a number of reports produced by the All Party Parliamentary Group on Skin. We would see a dramatic reduction in the numbers of obviously benign lesions being referred up and a reduction in consultant workload which could be shifted back towards the care of patients with chronic skin problems. Of course, this does not mean that all patients with psoriasis should be referred to a consultant!

Psoriasis care in the community could also be improved by better education for all members of the primary healthcare team. Recognition and diagnosis of psoriasis are relatively straightforward and the topical preparations available are not too numerous to allow for easy familiarity with their use, so skill levels and confidence could easily be boosted. I do believe, as mentioned above, that the best way to improve the overall management of patients is to use these skills in the context of an organised clinic with real protected time for the patient.

Once the diagnosis has been made, a patient will need time to understand the implications and the potential for chronicity – this is where a proper skin clinic would be ideal. If we look back at the original guidelines for setting up a chronic disease management clinic for diabetic patients, it can be clearly seen how such an approach could provide benefit to patients with psoriasis.

Maintaining an accurate disease register

A good record of patients with psoriasis allows for accurate call–recall to encourage attendance at regular reviews and to find patients if there are any new developments in drug therapy, to identify any concerns relating to side-effects and to assist in any new initiatives or research projects in secondary care. One spin-off from keeping accurate registers will be good statistics for primary-care organisations when it comes to decision-making about allocation of resources for training and when looking at the possible impact of changes in prescribing and the use of new drugs.

Education for newly diagnosed patients and continuing education

All newly diagnosed patients should be given appropriate education and advice about the disease and its possible effects on their lives. This should include information sheets and details of patient support groups such as the Psoriasis Association and Psoriatic Arthropathy Alliance. Such an education programme should also examine any existing knowledge about the disease, correct any misconceptions and begin to address any concerns that patients may have. An example of this concerns a particularly horrified patient of mine whose only previous experience of psoriasis involved her grandmother and the long-term use of very messy tar preparations. She could not see beyond this prospect until we had spent a considerable amount of time discussing the modern management options that were available. Continuing education can also determine whether patients have retained the information initially given and, for example, whether they have followed up on contacting patient support groups. It also allows for discussion about the triggers of exacerbations that may be particular to that individual, and the methods available to avoid them.

> All newly diagnosed patients should be given appropriate education and advice about the disease and its possible effects on their lives.

Individual patient management plans

I feel that individual patient management plans are critically important. Each individual patient must have a chance to choose a regimen that fits into their lives and meets their own ideas about successful management. However, their expectations may not match up with the GP's or nurse's ideas and may not involve full clearance of the skin. If this mismatch is not corrected, the management will fail. Patients vary greatly in their ideas of success and the amount of effort they might need to put in to achieve it. Some have very unrealistic expectations of a quick fix whilst others are prepared to comply with complex treatment regimens if success is guaranteed. Whilst looking at quality of life issues in psoriasis, Andrew Finlay in Cardiff found that half of the patients in one group were prepared to spend 2–3 hours a day on treatment if it would clear their skin and keep it clear for the rest of the day.

The pattern and distribution of the psoriasis will also affect the management plan. For example, a patient with chronic plaque psoriasis that affects both the trunk and the hands may accept a simple reduction in itch and scaling on the covered parts of the body as success, but would accept nothing less than complete clearance from the hands, particularly if their job involves dealing with the public or shaking hands a lot.

Review of general health

An overall review of a patient's general health should take place on diagnosis and again at an annual review. It may not be important for many patients with psoriasis but, even then, it is still an excellent opportunity for general preventive healthcare and advice. For some patients with more severe disease, it is very important to make sure they are not suffering from, or are prone to, any blood, liver or kidney disease that might limit the choice of potentially toxic second-line therapies. A well-established primary-care clinic could also take over a share of the monitoring of patients on second-line drugs as highlighted under the 'Enhanced Services' section of the new GMS contract. Patients with hypertension or heart disease should also be made aware of the potential of β-blocking drugs to exacerbate psoriasis.

General health questions should also focus on early signs of arthritic problems as psoriatic arthropathy can affect up to 7% of patients with the skin disease. As patients may not be aware of this, they might not think to mention any aches and pains in their joints!

Professional links

Anyone involved in the running of a psoriasis clinic should work together with other healthcare professionals who might be treating patients with psoriasis. In primary care this would include podiatrists involved in treating psoriatic nails or hyperkeratotic feet, and other colleagues with a less direct involvement. Midwives might need some support and education when faced with a pregnant mother, and nurses or doctors advising on travel matters would need to be aware of the adverse effects that antimalarial drugs can have on psoriasis.

Referral policies

A well-run primary-care clinic should be established with advice and guidance from local secondary-care providers. This should include a policy on referrals with a view to encouraging rapid access for trouble-shooting from consultants so that patients are not kept waiting for weeks or months with unstable or unresponsive disease.

Record keeping

The need for good record keeping almost goes without saying, especially as most GP surgeries are now computerised. I feel it is important that all those involved with patients in the primary-care setting can put notes onto the GP system to create a complete record, which should be augmented by information from secondary care and any other local providers. If second-line drugs that need monitoring are being used, the record system should also provide ready access to sequential blood test results.

Clinical audit

It is difficult to get away from audit these days! The care of patients should certainly be subjected to audit against the above criteria and there is also benefit to be had from looking at prescribing issues. Topical steroids are widely used in psoriasis, and so the length of treatment and the amount prescribed should be audited to minimise the chance of side-effects such as skin thinning. The use of emollient preparations could also be audited as this could be seen as the minimum level of care that patients should receive.

Conclusion

In summary, I hope that I have shown the added value that could result from better education of the primary healthcare team and a more co-ordinated approach to the provision of care. Individual practices and local primary care organisations need to acknowledge the prevalence and impact of chronic skin disease. Indeed, much of what I have set out for psoriasis could equally apply to patients with chronic eczema or acne. Depending on the size of the practice, it may make much more sense to include all three diseases when setting up an extra practice clinic as this would make the most of any educational courses undertaken by staff.

For GPs wanting to become confident in many aspects of skin care, I would recommend the Diploma in Practical Dermatology offered by the University of Wales College of Medicine. This is an academic year of weekly assignments which is now very much based on 'e'-learning through computer internet links between the college staff and other doctors on the course, with plenty of opportunity for interaction and the sharing of ideas. Similar courses are being developed for nurses with funding from the Skin Care Campaign (*www.skincarecampaign.org*) and the British Dermatology Nursing Group (*admin@bad.org.uk*). These groups and the Primary Care Dermatology Society (*pcds@pcds.org.uk*) can all provide more information on educational courses and regional meetings throughout the country and are well worth joining.

Key points

- Currently there is a lack of service provision, a lack of education and a lack of awareness of the impact of chronic skin disease in primary care.

- There are many myths and misconceptions among patients about the nature of the condition, and many are dissatisfied with their care. Much of this dissatisfaction relates to a lack of general support and an overall management plan.

- Establishing chronic skin disease clinics in primary care will go a long way to optimising patient management and should involve advice and guidance from secondary-care providers. Existing clinics, such as skin clinics for those with asthma and diabetes, can serve as models for psoriasis clinics.

- Improving education for all members of the primary healthcare team will also improve psoriasis care in the community. Patient education is also essential to allow individuals to understand the course of the condition and its potential impact on their lives.

- Implementing individual patient management plans is vitally important to ensure that management does not fail.

- An assessment of overall general health is important, particularly in determining potential problems if patients require second-line treatment.

- Clinical audit is useful to monitor the use of corticosteroids and ensure that minimal standards of care are being attained.

28. Schizophrenia

Dr Jill Rasmussen MB ChB MRCGP FFPM
General Practitioner, Merstham, Surrey
Director, UK National Neuroscience Research Institute
Royal Holloway, University of London

Summary

The increased use of atypical antipsychotics has led to more patients being managed in the community rather than as inpatients in hospitals and institutions. Thus, a greater burden has fallen on primary care. GPs should use their frequent contacts with schizophrenic patients to play a greater role in monitoring drug treatment and both the mental and physical state of people with schizophrenia. A greater degree of collaborative working between primary and secondary care is desirable. Atypical antipsychotics should be used as first-line treatment for all new cases of schizophrenia. Current labelling of atypical antipsychotics in the UK indicates an increased risk for diabetes and association with ketoacidosis. Screening for diabetes and cardiovascular disease and identification of risk factors, weight and lifestyle programmes should be an integral part of the management of patients with schizophrenia.

Introduction

Schizophrenia is a major challenge to the National Health Service (NHS). Schizophrenia has a prevalence of up to 1%, and so most GPs will regularly encounter patients on their own list with this serious mental disorder. However, most GPs have little previous experience of managing these patients' problems, many of which are ongoing due to the chronic or episodic nature of this disorder. The prescribing of the new 'atypical' antipsychotics has until recently been a controversial issue as they are more expensive than older antipsychotics but (it is claimed) they are associated with improved side-effect and efficacy profiles. Other issues have included drug-rationing procedures in some areas and a lack of clear, up-to-date guidelines. Now that the National Institute for Clinical Excellence (NICE) schizophrenia clinical guideline (available from *www.nice.org.uk*) has unequivocally recommended the use of atypical antipsychotics as first-line medication at least some of these issues have been resolved.

Increased responsibility for primary care

Regardless of guidelines and recommendations, the increasing use of atypical antipsychotics has led to more patients being managed in the community rather than as inpatients in hospitals and institutions. As such, substantial prescribing costs have transferred from secondary to primary care. Clearly, a greater burden has fallen on GPs and thus we should be sure about our responsibilities in respect to our patients. In fact, the best place to manage patients with schizophrenia is often as near to home, and friends and family as possible. They can provide help and support, and enable the person to have a happier and more normal lifestyle. With the right support and help, families and friends of people with schizophrenia can contribute to the recovery. Hospital acute-care beds can then be reserved for just such a purpose – those with acute symptoms. However, those with additional problems (dual diagnosis) and those with more severe, ongoing or resistant symptoms may require longer periods of inpatient care than other patients whose schizophrenia is less severe or more responsive to antipsychotic treatment.

Many patients with schizophrenia have very low expectations of their health and quality of daily life, a few are in sheltered employment, but many lead rather isolated lives on state benefits and are not in touch with a health professional. For example, the incidence of schizophrenia is disproportionately high amongst the homeless.

The public perception of schizophrenia is poor. Common misconceptions are that people believe that those with schizophrenia have a 'split personality' and are likely to be violent. GPs too, are often apprehensive about dealing with schizophrenia, and often take a fairly passive role. Few are comfortable altering dosing of antipsychotic medication independently of secondary-care opinion and are generally not confident in making clinical decisions regarding this disorder. This is in marked contrast to the diagnosis and management of other conditions, even within the sphere of mental health. A survey in 1997 by Bindman *et al.* found that 57% of Inner London GPs were unclear about their role in treating schizophrenia and 71% saw their principal role as providing repeat prescriptions for psychotropic drugs. The main challenge for primary-care physicians is to become more confident in taking responsibility for prescribing antipsychotic medication. They need to build-up a good knowledge and experience in this area. Furthermore, as the primary point of contact for most patients with schizophrenia GPs need to provide effective monitoring of physical well being of this group of patients and audit the results accordingly. With more optimal management many more people with schizophrenia will be able to lead healthier and more productive lives in the community.

Improving practice

Integration of primary and secondary care

In many cases GPs may be the only consistent care provider for patients with schizophrenia. In a survey by Kendrick *et al.*, 93% of long-term mentally ill patients had been seen by their GP in the previous 12 months, on average eight times, but over one-third of patients had no current contact with psychiatric services. GPs could (and should) use their frequent contacts with schizophrenic patients to play a greater role in monitoring drug treatment and both the mental and physical state of people with schizophrenia. Although schizophrenia is a severe mental illness that will require input from secondary-care services, the increasing role of care in the community requires a greater degree of collaborative working between primary and secondary care. Clearly, more links with mental heath services (community psychiatric teams, assertive outreach) and back-up from consulting psychiatrists are required to allow GPs to meet these requirements.

> More links with mental heath services and back-up from consulting psychiatrists are required to allow GPs to meet these requirements.

The World Health Organisation (WHO) has long argued for the integration of mental health into primary care, but what are the reasons for more integration?

- The opportunities for early recognition of the symptoms of schizophrenia are increased as it is likely that GPs will be the first point of contact for these patients.
- To ensure physical healthcare needs are not neglected as frequently physical and mental disorders are comorbid. Exclusive preoccupation with psychological aspects to the exclusion of physical disorders could be disastrous.
- GPs are well-placed to provide long-term follow-up and support to patients and their families and carers. There may be less stigma for a patient if their long-term care is provided in a primary-care setting.
- People with psychoses are more likely to consult with their GP than other healthcare professionals on a regular basis. For example, the national psychiatric morbidity surveys of Great Britain reported that 12% of adults with a psychotic disorder living in the community consulted with their GP in the last 2 weeks and the majority consulted in the last year.

There are several potential mechanisms for better integration between primary and secondary care. The attachment of 'specialists' and GPs with a special interest in mental health to primary care teams is an effective method for improving integration. The last decade has seen a greater targeting by community psychiatric nurses (CPNs) of patients with severe mental disorders. In 1990, about three-quarters of CPNs had no patients with schizophrenia on their books but by 1994, 80% of their case load consisted of patients with severe mental illness where they received referrals from psychiatrists. Clearly, the effective utilisation of CPNs is an essential part of the mechanism for helping schizophrenia patients in the community. Furthermore, many psychiatrists see patients in outreach clinics in primary care. Where GPs and specialists are able to meet regularly, the opportunity to discuss cases can result in mutual learning. Social workers and psychologists also have a critical role to play in supporting patients with schizophrenia in the community.

Improved collaborative working between psychiatrists and GPs is key to improving the provision of services for patients with schizophrenia. However, as there are approximately 2000 consulting psychiatrists in the UK and about 30,000 GPs, then each psychiatrist will need to have close links with 15 or more GPs. Thus, a fair and equitable distribution of these groupings is paramount.

It is important to develop service structures that are appropriate to local requirements and resources. The timescales for the implementation of any changes and training needs for primary care staff need to be considered before clinically effective interventions are implemented.

Specialist care duties

What are the duties of specialist care in relation to primary-care services for the integrated treatment of schizophrenia?

- Develop and agree with GPs and the primary care team a communication and cross-training strategy and a protocol for clinical responsibilities.
- A comprehensive assessment of referred patients.
- The nomination of a key worker to act as the key point of contact with primary healthcare providers.
- The provision of a care plan (including assessment of mental, physical, social needs and a risk assessment) and allocation of clinical responsibilities for each patient.
- Provide the primary-care team with a resources directory of the specialist and other mental health services, and agreed criteria for referral.
- Provide a mechanism for the rapid assessment and treatment of patients with acute symptoms.
- The employment and supervision of attached psychologists, CPNs and counsellors.

The NICE guidelines now recommend that patient care is co-ordinated through a care programme approach (CPA) and the appointment of a named 'care co-ordinator' from the secondary-care mental health team. They should develop a care plan based on financial, social, psychological, medical and cultural needs, as well as accommodation and work requirements.

Primary care responsibilities

- Ensure that patients with suspected schizophrenia are identified and urgently referred to secondary mental health services for assessment and development of a care plan as early treatment improves prognosis.
- Referral to early intervention services, or in more severe and/or chronic cases, referral to crisis resolution or home treatment teams, acute day-hospitals or inpatient services.
- If acute symptoms of schizophrenia are apparent then GPs should consider the prescription of antipsychotics at the earliest opportunity – before the patient is seen by a psychiatrist if necessary, though wherever possible this should be following a discussion with a psychiatrist.
- Good liaison with secondary-care services.
- Compilation of an up-to-date practice case register for all patients with schizophrenia that includes risk factors for and monitoring of patients' physical and mental health.
- Joint agreements with secondary care regarding care plans and allocation of clinical responsibilities for each patient (e.g. frequency of regular physical healthcare reviews, areas of concern).

If acute symptoms of schizophrenia are apparent then GPs should consider the prescription of antipsychotics at the earliest opportunity.

Where appropriate the decision to re-refer to secondary care should take into account the views of the patient and their carers. Whenever possible re-referral should be undertaken before crises arise, and particularly in the following cases:

- lack of patient compliance
- poor response to treatment(s)
- if comorbid substance abuse is suspected
- if the level of risk to self and others increases.

An algorithm outlining decisions faced by primary care and their interactions with secondary care services when treating schizophrenia is shown in Figure 1.

Integration with social care

It is essential that case management and social outreach functions are available in order to achieve the best clinical and social outcomes for patients with schizophrenia. There is a particularly high proportion of

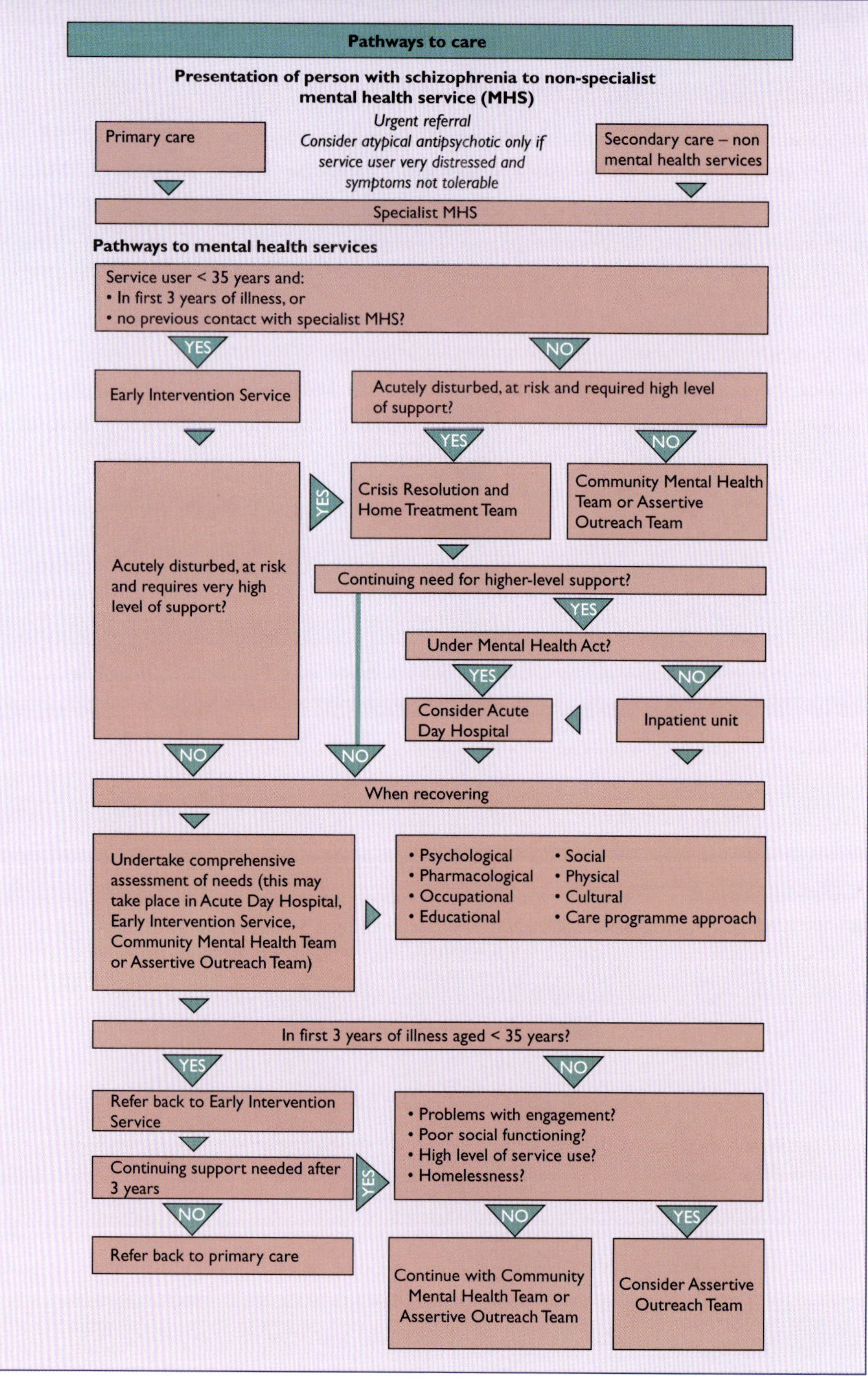

Figure 1. Pathways to care for patients with schizophrenia. Adapted from Schizophrenia. Core interventions in the treatment and management of schizophrenia in primary and secondary care. Clinical practice algorithms and pathways to care. December 2002.

people with schizophrenia living alone in cities. In these cases, a dedicated specialist case management and outreach team can provide the best care. These teams should liaise with local primary-care teams through the establishment of joint case registers and regular joint review of care plans.

Audit

The stages for a successful audit should involve:

- the development of an audit strategy and a team to carry out the audit (e.g. a lead GP, community psychiatric nurse and other team members to assist with the collection of data)
- identification of patients with schizophrenia from practice records
- establishing or updating the practice schizophrenia register and assigning audit numbers to maintain patient confidentiality
- performance of the data to be audited either 'in-house' or using an appropriate external audit body
- feeding back results from the audit to all healthcare team members to encourage better practice, setting targets with deadlines and a date for re-audit (e.g. annually).

A sample questionnaire is shown in Figure 2. The recent NICE schizophrenia guidelines recommend that clinicians audit their own compliance with these guidelines by having management plans for each patient. These guidelines also go into considerable detail regarding criteria for audit. Criteria that should be considered for audit by primary-care teams are:

- have family interventions been offered to any family who lives with or is in close contact with a family member with schizophrenia?
- has cognitive–behavioural therapy been offered to the patient?
- are assertive outreach community psychiatric teams being used?
- are the patient care plans comprehensive and appropriate?
- have patients and their carers received written educational materials about schizophrenia?
- have patients' occupational needs and status been assessed?
- are patients on the practice case register?
- has a frequent physical health check been performed?

Drug treatment

The recent NICE schizophrenia guidelines now recommend that GPs should consider prescribing atypical antipsychotics early if a patient has acute symptoms of schizophrenia, even before a patient has seen a

Figure 2. A sample questionnaire for the audit of patients with schizophrenia in primary care. Adapted from the Lothian integrated general practice quality group audit package for the primary care of people with schizophrenia.

SAMPLE QUESTIONNAIRE

INTEGRATED GENERAL PRACTICE QUALITY GROUP

PRIMARY CARE OF PEOPLE WITH SCHIZOPHRENIA

PRACTICE NO

PATIENT AUDIT NO

CURRENT CARE

Patient details

Age ___________

Sex   Male ☐   Female ☐

Ethnicity ___________________________

1. Diagnosis

Is the recorded diagnosis of schizophrenia correct?   Y ☐ N ☐

IF DIAGNOSIS IS <u>NOT CORRECT</u>, DO NOT FILL IN THIS QUESTIONNAIRE FOR THE PATIENT

2. Registers

Is the patient's name and / or ID recorded on either a manual or computerised practice Schizophrenia Register?   Y ☐ N ☐

3. Involvement with Mental Health Team (in last year)

Is there a record of care having been received within last year from Community Mental Health Team?   Y ☐ N ☐

If Y, was this: (Tick all boxes that apply)
Community Psychiatric Nurse   ☐
Psychiatrist   ☐
Other Mental Health Professional   ☐
Care Programme Approach   ☐

4. Hospital Admission (in last year)

Is there a record of the patient having been admitted to hospital for schizophrenia within the last year?   Y ☐ N ☐

If Y, is there a discharge care summary in the notes?   Y ☐ N ☐

If Y, is there a record of the patient having been on Mental Health Act Section in the last year?   Y ☐ N ☐

5. Accommodation Status (in last year)

Does the patient live: Alone?   ☐
                        With family?   ☐
                        With friends?   ☐
                        In supported accommodation?   ☐
                        Not known   ☐

6. Medication

Is the patient on antipsychotic medication?   Y ☐ N ☐

If Y, please specify ___________________________

QUALITY OF CARE

7. Review (in last year)

Is there a record of the patient having been reviewed in the last year?   Y ☐ N ☐

If Y, was this by: (Tick all boxes that apply)
GP   ☐
Consultant Psychiatrist   ☐
Other Mental Health Professional   ☐
Care Programme Approach   ☐

IF REVIEW UNDERTAKEN, PLEASE COMPLETE THE FOLLOWING SECTION ON REVIEW

8. Review (in last year)

Is there a record of:
Symptoms being assessed?   Y ☐ N ☐
Continued use of antipsychotics being assessed?   Y ☐ N ☐
Side-effects of medication being assessed?   Y ☐ N ☐

If side-effects were present and recorded, is there a record of how they would be managed?   Y ☐ N ☐

9. Health Screening Assessment (in last 5 years)

Do the records show the following having been assessed within the last 5 years? (tick not known [NK] if records not available for the whole 5-year period)

BP   Y ☐ N ☐ NK ☐
BMI   Y ☐ N ☐ NK ☐
Smoking Status   Y ☐ N ☐ NK ☐
Alcohol consumption   Y ☐ N ☐ NK ☐
Family history of diabetes   Y ☐ N ☐ NK ☐
Family history of cardiovascular disease   Y ☐ N ☐ NK ☐

FEMALES (under 60 years)

Cervical screening within the last 3 years?   Y ☐ N ☐ NK ☐

psychiatrist, though this should be following a discussion with a psychologist wherever possible and a referral should be a matter of urgency. First-line treatment for all new cases of schizophrenia is oral atypical antipsychotics (amisulpride, olanzapine, risperidone, quetiapine and zotepine) at the lower end of the standard dose range. Furthermore, oral atypical antipsychotics should be considered as treatment options for those currently receiving typical antipsychotics who:

- are experiencing unacceptable side-effects
- relapse
- have previously had unsatisfactory management of their symptoms and/or have had unacceptable side-effects.

GPs should be aware of the spectrum of side-effects associated with antipsychotics and the symptoms of schizophrenia. They should have the confidence to be able to change the dose of medication and even switch antipsychotic, though understandably, liaison with a psychiatrist may be warranted.

> GPs should have the confidence to be able to change the dose of medication and even switch antipsychotic.

Schizophrenia, type 2 diabetes and weight management

Research shows that patients with schizophrenia and their families have 4–6-fold increased rates of type 2 diabetes compared with the general population. Screening results also show that the incidence of diabetes and IGT in patients with schizophrenia is grossly underestimated. Whilst treatment-naive patients have a higher risk of glucose dysregulation, typical and atypical antipsychotics are also associated with factors that increase the risk of diabetes – increased weight and glucose dysregulation. In patients this effect is largely independent of which antipsychotic medication is prescribed. Antipsychotics are one of a range of factors that not only increase the risk of diabetes but also increase the risk of metabolic syndrome or syndrome X. Other risk factors are:

- age
- gender (male)
- ethnicity (higher in Asians and Afro-caribbeans)
- family history
- obesity.

In addition to glucose dysregulation and insulin resistance the metabolic syndrome includes potential for raised cholesterol levels, and as a consequence, an increased risk for cardiovascular disease.

A recent evaluation of the relationship between schizophrenia, type 2 diabetes and antipsychotics has recently been undertaken by the US regulatory authorities, the Federal Drug Administration (FDA). They concluded that:

> "Assessment of the relationship between atypical antipsychotic use and glucose abnormalities is complicated by the possibility of an increased background risk of diabetes mellitus in patients with schizophrenia and the increasing incidence of diabetes mellitus in the general population."

> "…patients with diabetes who begin taking atypical antipsychotics should be monitored for a worsening of glucose control, and those with risk factors for diabetes (e.g., obesity, family history of diabetes) should undergo fasting glucose testing at baseline, and periodically throughout treatment."

The text "Any patient developing suggestive symptoms during treatment with an atypical antipsychotic should be tested for diabetes", has been added to the labelling of all atypical antipsychotic drugs in the US, and other authorities are known to be considering this evidence. Current labelling in the UK indicates an increased risk for diabetes and association with ketoacidosis for some of the atypical antipsychotics drugs. The NICE guidelines specifically advise about monitoring for:

- endocrine disorders, such as diabetes and hyperprolactinaemia
- cardiovascular risk factors, such as blood pressure and lipids
- side-effects of medication
- lifestyle factors such as smoking.

Results of weight and lifestyle management programmes with schizophrenic patients have demonstrated positive results with respect to weight control and weight loss in the obese and improvement in lifestyle. These programmes have utilised relatively simple measures such as:

- sugar substitution
- lowering fatty and 'fast food' intake
- encouraging gentle exercise – walking, climbing stairs.

An additional benefit has been an improvement in patient self-esteem and in the care-team–patient relationship.

Key points

- The burden of schizophrenia has, to a great extent, shifted from secondary to primary care.

- Most GPs will regularly encounter patients on their own list with schizophrenia and are often best placed to ensure that an early intervention occurs, which can improve prognosis.

- Rapid referral to a psychologist to confirm a diagnosis and to produce a care plan for each patient is essential.

- Greater integration of primary- and secondary-care services allows for the better management of the mental and physical health needs of schizophrenia patients in the community.

- The development of an audit strategy and case register will help to improve standards in primary care practices and aid in the management of individuals with schizophrenia.

- Screening for diabetes and cardiovascular disease and identification of risk factors, weight and lifestyle management programmes should be an integral part of the management of patients with schizophrenia.

- Failure to treat a patient because of the risk or complications of diabetes places the patient at a higher risk for more serious problems.

Notes

Notes

Notes

Notes

Notes

Notes

Notes

Notes

Notes

Notes

Notes

Notes